The R

Travels through 22 former Soviet Republics

By Jason Smart

Published by Smart Travel Publishing

To Angela, Phil, Michael & Jon

Prologue

"Zis your first time in Russia?" asked the woman behind border control at Moscow's Domodedovo Airport. She seemed grimly official and looked like she had not smiled since 1989. I nodded and passed my passport through the narrow gap. The thin-lipped security officer took it without comment, scrutinising my visa and immigration card as if expecting to find microfilm. Eventually she looked up and studied my face. I kept it as neutral as possible. Looking cheerful was not the correct protocol at passport control in Russia - it was a sign of something to hide.

"I vill ask again. Is zis first time in Russia?"

Under the woman's steely gaze I cracked. My mouth formed into a nervous smile. "Yes... and it's hot."

I was referring to the heat wave. It was thirty-nine degrees Celsius in the shade. Reports of drunken vagabonds cooling themselves in the city's fountains were beginning to hit the British press because some had drowned.

The customs official didn't understand. Her eyes narrowed a fraction. "Hot? What you mean...hot...?"

Around me, my fellow passengers averted their eyes. Swallowing hard, I gripped the metal bar in front of me to steady myself. "The weather is hot..." I stammered. "Moscow is hot."

Time stood still. The woman stared without blinking. Finally she spoke. "Yes, I think I see...Moscow is hot." She stamped my passport and ushered me through. I had infiltrated Russia, but it had been a close shave.

1. The Quest Begins in Snowy Latvia

Interesting fact: The national airline of Latvia, Air Baltic, does not serve curry.

"Why do you want to go to Russia in February?" asked Phil as he put his pint down. "All you'll see are turnips and tractors. And it'll be freezing."

Phil and I had been friends since university. In the decade and a half since then, we'd both become teachers and got married. Not to each other. But we still found time to meet for a few pints on a Thursday evening.

I shook my head. "For a start, Phil, Latvia is not Russia. And anyway, it's meant to be nice."

"*Latvia!* That's even worse. Who goes to Latvia for their holidays? What's wrong with Barcelona or Paris? Latvia will be grey and full of concrete. Arms dealers will mug you, and sex traffickers will hound you. You'll queue ten hours to get a loaf of bread."

I took a sip of my lager and smiled. "What you're describing is Eastern Europe from thirty years ago. Latvia is modern. It's been an independent country for about twenty years. It's part of the EU for God's sake! Why wouldn't I want to go there?"

"Err, what about the language?" stated Phil bluntly. "Can you speak Russian or Latvian or whatever the hell they speak over there? What about hotels? They'll all be bugged. You'll get arrested by the KGB!" Phil laughed at his own mirth. "And what about Angela? What does she think about going to Russia in the middle of winter?"

My shoulders slumped. Phil had hit upon the only real obstacle in my plan, namely my wife. Not that Angela had anything against Latvia, but I knew it would be a tall order to convince her to go in the depths of a February winter.

"She doesn't know, does she?" said Phil grinning an evil grin. "She has no idea of your mad plan to go turnip-spotting in Russia? You're an idiot! I can't wait to find out what she says!"

2

"Where's Riga?" asked Angela.

It took me three days to pluck up enough courage to broach the subject of jetting off to the Latvian capital for a two-day city break.

"It's the capital of Latvia," I answered calmly. "It's near Russia, and I've-"

"Russia! You want me to go to Russia in February! You're not being serious are you?"

Inwardly I grimaced but outwardly I smiled. "Yes."

"No," Angela said turning back to the TV.

An hour later I tried again. Taking a deep breath, I told my wife about Riga's medieval centre, and the modern bars and restaurants that surrounded it. I described the parks and monuments, and I then showed her the ace up my sleeve, a photo of a hotel I'd found, the tallest building in Riga, no less. Angela took it reluctantly but then looked impressed. I pressed home the advantage. "It's got a bar on the top floor which overlooks the city."

Angela's eyes widened when I passed her the photo of the bar. "Okay...that does look nice. Very modern." Then her face furrowed. "But it'll be freezing in February."

I nodded. She was right. Riga would be freezing. In fact, the previous February it had been down to minus 28°C.

"Look," I said, passing her a photo of Riga's medieval centre. "It will be cold - there's no getting away from that - but if we wrap up warm, we'll be fine. And besides, the snow might add to the trip. Everything will look really Christmassy."

"Christmassy...?"

"Yeah I'm sure of it."

~ 4 ~

Angela looked at the photos again. I waited for her decision. She was flicking between the picture of the bar and another one showing some medieval guild houses. "So what do you think?" I asked.

Angela put the photos down. "Somehow, I think you've convinced me."

I whooped with joy! We were going to visit a former Soviet republic! And deep inside my brain, neurons were buzzing with excitement. An insane mission that would see me traversing half the planet had been kick-started into life.

3

Touching down at Riga Airport well after sundown, we stared at the snow and ice outside. Nowhere looks warm and inviting in the dark, even less so in a snow blizzard, and with an aeroplane from Uzbekistan parked at the next gate.

"Where have you brought me?" asked Angela, peering towards the terminal.

"Somewhere exciting, somewhere different," I answered. "Somewhere none of our friends have ever been!"

"Mmm…there might be a reason for that."

After passing through passport control, we entered the modern-looking airport lounge. We saw a café selling trendy lattes, and chic people buying the latest perfumes. Latvia, or at least its international airport, seemed modern and vibrant. I wondered what Phil would make of it. I was impressed and could see that Angela was too.

As soon as we stepped outside, the freezing temperature hit us - a blast of ice instantly enveloping every exposed inch of skin. We ran through the snowstorm for the nearest taxi and were soon on our way. With a sudden veer to the right, the driver joined a two-lane highway, snow whooshing across the lanes in icy flurries. Over the radio, a woman sang a western song in a foreign accent.

Ten minutes later, we pulled up outside the hotel. The rest of the evening was spent in the bar watching the snow build up outside.

4

Angela and I were up early. After a quick peer between the curtains, I regarded the snow. It covered every rooftop and weighed down every tree branch. Did it look Christmassy? I wasn't sure, but at least it had stopped actually snowing.

Angela joined me at the window. "Oh wow," she cooed. "It looks so pretty! That church looks amazing."

Wrapped up like Eskimos, we prepared ourselves for the arctic conditions outside. The temperature was a bone-rattling minus nine. "Here goes," I said.

Needles of ice stabbed our exposed skin, making us pull our hats tighter as we headed along Brivibas Bulvaris, a long, straight road that led to the old town. A blanket of white coated every building, but the roads and pathways were clear. The snow cones at various intersections suggested that snow shovellers had been busy before dawn.

The people on the street with us were all wrapped up warm and snug, some waiting at tram stops, others walking briskly with collars turned up against the chill. Some even wore big furry hats. We hurried on towards the Freedom Monument.

Built in 1935, and regarded by many Latvians as a national shrine, Mother Latvia sat on top of the Freedom Monument's thin column. She held aloft three golden stars. A thin layer of snow coated her green, coppery head. Mother Latvia had once looked down upon a group of protesters. They had gathered to lay flowers.

5

In 1987, five thousand people came to place flowers at the base of Mother Latvia. It was brave of them because the Soviets had made it clear they would not tolerate the flowers because of what they represented – victims of Soviet deportations. Nevertheless, people still came; each armed with handfuls of blooms.

Instead of crushing the demonstration by force, the Soviets came up with a more subtle plan - they organised a bicycle race. With party workers zipping around the statue, protestors found it difficult to lay flowers, so the demonstration petered out.

Two months later another flower laying protest was organised, this time with even more people. Yet despite the success with the bicycles, the Soviets responded with their usual hob-nailed boots. They fired water cannons at the protesters. This put an end to the flower laying in Latvia, but beneath the surface, the Latvian independence movement had begun.

6

Angela and I stared at the two soldiers standing to attention at the base of the Freedom Monument. Both looked freezing. Then like the flip of a switch, they started moving in a peculiar manner. Each movement was exaggerated and in slow motion. It was the changing of the guard.

"We're lucky to see them," I said as we watched them march away. In the distance, another couple of guards were already coming to replace them. "They don't work if the temperature is below minus ten."

"Look at the ducks!" Angela said, pointing to the right. I turned, noticing a small park with a thin river running through it. Snow covered the frozen stream, and on it, about thirty ducks sat huddled together, as if trying to fathom where their river had gone.

We wandered further down Brivibas Bulvaris, passing upmarket department stores until we came to a temporary ice rink. Some beautiful chocolate-box buildings were just beyond it, quaint and colourful in equal measure. Skaters moved across the ice, scarves flowing behind them. The whole scene looked like it belonged on a Christmas card.

The strangely named House of Blackheads was a popular tourist attraction in Riga's old town. Icicles hung from its pointy awnings, and slippery cobbles lay around its entrance. The building's exterior was a patchwork of red and white. It was highly distinctive.

Dating from the 14th century, the House of Blackheads had been the abode of unmarried merchants. The men wore black caps (thus the name) as they indulged themselves in mad banquets and drinking sessions. Today the House of Blackheads is a museum.

"So are you glad we came to Latvia?" I asked Angela.

Tightening her scarf, Angela smiled. "You know what? Yes. I didn't know what to expect, but it's really pretty. You've done well, Jason. I like it."

The museum was closed, we discovered, so we walked away, leaving footprints in the snow. "See that spire over there?" I asked. Around our heads, snowflakes lazily drifted downwards in the dense cold air. "It's called the Church of Saint Peter, and there's an interesting story behind it." Angela listened as I began to tell the tale.

The spire had fallen or burned to the ground so many times that Peter the Great, visiting Riga at the time, ordered a proper rebuild. The newly designed church was eventually completed in 1746, and in celebration, the architect in charge (with his entourage) climbed to the top to have a few glasses of wine. After quaffing the booze, the architect threw his empty glass over the side, telling everyone that the number of shards it broke into would signify how many centuries the spire would remain standing. They all rushed down to have a look. They weren't happy with what they found though. The glass only broke into two pieces. It landed in a pile of hay.

"So did the spire fall down?" asked Angela.

"Yeah, nearly two centuries later. During the Second World War, a bomb hit it!"

In a small square near House of the Blackheads was a dark and sombre building that housed the Occupation Museum of Latvia. The museum chronicled Latvian life during the Nazi and Soviet regimes. The communists had deported thousands of Latvians to Gulags, but the Germans had done worse.

In 1941, after the Nazis had taken over Latvia, special units began scouring the land searching out undesirables. These included gypsies and the mentally ill, but were mostly Jews.

A ghetto was quickly established in Riga. Jews couldn't leave their homes in the evening, visit cinemas or parks, ride on trams, or even walk on pavements. A non-Jew could also assault a Jew with impunity. Against this backdrop, the Latvian Holocaust began.

The worst atrocity happened in November 1941. Twelve kilometres south of Riga was a small train station called Rumbula. It was the ideal location for transporting equipment required for the upcoming massacre.

Not far from the station was a large hill covered in pine forest. The soil the trees grew in was ideal because it was sandy and soft. It was easy to dig the six execution pits needed. Each pit was big enough to hold thousands of bodies.

Back in the Riga Ghetto, able-bodied men were separated from their families and then murdered. At 4 a.m. on the 30 November, Nazi troops tore into the ghetto, rounding everyone else up, murdering hundreds in the process. Next, they organised Jews into columns, forcing them to march out of the ghetto.

As dawn broke, the columns kept leaving. Most of them contained women, children, the elderly, and the disabled. If a person fell, a never-ending stomp of feet would crush them to death. Nazi guards would whip and shoot anyone who stopped to help. By lunchtime, the columns finally left Riga. They left behind a trail of corpses, and a river of blood.

After three hours of constant marching, the first column reached the hill near Rumbula Station. Guards made each person hand over their belongings before making them strip naked.

Ten people at a time were ordered to walk down ramps that led into the first pit. Guards forced them to lie face down in the dirt so that marksmen could deliver a single bullet to their heads. Then the next ten came for the same fate. By the time night had fallen, 13,000 Jews were dead. By the end of the week, 25,000 people were dead.

The Nazi leader in command was Friedrich Jeckeln. When the Red Army liberated Latvia, they captured him, along with some of his underlings. A Soviet military court found them all guilty of war crimes. Jeckeln was hanged in Riga on the 3 February 1946.

9

Angela and I left the Occupation Museum, and turned left along a main road running parallel to the Daugava River. A few minutes later, we came to a side street. The scene in front of us looked bleak and Eastern Bloc - graffiti was everywhere. Somehow, we'd stepped into an unsavoury part of Riga without even realising it.

We walked forward, trudging through slush and cigarette ends, hoping to get back to civilisation. Just then, about a hundred metres in front, two men stepped into the street. They stood watching us, lighting cigarettes through cupped hands. Both were in their early thirties and looked hardened to the bitter, wintry weather.

As we got nearer, I steeled myself for a confrontation of some kind. Twenty feet, fifteen, and I could hear one of the men speaking to the other in a deep, rasping, unrecognisable accent. Ten feet, five, and then it was all over. We passed them without incident. One of the men even nodded in acknowledgment as we'd walked by.

Thirty seconds later, the street opened into a wide area of tram stops, billboards, and, more importantly, people. We were back in safe hands, if we'd ever left them in the first place.

10

Angela and I were browsing through the stalls of an outdoor market. They sold mainly fruit and vegetables (including plenty of root produce), and I could imagine Phil nodding at the scene. Rotund women with wide pink faces wrapped in headscarves were in charge of the stalls. I was almost temped to buy a turnip to take back to Phil.

Just beyond the stalls was the largest indoor market in Europe. Constructed inside five former zeppelin hangars, we entered one to find stalls selling every kind of meat imaginable. Sausages seemed the main item, but huge shanks of meat, small cuts of steak and even red-tinged strips of white fat were on sale too. Angela and I wandered up and down the aisles until we came out the other side. The next zeppelin hangar contained just fruit and vegetables. It was as vast as the meat market.

"Come on," I said after passing yet another turnip stall. "Let's get some lunch."

11

Lunch turned out to be a cheap self-service cafe full of local people on their work break. Afterwards, warmed with hearty East European food, Angela and I found ourselves standing outside the Powder Tower, a large cylindrical structure rumoured to have stored gunpowder during medieval times. It deserved a place in a *Harry Potter* movie, I thought. Just then, a gorgeous girl wandered past.

Beautiful women were everywhere in Riga. They stood at tram stops, sat on buses, served in bars, and passed by on busy streets. Even Angela noticed how pretty they were. The blonde girl passing the Powder Tower was wearing a thick fur-collared coat and high heels. She negotiated the cobbles with practised ease.

"What is this Black Balsam stuff?" asked Angela as we passed another shop window full of the distinctive dark, ceramic bottles.

I shrugged. "I'm not sure, but I think we should buy some."

"Iz traditional Latvian liqueur," the woman behind the counter told us, retrieving a bottle for us to study. "Here is leaflet to read if you like. It will explain many things."

We bought a medium-sized bottle of the stuff and thanked the lady for her help.

Outside, we found an alcove in a frost-coated doorway, and opened the bottle up. "You first," said Angela.

I nodded and took the tiniest of sips. The effect was immediate. My throat contracted, and my mouth grimaced. Angela doubled up laughing as I tried to spit what remained of the vile brew from my mouth. Riga Black Balsam was truly disgusting, one of the worst things I'd ever tasted. It was like drinking bitumen. But at least it made me forget about the cold.

"I think I'll try some later," laughed Angela. "...If I ever do. Is it that bad?"

I nodded and fished the leaflet from my pocket. It told me that an 18th century pharmacist from Riga had invented the stuff. He'd mixed twenty-four different ingredients (including herbs, flowers, roots and berries) into vodka. "Listen to this," I said. "People actually put this stuff in coffee or on ice creams!" The aftertaste was still curdling my throat, so I put the black bottle away for later.

12

We found ourselves in Dome Square, right in the heart of the old town. Its centrepiece was Riga Cathedral, an enormous building that the Soviets had once converted into a concert hall. As we tightened our scarves, more snow flurries began to fall in circles around us, creating a fresh layer of white.

In the early hours of the 13 January 1991, the area around Dome Square wasn't quite so peaceful. At 4.45am, a broadcast by a pro-independence group resulted in a crowd gathering in the square. They were responding to communist forces attempting to restore a Soviet-style government. By that afternoon, 70,000 people gathered.

The Soviets dropped leaflets from helicopters ordering the protesters to desist and leave. Everyone ignored them and began building barricades from anything they could find. Trucks, logs, concrete blocks and coils of wire were erected all over the city, but especially in the area around Dome Square. Behind these makeshift barriers, people formed human shields.

The Soviets had a rethink and decided that force was the best way forward. They sent in the troops, the upshot of which was the death of one protester.

A violent demonstration followed, and the Soviets, worried that things were spiralling out of control, stormed the barricades. They killed five more people, including a schoolchild. World reaction was devastating, and the Soviets had no choice but to back down. Six months later Latvia was an independent country.

13

"Iz beautiful church, yes?" said an elderly man who must have noticed us staring at Dome Cathedral. He'd originally tried speaking to us in Latvian but quickly turned to English when he'd seen our uncomprehending looks.

He was wearing a thick coat, and his warm breath spilled into the air as he spoke. I wondered whether he had been part of the demonstrations. "Can I ask which country you are from?"

"England," I answered.

"England? You have come to Latvia at strange time!" He was smiling and gesturing at the snow. "Most England people come in summer. Most of them loud, young men causing nuisance for Riga. But you are not like that. You are most welcome in Riga!"

We thanked the old man and wandered away.

14

Riga at night looked just as appealing as during the day. And curiously, the temperature had gone up: a positively balmy -7° C.

We decided we liked the sound of the Livonija, described as a medieval restaurant. It was located below the Small Guild Hall. One thing worried us though - it was Valentine's Day. All evening we'd seen young men carrying single red roses in their teeth, clearly the way things were done in Riga.

We found the restaurant easily enough, and as we approached the door, a large middle-aged man stepped out from the entrance. He addressed us in Latvian.

I spoke up first. "Erm...we're from England. Do you speak English?"

The man nodded and smiled. "Of course. Welcome to Livonija. We don't get many persons from England here at restaurant. In fact, you are only second ever. You have reservation, yes?"

I shook my head and pulled an imploring face. "No, sorry. But we read that your restaurant is so nice we thought we'd try it anyway.

The man rubbed his chin, then grinned. "I think we squeeze you in. Follow me, please."

As we descended some stone stairs into the cosy warmth of the place, the man asked us how we'd heard of his restaurant.

I told him I read about it in our guidebook and showed him the page. The man looked at the review in open astonishment and then broke into hearty guffaws. "Livonija in English guidebook! How this happen?"

At the bottom of the stairs, we entered a large brick-covered cavern laid out with tables and chairs. It was almost full, but as promised, the man found us a table. Tempting smells emanated from the kitchen, and as Angela and I took our seats, we took in the atmosphere of the place. It was like being inside an old tunnel, or possibly a dungeon. A big, warm dungeon though, and when the food turned up, it was excellent.

As I took a sip of Aldaris lager, I looked at Angela. "So," I said. "You've loved Riga. Do you fancy anywhere else in Eastern Europe?"

Angela picked up her glass of wine and took a small sip. "Maybe."

"Okay. How about Estonia or Hungary…?"

Angela put her glass down. "I don't know anything about those places."

"You didn't know anything about Latvia, but you enjoyed it."

"True."

"You'll love Estonia. Its capital is gorgeous."

Angela still looked doubtful. "Let's wait and see, shall we. When we get home you can show me some pictures."

I nodded. That was about as good as it was going to get, I supposed.

The next day we checked out of the hotel and caught a taxi back to the airport. Our trip to Riga was over, but in the back of my mind, the tiny spark was smouldering.

2. Onwards to Estonia

Interesting fact: Estonia is the least religious country in the world.

Estonia had a rather unique way of gaining independence. They sang for it.

In 1987, what started as spontaneous singing of national songs eventually led to a huge festival called *Song of Estonia*. In it, a quarter of the population gathered to croon. This singing revolution continued on and off for the next two years, until the final showdown.

With Soviet tanks rolling in, the people of Estonia formed human shields around TV and radio stations, singing and humming as they did so. Then the unexpected happened, because the Soviets backed down. The singing worked. Estonia became the only Baltic nation to gain independence without bloodshed.

Since then, Estonia has done okay for itself. It quickly established itself as the wealthiest of the former Soviet republics. It became a world leader in electronics and IT (an Estonian company developed Skype). Not bad for a country almost brought to its knees during the communist regime.

2

It took a few weeks of gentle persuasion for Angela to agree on another Eastern European jaunt. But with Riga safely under our belt, I knew Estonia would be easy, especially with the weather in May more or less guaranteed to be good.

Phil was also interested in our plans to visit Estonia. "I've got to say," he told me. "I didn't think you'd pull it off. Going to Turnipland in the middle of winter - fair play to you. I'm not sure I could convince Julie to go somewhere like that. Anyway, what's Tallinn like?"

"Really nice," I said. "Some people say it's the new Prague. It has medieval buildings, cosy bars, lots of cafes, a nice little harbour and an old castle. I can't wait."

"Are you sure you're not joining MI5? The White Stork flies at midnight, and all that shite?"

3

We arrived in Estonia on a gloriously sunny day. Angela and I began our sightseeing by walking to Viru Gates, a pair of medieval towers. They looked like the producers of *Lord of the Rings* had placed them there, all turret-like with orange pointy roofs. As we headed underneath, we saw the McDonald's restaurant on the other side.

We ambled along a cobbled street until we came to the Town Hall Square. It was a delicious part of Tallinn that was comprised of more pointy-roofed buildings and a whole line of outdoor cafes. The town hall stood proud at one end of the square, a prime landmark because of its spindly spire.

The square was teeming with people. Most were wandering about looking at the town hall, or else sitting in the cafes. Parked at one edge of the square was a tourist train waiting for its carriages to fill up. Angela and I sat down for a coffee.

During its 700-year history, Tallinn's Town Hall Square had served as a medieval market place, a site for tournaments and a place for public executions. One notable beheading involved a priest called Panicke.

Panicke was a man of the cloth in sixteenth-century Tallinn. One evening, whilst drunk, he decided to order a pancake from an inn. After tasting it, he deemed it horrible, describing it as being 'as hard as a shoe.' He told the serving girl to fetch him another.

Panicke didn't like the next one either, and started to lose his temper. When the third one wasn't to his liking, the priest blew a fuse. He grabbed an axe and slaughtered the poor girl. The authorities sentenced Panicke to death. They chopped his head off near the edge of the square.

4

Angela and I were staring inside a shop window just off the square when we heard a male voice. We turned to see a middle-aged man sauntering towards us. He resembled the bearded one from Abba, but instead of carrying a guitar, he carried a couple of bags of beer.

The man was a bit tipsy. He spoke again, but of course, we couldn't understand him. He soon realised this, and addressed us in English.

"Do you know where the harbour is?" His words were slurred, but he was clearly in a jovial mood.

We didn't, and informed him of this.

The man shrugged. "Oh well, I am sure I will find it eventually. Can I ask where you are from?"

"England," said Angela. "Are you from Tallinn?"

The man shook his head and wobbled slightly on his feet. "No, I am from Helsinki. I arrive in Tallinn to buy alcohol. In Finland, it is expensive. It is cheaper to get ferry, buy alcohol from a supermarket in Estonia, and then go back. Ferry only takes two hours and I get to see this beautiful little city at the same time. But I must get to harbour. I have boat to catch!" And with that, he traipsed off, cans of lager swaying with each of his unsteady movements.

5

"Do you know something?" said Angela as we headed along a cobbled hill. "I think I prefer Tallinn to Riga. It's a fairy-tale, medieval town. They even have horses and carts selling roasted chestnuts for God's sake! But the thing I can't get over is that six months ago we'd never heard of the place."

We came to a building called the House of the Brotherhood of Blackheads. Like the similarly named building we'd seen in Riga, the house had been a guild of young, unmarried merchants.

The Blackheads had held fair sway in medieval Tallinn. They organised celebrations and tournaments, and sorted out the city's defences. Not only that, the Blackheads were responsible for the first ever Christmas tree in the world. They put one up in Town Hall Square, but instead of adorning it with baubles and tinsel, the Blackheads danced around it then set it on fire.

The Blackheads had some strange rules. For instance, any member of their guild who cursed a fellow member had to pay a one-mark fine. If he hit a fellow Blackhead's ear, the fine was two marks. The largest fine, five pounds of wax (a valuable commodity during the Middle Ages), was for the heinous crime of flinging beer in a Blackhead's face.

We stood in front of the building, our eyes drawn to the wooden door. It was big and arch-shaped, adorned with green and red stripes. It was finished off with an impressive iron knocker.

"I bet there were some strange things going on behind that door," I said to Angela, secretly wishing I'd been a Blackhead.

Angela nodded. "But why would they want to burn a Christmas tree down? That's awful."

6

Saint Olav's Church was along Pikk Street. Five hundred years previously, its massive spire made it the tallest building in the world. The spire also made an impressive lightning rod. The church burned to the ground three times before the authorities finally decided to build a smaller spire. Even so, it was still tall enough for the KGB to use as a radio communications antenna.

"Listen to this," I said to Angela as we sat in another street cafe. "According to legend, when they started building the spire, local merchants decided they needed a proper builder to complete the work. There was a problem though - the town had no spare cash. Luckily, out of nowhere, a strange man appeared. He said he'd build the church for free, but on one condition - the town had to guess his name before the work ended. If not, they had to give him all the town's gold."

With the odd deal struck, the stranger began work on the spire, while people rushed hither and thither trying to guess his name. But it was to no avail, no one was even getting close. He laughed at their pathetic attempts, and as the spire neared completion, the merchants began to get worried. They resorted to underhanded tactics. It involved, as it often did, a dastardly spy.

Creeping furtively, the spy arrived at the temporary home of the strange builder and his wife. Within minutes, the hidden scout heard a woman singing to a baby. *Sleep, my baby, sleep*, the woman sang, *Olav will be home soon, with enough gold to buy the moon.*

With the man's name now known, the spy rushed back to his merchant overlords. Victoriously, they hurried to the church and found the stranger at the top of the spire.

'Your name is Olav!' they boomed. 'Your name is Olav, you fool!'

Upon hearing his name, Olav lost his balance and fell. He died at the scene, and the town didn't have to pay up.

"What happened to his wife?" asked Angela.

"The townsfolk threw her down a well. The baby too."

Angela looked shocked. "You're joking!"

I laughed and nodded. "Yeah. Just made that last bit up. It doesn't say what happened to her." We finished our drinks and left the cafe.

There was a building down the road from the cafe. It once was the most feared establishment in Tallinn. As Angela and I approached the old KGB headquarters, we realised we had actually walked past it twice already, so nondescript was the building. One feature was particularly ominous though. Unlike every other building along the street, the ex-KGB Headquarters had its cellar windows bricked up. It wasn't hard to guess why.

7

According to our guidebook, Olde Hansa, just off the town square, offered medieval-style Estonian cuisine. We decided to try it, even though we knew it would be expensive.

Inside was suitably dark, lit only by candles. Draped over wooden benches were animal skins, and in the gloom, serving wenches carried jugs of ale and plates of meat. As we sat down, a waiter handed us wrapped napkins that contained cutlery.

"Here are your weapons!" she boomed. "Enjoy Olde Hansa!"

As a starter, I ordered dried elk meat. It came in a cloth bag tied with a piece of string. I stared at the contents. "Do you want a bit?" I said to Angela, as I put a strip of meat into my mouth. I began to chew on the tough leathery piece of elk, which tasted vaguely of beef. It wasn't really my cup of tea.

My main meal was even stranger. It was elk, boar and bear sausages, with an unusual side accompaniment of things from the forest. Brandishing my pronged weapon, I prodded them. We worked out it was a mixture of red berries, sauerkraut, turnip, and something unrecognisable with ginger in it. It was a truly hideous concoction. Where was Panicke, the pissed-up priest when we needed him? Perhaps a public execution might put a stop to this madness. I ate the sausages (which were actually really tasty) and the turnip, but left the rest. I washed it down with a bizarre tasting herbal beer, a meal of truly strange proportions. Nevertheless, I was still happy with my choice. It wasn't everyday a person got to eat elk, boar and bear in the same meal.

8

The next morning was our last in Estonia, and Angela and I decided to climb the town hall tower. At nearly two hundred feet, getting to the top would mean a gruelling clamber up a spiralling stone staircase. Regardless, we paid the entrance fee and then stopped to read the sign. *Entrance is at Your Own Peril*, it read. We climbed the first step.

At the half way stage, on a small platform, we stopped to catch our breath. I felt quite light-headed and could tell Angela was feeling the same. My thighs were burning, and my head was pounding.

We soon reached the summit though. Five or six people were already there, and all looked on the verge of cardiac arrest. Angela and I stopped at one of the viewing points and looked out across the red-roofed buildings of the old town. Tallinn was a truly beautiful little city. From where we stood, Estonia's capital was a hearty mixture of medieval Europe and imperialist Russia, all sprinkled with a hint of Scandinavian. The Russian element came mainly from a glorious cathedral with black and gold onion domes.

I stared down at the square, watching tiny people scurrying about. Then I raised my eyes to the more modern part of Tallinn, a section of the city we'd not even visited. Skyscrapers were shooting up, and shopping centres were opening everywhere. The cranes littering the horizon proved that Estonia was in a boom time.

"Not bad, is it," I said to Angela, "for a once forgotten outpost of the Soviet Union?"

After a few moments of gazing at one of the prettiest old towns we had seen, we headed back to the hotel to pack.

9

A few days later, I was sitting at home with a map of Europe in front of me. I wanted to research the next port of call on our adventure. Hungary was a possibility, as was Bulgaria, but the country that jumped out most was sitting over on the eastern portion of the map, tucked under Latvia. The country's name was Lithuania, the third of the Baltic nations.

After I'd priced up a few flights and hotels, I put my plan to Angela. She was reluctant at first, but finally agreed.

Secretly, I wondered how many former Soviet countries we could visit before Angela got sick of them. Perhaps six or seven would be a good number to aim for. But I decided to keep these thoughts to myself for the time being.

However, behind the scenes, something was brewing, which would take me off to another country first. A country that had not even existed before 1993. A country called Slovakia.

3. Four Men in Bratislava

Interesting fact: In 2000, George W. Bush mixed Slovakia up with Slovenia.

"Slovakia? Is that where that horrible movie was filmed?" asked Angela when I told her I was heading off to Bratislava for a two-day break with the boys.

Angela was right. *Hostel* made headlines for two reasons. One, because of its use of gratuitous violence, and two, it was supposedly set in Bratislava. The movie depicted Slovakia as a bleak, poor country, even though filming had taken place in neighbouring Prague. So disgusted were the Slovak tourist board that they offered an all-expenses paid trip for Eli Roth, the movie's writer and director, to visit their country, so he could see for himself how untrue his portrayal was. Roth declined.

It had been Phil's suggestion that we go off on a lads' holiday. He'd suggested somewhere cheap and off the tourist trail, and when I'd proposed the capital of Slovakia, he'd looked sceptical, accusing me of ticking countries off my turnip list. He quickly came around when I told him it was only two hours away from the UK, and a pint of beer would be less than a pound.

"What could be better?" I said to him.

Well, the plane for a start.

2

The four of us knew our budget airline flight would not epitomise comfort and luxury, but we did not expect vomit as part of the package. With no allocated seating, it was a free for all as everyone rushed up the aircraft's stairs in a mad dash to bag a decent seat. "Hurry up, lads," yelled Phil over the melee. "Push your way through. Every man for himself."

Ahead of me, my friend Michael bagged a window seat near the front. He flopped down, and Jon grabbed the seat next to him. Phil was about to get the third seat in that row, but was barged out of the way by a woman carrying a large bar of chocolate. In desperation, he lunged for the row behind, and managed to secure himself the window seat. I quickly followed, stamping my rear into the middle seat. A middle-aged man plopped down next to me. All around, people were rushing dementedly, pushing, banging, kicking and twisting as they fought their way along the scrum. A minute later, the madness subsided and the plane was full to capacity. A post-traumatic calm descended over the cabin.

"Shit!" exclaimed Phil, raising himself upwards because of something on his seat. When he'd hoisted himself sufficiently, we both looked to see. And there it was - a damp patch of fresh vomit. His window and armrest were splashed with the vile bile.

"Fuck's sake," he said as he slumped down.

3

Our hotel had a strip club on the top floor.

"Look," said Jon, ever the pragmatic. "Let's make a pact right now. We will not visit the top floor of our hotel. It's sad and seedy, and they'll rip us off anyway. Agreed?"

We all nodded, and with that decided, we went out for a night on the lash, delighted to find a plethora of friendly bars serving cheap bottles of Zlaty Bazant, the local brew. Three hours later, we were in the strip club.

We were sat by ourselves in a section of the dimly lit lounge. We had our own private stripper. We hadn't requested her presence, of course, but later found she was included in the hefty entrance fee we'd shelled out.

The young blonde gyrating in front of us was in the process of removing her bra, and I could see that Michael's lenses had already steamed up. By the end of the dance, a pair of flimsy knickers would be dangling from them.

4

Slovakia had never been a Soviet republic. Instead, it was a member of the *Warsaw Pact*, a six-country alliance that formed a buffer zone between the Communist East and the Capitalist West. The western borders of these nations formed the infamous Iron Curtain. All six were puppet states of the Soviet Union.

Slovakia had been one half of Czechoslovakia. When Germany took over parts of Czechoslovakia during the Second World War, they allowed Slovakia to become an independent country for the first time. Jozef Tiso became head of the newly created Slovak Republic.

Tiso was a Slovak who, in his early years, had trained to be a priest. He'd even served as a field curate during the First World War. Yet despite his early years as a man of the cloth, Tiso quickly became a loyal disciple of Adolf Hitler.

He wasted no time in enacting a law called the *Jewish Code.* In it, Slovak Jews could not own property, could not take part in sporting events, and could not attend secondary schools. When the order came from Germany to deport Jews to the death camps, Tiso signed it immediately. He even provided payment for their transportation.

By 1942, over fifty thousand Slovakian Jews had been deported, most of them to Auschwitz. Then suddenly, the movement of Jews stopped. There were a few reasons that explained this. One had to do with the Vatican. The Pope directly asked the Slovak authorities to stop the deportations. Another reason was the mass bribing of officials within Slovakia, orchestrated by groups of rich Jews. With cash in their hands, Slovak guards turned a blind eye when Jews escaped. A further cause was the presidential exemptions signed by Tiso himself. According to some reports, these numbered in the thousands. Public protests added to the mix too. When Slovak citizens found out that Jews were actually being killed, as opposed to being put to hard labour, many were horrified.

~ 27 ~

When dissent grew strong enough, Tiso ordered a halt to the deportations. Slovakia became the first Nazi-controlled state to do so.

The respite didn't last long. Angered by Tiso's meddling, Germany quickly annexed Slovakia and resumed the Jewish deportations. They allowed Tiso to remain in office, but his role diminished to that of a man signing papers and waving at crowds. When the Red Army conquered Slovakia in 1945, the Soviets arrested Tiso and charged him with Nazism. His only defence was that he did try to end the deportations, but this wasn't enough to save him. As the Soviets pointed out, Tiso was the only European leader to pay the Nazis to deport Jews. In April 1947, Joseph Tiso wore his clerical clothes for the last time as he headed for the gallows in central Bratislava.

Following World War II, Slovakia united with the Czech Republic to become Czechoslovakia. They remained together throughout Soviet rule and even for a short time afterwards. Both nations went their separate way in 1993, making Slovakia one of the youngest countries in the world.

For the four of us, we woke up on our first morning in the Slovakian capital nursing hangovers from hell.

5

We made our way to Saint Michael's Gate - the only medieval gateway that remained in the old town. It actually looked more like a clock tower to us.

"Jesus!" exclaimed Jon. "It's bloody hot!"

Jon suffered with the heat at the best of times. It probably had to do with the huge shock of black hair on his head. While the rest of us had begun (or in Michael's case finished) the process of going bald, Jon's hair was still sprouting in thick bushy waves from his skull, overheating his brain. With the July temperature already in the mid to high thirties, we knew he was going to suffer, especially when combined with his hangover.

"This gate is boring," said Phil, never one to appreciate the culture of a new city. But I happened to agree with him, and so instead, we headed for the central square.

Bratislava's central square was small but perfectly packaged, just like a medieval town ought to be. I could easily conjure up images of horses and carts passing through, or perhaps peasants haggling over bags of turnips with their hard-earned groats. The square's centrepiece was the Roland Fountain, commemorating a famous knight of the town. Later that evening, the area around the fountain would become home to various street performers, including jugglers, jazz musicians and dancers, but for now, we had the square more or less to ourselves.

The tallest building in the square was the town hall. It had a cannon ball embedded in its front wall, left as a reminder of the Napoleonic attack of 1809. Inside was a museum.

"Let's go in," suggested Michael, always one to seize the opportunity for a museum visit. "We might be able to get into the clock tower."

6

Old women ushered us around The History of Bratislava Museum, even though we hadn't asked for their assistance. Each of them said in thick accents that taking photos was against the rules. As we perused ancient pots, coins, manuscripts and stoneware, Phil turned to me. "As if I want to take a photo of this old shite."

We spotted some stone steps leading up to the actual tower, and left the pots behind. The women waited at the bottom, clearly not relishing the climb, and a few minutes later the four of us were enjoying some spectacular views of the central square. Pastel coloured buildings with large sweeping roofs graced the square, and behind them stood the spindly spire of Saint Martin's

Cathedral, the city's largest church. After catching our breaths, we headed down into the dungeon.

Medieval pits and cells were the first things we saw. Thankfully, the women decided to leave us alone again. We quickly came to a set of exhibits showing gruesome torture implements. "Look at this thing here," I said, pointing at a metal device resembling a pair of kitchen tongs with rounded cups at the end. "What do you reckon these were used for?"

"Squeezing testicles?" Phil quipped.

"No, the cups were probably filled with molten lead and then poured onto people's feet," stated Michael with an air of authority. His knowledge of historical titbits was legendary. We accepted his comment as Gospel.

All around the room were artists' impressions of torture, dismemberment, boiling and stretching, but the worst was of some wretched soul hanging upside down, legs suspended into a hellish V-shape. The demented artist had drawn the image with ghastly skill. It depicted a torturer armed with a saw, slicing his victim down the middle. Thank God it was in black and white. Besides, the terrible image led us to discuss how long a person could stay alive under such torment.

"Not sure," admitted Michael. "But during the French Revolution, someone did an experiment on how long a severed head could remain aware of its surrounding. It was about half a minute. Mind you, according to records kept, the person doing the investigation had to keep slapping the head to make the eyes open."

"Jesus wept!" Phil exclaimed. "I need some fresh air."

7

The 18th century Primate's Palace was located just behind the town hall. The pink building was famous for its Hall of Mirrors. It was where Napoleon and Emperor Francis had signed the Peace of

Pressburg treaty in 1805, an agreement putting an end to the Holy Roman Empire.

Phil spoke before I got the chance. "Look, Michael," he said. "I don't mind museums full of torture implements, but one full of tapestries and mirrors – I don't care!"

I nodded in agreement and so did Jon.

"Okay, how about the Blue Church?" asked Michael, studying the guidebook.

"And why is it called the Blue Church?" Phil asked with a sigh.

"Because it's blue," answered Michael. "You'll like it, I promise."

8

After a hefty hike, we reached the Church of Saint Elizabeth, more commonly known as the Blue Church. Built in the early twentieth century as a memorial to the daughter of a Hungarian King, it was covered in gorgeous pastel blue paint. Inside was just as good, blue everywhere, and we had to concede that Michael had been right about visiting it. Just above the entrance was a picture of a woman with some roses. It was Saint Elizabeth.

Elizabeth had been born in 1207, and was Bratislava's most famous Saint. Tending to the sick and needy of the city, she decided to convert her castle into a hospital. This really annoyed her family, especially her husband, Prince Louis of Thuringia, who thought it not fitting for a woman of Elizabeth's stature to be mixing with the poor. One day, he caught his wife with something hidden in her apron, and demanded to see what it was.

"It's only roses," Elizabeth said, even though it was bread for the poor.

"Show me," demanded Louis.

With no way to escape the situation, Elizabeth revealed the contents expecting the worst. Miraculously though, the bread changed into red roses. Thus the legend was born.

Despite the heat, the four of us made our way up to Bratislava Castle, a huge rectangular building with some pointy towers at each corner. The view was great, spanning the River Danube as well as the terracotta roofs of the old town.

During the summer months, tourists often took boat trips along the Danube to Vienna. It only took an hour, and if time had been on our side, we might have taken advantage of this. Instead, we left the castle and walked across the New Bridge towards the UFO Cafe, a gangly construction resembling a flying saucer set on top of a giant tripod. The Soviets had constructed it in the early seventies, but it was now a chic restaurant with amazing views of the city.

"The toilets are interesting!" said Michael.

"Why?" asked Jon, studying his bottle of Zlaty Bazant.

"See for yourself."

I was intrigued, and set off to investigate.

The three urinals consisted of steel buckets plumbed into the floor. The large window above the buckets offered an expansive vista of southern Bratislava (mainly dull apartment blocks), and I couldn't shake off the notion that if someone wanted to, they could use binoculars to view me at work. I quickly finished my tinkling, and peered suspiciously at the apartment blocks. I was looking for the telltale sign of sun glinting off a telescopic lens. Thankfully, I couldn't see any.

That evening as we sat enjoying another Zlaty Bazant, we pondered our trip to the Slovakian capital. The consensus was that we'd had a great time. And the general lack of mass tourism was the most appealing aspect of all. None of us saw any louts or drunken fools. In fact, there was a noticeable peacefulness about town. Not once did we hear the drunken wail of the Brit on holiday. It was all so much nicer than that.

Phil turned to me. "So where are you going next on your turnip tour?"

"Lithuania."

Michael nodded. "Yeah, these Eastern European countries are pretty good. Cheap and easy. Bratislava is better than I expected."

"Except for the flight in!" said Jon.

"Don't remind me," said Phil. "Vomit Air."

We finished our evening in a few more bars. I'd just crossed country number three from the list with number four soon to follow. It was like a mini quest, I thought. I could even give it a name, perhaps something like the Red Quest.

"Here's to Slovakia," said Phil, bringing me out of my musings.

We clinked glasses as the sun began to set on a gorgeous summer evening in Bratislava.

4. The Last of the Baltic Three

Interesting fact: Lithuanian children believe in the Easter Granny, the bunny only helps to paint the eggs.

I am nine-years-old, sitting in my classroom, waiting for the teacher to give out atlases. He tells us to open them onto the double-page spread showing Europe. When I do so, I see lots of peculiar countries with even stranger-sounding capital cities: Warsaw, Budapest, Bucharest, Minsk and Vilnius, all of them sounding mysterious and decidedly off-limits. But the most prominent feature is the thick black line splitting the map down the middle.

Mr McDermott tells us it is the Iron Curtain, and it separates the communists from the rest of us. I run my finger along its length, noting the countries on both sides, feeling a peculiar sense of excitement as I do so.

"The red countries," Mr McDermott explains, "are controlled by the Soviet Union. The likes of us will never be allowed to visit them."

How wrong that turned out to be. When the USSR formally dissolved itself on Christmas Day 1991, it marked the end of the Cold War, and the speediest loss of territory of any state in the history of the world.

2

I asked the middle-aged Lithuanian taxi driver parked outside Vilnius International Airport how much it would cost to go to the town centre.

"Sixty litas," he answered in deep Eastern European tones, his eyes not flinching a fraction of an inch.

I frowned. Sixty litas was about twelve British pounds, well over the odds for the short fifteen-minute journey. I decided to try haggling. By my side, Angela rolled her eyes.

"Thirty litas," I said with an air of feigned authority, doing my best to give the impression that trifling with me was a pointless endeavour. With my top lip arched theatrically, I awaited the man's answer.

"Sixty litas," he stated again. "That iz price." He turned back to his newspaper.

We got in, humbled by the presence of a master haggler, evidently trained in the fabric bazaars of deepest Marrakech.

3

Lithuania, the largest of the three Baltic nations, was the first Soviet Republic to declare independence.

In the early hours of 13 January 1991 (the same day that Latvian protestors were setting up barricades around Dome Square), Lithuanians gathered around Vilnius TV tower. The Soviet authorities sent in some tanks and soldiers to disperse them. The crowds refused to budge, and so the tanks fired blank rounds at them. That didn't work either, but some of the ammunition did manage to shatter some windows and deafen a few protesters.

Wondering what to do next, Soviet troops stood and watched as more people arrived. Then the order to fire live ammunition came.

At first, the Soviets fired above the crowd, but this simply caused the mob to surge forward. In response, tanks drove towards the protesters, crushing a 51-year-old local butcher and a 23-year-old woman to death. In the resulting melee, troops lowered their guns and fired into the crowd. Twelve people were killed, including two 17-year-old students.

Fearing news would get out about what they had done; the Soviets stormed the TV tower and shut down all transmissions.

However, sixty miles to the west, in the town of Kaunas, a local reporter caught wind of the events in Vilnius. He powered up his TV station and began broadcasting. Across the sea, a Swedish radio station picked up the transmission. After they heard it, they passed the news onto their central news agency. Soon after, the whole of Sweden knew what had happened, as did other Scandinavian countries. The news spread to Western Europe and America.

Meanwhile, in downtown Vilnius, thousands more people gathered. Many of them began building anti-tank barricades. By daybreak, 50,000 protesters were in place, singing and chanting independence songs. When the rest of the world woke up and found out what had happened in Vilnius, the Soviets had no choice but to back down. Less than two months later, Lithuania was an independent country.

4

It was a late October evening when Angela and I arrived in the Lithuanian capital, the start of my half-term break. After checking into the hotel, we wasted no time in heading outside. Walking along a side street towards the old town, we passed peeling, graffitied walls and the dirty window panes of sleazy strip clubs. "I'm not impressed so far," said Angela. "This looks seedy."

We passed another crumbling brown building and hurried onwards. From behind, we could hear the sound of a trolleybus making its way through the road system, but then quite suddenly, the graffiti thinned, and we entered a large square dominated by the town hall.

Amber shops, cosy-looking bars, and a whole line of restored buildings filled one side of the square, and Vilnius looked better.

"Okay...," said Angela. "This is looking more promising."

Further in the old town, we came to a Russian Orthodox Church, supposedly the resting place of some fourteenth-century Vilnius Martyrs.

The martyrs had been a trio of brothers caught preaching in a city full to the brim with pagans. Their punishment was to eat a pile of meat, even though it was an Orthodox fasting period. The men refused, and were duly tortured. After failing to repent their ways, the pagan hordes hanged the first brother and gave the remaining two the chance to give up their religion. They refused, and so they strangled brother number two and hung him from the same tree as his brother.

The third brother still refused to recant his Christian vows, and so the pagans dragged him into the wintry streets of Vilnius. There, they beat him with metal rods. Then they stripped him naked and poured ice down his throat. As if this wasn't bad enough, his ankles were broken and his ears and nose cut off. But still, the Christian would not die, and so they began to peel the skin from his head. This did the trick, and he finally stopped breathing.

Me, I'd have eaten the meat.

5

Angela decided she needed some tissues, so we entered a small general store just down from the Orthodox Church. Inside were a few people, one of whom was clearly drunk. In his late-twenties, the man was looking at a bottle of vodka. I stood near him while Angela perused some of the strange liqueurs on display. After swaying at the counter for a moment, the drunkard turned and spotted Angela.

He immediately lumbered towards her, mumbling something entirely incoherent. Without pause, I took action, inserting myself between the Lithuanian Lagerhead and my wife, and shoved him away. Simultaneously, the woman behind the counter began shouting at him. Bleary-eyed and grizzle-chinned, the man looked around in a confused manner before staggering towards the door. I puffed out my chest and watched his exit as testostcrone flowed through my mighty veins.

"Let's get a drink," I suggested as we left the shop. "I think I need one after that."

We settled on a bar along Pilies Street. Svyturys was the brand of lager, and costing 90p a pint, it tasted good: a fitting drink for the hero of the hour.

"To Lithuania," I toasted. "Country number four of the quest!"

Angela looked at me. "The quest?"

Shit, I thought. The altercation in the shop had clearly affected my brain. I put my pint down and looked up. "What?"

"You said: country number four of the quest."

I shrugged. "Did I? Well, you know what I mean. We've been to a few places in Eastern Europe, and it's like an adventure."

It was a pathetic attempt at deflection, and I could see Angela looked sceptical. She stared at me with a quizzical look on her face. "Come on," she said finally. "Let's get something to eat."

6

The next morning, it was time to see the sights of Vilnius properly. Thankfully, since my foolish outburst the previous evening, there had been no more talk of the quest. For that, I was grateful.

After wandering past an outdoor market selling plastic flowers, we came to the 16th century Gates of Dawn. Inside was a chapel containing an icon of the Virgin Mary that supposedly had mysterious healing powers. A line of worshippers was waiting to see it.

"What sort of miracles did it do?" asked Angela as we stared at the golden icon.

"The first had to do with a two-year-old boy," I answered. "He fell from a top-floor window and was badly hurt. His parents prayed to Mary, and lo and behold, a few days later he was cured."

"Hmm," said Angela. "Not very convincing."

"What about this one then? A few hundred years ago, some Swedish troops took over the city. A few of them mocked the painting, and one soldier shot it. It still has the hole in it somewhere. Anyway, not long after, some gates fell down and crushed some soldiers. The painting was getting its vengeance. A clear miracle."

Angela thought about this. "So the soldiers who got crushed, were they the ones who'd shot the picture?"

"No, just some random Swedish ones."

"So it's a rubbish miracle."

I called Angela a pagan.

7

We walked along Pilies Street until we came to Cathedral Square, home of the city's prime sight – Vilnius Cathedral. Constructed on the site of a pagan altar, it was large and white, with a huge bell tower just along from it. The Soviets had used the cathedral as a warehouse.

"What's going on over there?" I said to Angela. She quickly spotted the strange flower arranging competition. From what we could gather, each person had a small rectangle of soil to position flowers (and other vegetation) into whatever way took their fancy. One plot depicted a sun rising over a field. It looked effective. Another artist had utilised vegetables to create a picture of something that neither of us could work out.

On the eastern side of the square was a monument to the city's founder, Grand Duke Gediminus. He was wearing a fetching suit of armour and had a horse by his side. The Duke also had a tower named after him up a hill. We decided to go and see it.

Gediminus Tower was not big, but it was an important symbol for Lithuania, mentioned in numerous folk songs and poems. As we traipsed up the winding path towards it, we could see three white crosses on a nearby hill. According to legend, a bunch of pagans killed fourteen monks there in the 14th century.

"They should have called this city Paganville," I said. "I bet a day didn't go by without at least one Christian being boiled, hanged, pushed down a hill or cooked in a pot of molten lead."

The tower was three stories high and had a Lithuanian flag at the top. We climbed to the observation deck to have a look out across Vilnius.

"Look," I said. "We could have caught the funicular railway up here. All that hiking for nothing."

A few people were climbing out of the small carriage. None of them looked tired.

"The views are good though, aren't they?" Angela said, staring down over the northern side of the river. We could see skyscrapers, shopping malls, and a strange building with *Molesta* written on the side.

8

After catching the funicular back down, we walked to Lukiskio Square, which the Soviets had called Lenin Square. One side of the square featured a pleasant-looking white building that used to be the KGB Headquarters. Nowadays, it is the Museum of Genocide Victims.

It cost six litu each to enter the museum. Thick green doors with tiny spy holes formed the entrance to the cells. According to the information placards, there had been fifty cells originally, but by the 1960s, the KGB had reduced this number to twenty-three. Angela and I entered cell number one.

It was small, yet had once contained up to fifteen prisoners, all of them forced to sleep on the bare concrete floor.

"This is horrible," said Angela as we entered another cell called the confinement cell. The room was thin and dank-looking, coated in a hideous maroon-coloured paint scheme. A deep section covered most of the floor, except for the far end, which was slightly raised. Cold water had filled the recess, forming a shallow pool. This forced the near-naked prisoner to balance on the tiny dry section. If they slipped, or fell asleep, they would invariably fall into the freezing water.

Then we came to the padded cell. Inside, all the walls were padded and soundproofed. A black straight jacket hung on a stand near the back wall. We could only imagine the horrors going on when the room had been in operation. We headed down to the execution chamber.

9

The actual number of people shot to death by the KGB inside the execution chamber is believed to be over a thousand. Executioners killed the vast majority with a shot to the back of the head, but some prisoners had suffered badly before their deaths. Evidence from a mass grave discovered in the mid-90s, found dagger and axe wounds. Other bodies displayed head trauma caused by having their skulls squeezed between two flat, hard surfaces.

Most historians agree that most of the executions occurred between 1946 and 1960. For a short time in the 1940s, the KGB executed around fifty Lithuanian dissidents each day. These terror tactics worked well for the Soviets, because Lithuanian dissent soon subsided.

The execution chamber was a depressing concrete room. Some sections of the wall still had bullet holes in them, and a glass panel in the floor displayed some of the grim artefacts discovered in the mass grave - things such as glasses, shoes and bits of clothing.

"Well that was depressing," said Angela as we left the museum.

I nodded my head.

10

"Do you fancy seeing Frank Zappa?" I asked Angela after lunch.

"Frank Zappa? In Vilnius? Is he still alive?"

"I'm talking about his statue."

And so to lighten our mood, Angela and I took a detour through some decidedly dodgy backstreets of downtown Vilnius.

Erected in 1995, and designed by a sculptor who had once cast statues of Lenin, the monument to the American guitarist was in a run-down part of the city. Soviet-era apartment blocks filled the street, and once again, graffiti was everywhere. How the statue came into being was quite interesting.

After independence, Lithuania, like lots of former Soviet Republics, had a whole bunch of ugly communist statues dotted around. Most of them were removed, which left a job lot of nice plinths going spare.

A man by the name of Saulius Paulstys came up with a cunning plan for one of the plinths and founded the Lithuanian Frank Zappa Fan Club. With donations from his members, he commissioned the Zappa statue, and when it was ready to be unveiled, he organised a brass band to play some of the musician's hits. His statue became a hit, and Paulstys's fan club ballooned.

We stared up at the strange statue, featuring the musician's head set in a sombre pose. Both of us agreed it was a bizarre monument to have in Lithuania. Zappa was not even that famous in the country.

11

The next morning, we found a giant egg. In 2002, an angel supposedly hatched from it. The egg was in a small square around the corner from our hotel. It was sitting on a tall pedestal in its nest. Angela and I decided to find the angel.

It was in the Uzupis district of the city, just east of the old town. To get there, we had to cross over a small bridge with padlocks attached to the railings. Newly married couples had placed them there, symbolising that once the key had turned, no one could ever unlock the union. Angela thought it cute. We crossed the bridge and entered Uzupis, home of artists and romantics.

As well as coming up with the egg hatching insanity, every year, on 1 April, the residents of Uzupis declare their independence from Lithuania. With an army of twelve people, the Uzupis Republic sets up fake border crossings. 'Officials' check and stamp passports and everyone has a great time. The next day, the Uzupis Republic ceases to exist again.

We quickly came to the famous Angel of Uzupis. She stood upon a tall column, blowing a trumpet. We took a few photos, and then hatched a plan to see the ancient capital of Lithuania.

12

Angela and I approached the taxi driver. I gestured to my guidebook, and then pointed at a photo of Trakai Castle. I asked the man how much it would cost to get there.

The driver looked at the photo. "Trakai? I not sure. Iz long way." He rubbed his head. "But maybe I do it for one hundred and eighty litu. Take you there. Bring you back."

I looked towards Angela. I knew she wasn't keen on the idea of getting a taxi to some far-flung place in the middle of Lithuania. But a hundred and eighty litas was well within our budget.

"We want to stay at Trakai for two hours," I explained to the man. I showed him my watch and made a circular movement around the clock face twice. I wanted to be sure he'd come back at the right time. I dreaded to think how Angela would react if we missed our flight back to the UK. "And then you come back for us?"

"No, I wait in Trakai for you. Good, yah?"

Fantastic! We got in, our chauffeur putting the pedal to the metal. Half an hour later the taxi driver parked up, got his newspaper, and pointed to the castle. "Enjoy Trakai!"

Three lakes surrounded the castle. One of them, Lake Galve, translated as Lake Head. According to legend, it got its name after Grand Duke Vytautas, the founder of the castle, had decapitated an enemy and tossed the head into the lake. After that, the lake had supposedly developed a taste for human flesh. Nowadays, a narrow wooden bridge connects the island from the mainland. Angela and I were soon crossing over it.

The whole complex looked suitably medieval, all turrets and stony battlements. It was easy to imagine fair maidens spilling their golden locks from pointy turret windows, and noisy jousting going on inside the castle grounds. We were surprised to find we were the only people there.

After ambling around the castle, stopping every now and again to stare out over the tranquil lake, we headed back to the mainland, where we ordered some lunch in a nice restaurant.

"For our next city break," said Angela. "I was thinking maybe Naples. The weather in February should be okay, and it will be romantic. What do you think?"

Bloody hellfire was what I thought about that! I had to tread carefully though. Was Angela testing me to see what I'd say? Was her Italy idea really in response to what I'd blurted the previous day when I'd mentioned the quest? If so, then I couldn't say no to Naples, otherwise Angela would know I was developing a fixation with Eastern Europe. On the other hand, maybe her suggestion was genuine. And maybe once Naples was out of the way, the Red Quest would continue. I didn't know what to say.

"Well?"

I gathered my thoughts. "I think Italy would be great…" I said. "But so would somewhere like…oh, I don't know…Budapest. It's meant to be one of the most romantic cities in Europe." I had no idea whether that was true or not, but felt it was worth saying. "And it's famous for its cakes! Plus it will be cheaper than Naples

– you know what Italy's like for prices. I think we should save Italy for when the weather is really nice. But it's up to you. If you want to go to Italy, then I'm up for it."

Angela stared at me for a moment, and then looked down at her salad, absently moving it around with her fork. My innards coiled in turmoil.

Finally she looked up. "What is it about these Eastern European countries you like so much? I think you're getting a bit obsessed."

I snorted. "I'm not obsessed! They're just cheap. And they're different. And not many British people go to them. Plus, you've enjoyed them. I haven't heard much complaining from you."

"Yes I have enjoyed them. But that's not the point. What I'm saying is the only places you want to visit are in Eastern Europe. Why not Western Europe? Yes, they're a bit more expensive, but not by much. You nearly died when I suggested going to Italy. I could tell by your face."

I looked outside at the lake and castle. I didn't want Angela to see the blood draining from my cheeks. It was clear to me now that I could never tell Angela about the Red Quest. Not ever. Imagine her reaction if I came clean and said, *Yes I'm obsessed with Eastern Europe and in particular, the former Soviet states. Yes, I think I want to go to all of them. Is that all right, darling? A holiday in Belarus? Or how about Moldova? Oh, and by the way, we don't have time to visit places like Rome or Barcelona anymore. Not when Moscow and Minsk are there to visit.*

No, I couldn't say any of that and so instead kept silent. It was up to Angela now. The quest would continue, or the quest would fail. It was out of my hands.

"Tell me about Budapest," she finally said.

I breathed out slowly.

An hour later, we were at the airport for our flight back to the UK. The Red Quest was still on track.

5. Hungarian Goulash

Interesting fact: Hungary has the highest death rate by cancer in Europe.

The airport taxi driver was a pleasant young man. After chatting about our reasons for visiting Budapest, I noted his good English.

"I used to be a secondary school teacher," he told us. "I did three years and then gave up. I could not afford to live on money a teacher gets here in Hungary. So I became an au pair in London. I learn good English there. But then I return to Budapest to drive taxi. Here I am."

I asked about the recent demonstrations in Budapest. They had made the news in the UK. The taxi driver nodded. "The people don't trust the prime minister. They make protest around Parliament. It is a normal state of affairs in my country."

I nodded at his summing up. But at least the protests weren't as bad as the infamous uprising of 1956.

2

Unhappy with Soviet repression, 50,000 students, journalists and writers had marched upon Budapest's Parliament Building. The date was 23 October 1956.

The Soviet-backed leader of Hungary made a radio broadcast condemning the largely peaceful demonstrations. This spurred the crowds into taking more direct action. Soon 200,000 people were protesting, and some of them toppled a 30m high statue of Stalin. Only his hollow boots remained on the plinth.

Around the same time, another group of students entered a Budapest radio building. Once inside, they began broadcasting their demands to the communist government. The police stormed the building.

False rumours began to spread outside that the police had shot some of the students. With a hostile crowd on their hands, police units threw tear gas and began shooting for real. Quickly, they killed their first protester.

The crowd went berserk, setting police cars on fire and taking up arms. The police, unable to cope, retreated, leaving the city in anarchy. Hungary's government soon collapsed, and four days later, the leader of the rebellion, a man called Imre Nagy, formed an interim government. He organised a ceasefire. The world waited to see what the Soviets would do. They didn't have long to wait.

Red Army tanks rolled into Budapest a week later. The rebels didn't stand a chance. By the end of the week, more than two thousand people lay dead. Soviet forces captured and then executed Imre Nagy. Hundreds of other rebel leaders suffered the same fate. Fearing for their lives, thousands of Hungarians fled from their homes. In Budapest, the Soviets installed a new hard line communist government and then banned public opposition. They also prohibited any discussion of the uprising for thirty years. The Soviet's harsh actions quashed any burgeoning unrest in the other Soviet buffer states. No one would dare challenge the might of the Kremlin after that show of brutality.

3

The next morning was overcast and misty, giving the city a dull and listless hue. Angela and I left the warmth of the hotel and headed along Vaci Utca, one of the city's main pedestrian streets. As we walked towards the Danube, we noticed graffiti scrawled on many of the lampposts and walls.

"I really hate graffiti," Angela said as we passed a building covered in the stuff. Blue and purple scrawls and a crude painting of a robot kissing a dog made us shake our heads. Graffiti was an unpleasant fact in virtually every city we'd visited, and there was nothing we could do about it. But Budapest seemed worse than most. Wondering whether the Soviets had abided graffiti in their day, we continued walking.

The River Danube looked murky and cold. We stood and stared at its swells and currents before turning along a pedestrian footpath. A man was walking towards us. He seemed to be fiddling with his trousers.

I peered at the man, who was about thirty, wondering the same thing myself. I couldn't be sure what he was doing, but as he came closer, I saw he had his penis out. It hung limply in the cold weather. The man had a glazed expression on his face, and gave no indication that he was aware of our presence.

Angela spotted it too. "*Jesus Christ!* What's he doing?"

But it was obvious what the man was doing. The stream of urine was the biggest clue. He was covering himself in it, but seemed oblivious. He blithely walked past us without even glancing in our direction.

"Well that was nice," said Angela, looking back at the man.

"Needs must," I countered.

We walked on until we reached a large bridge spanning the Danube. It was the famous Chain Bridge.

4

The Chain Bridge is a major link between the two sections of the city. Buda is the hilly, medieval side, famous for landmarks such as Gellért Hill, the Royal Palace and the Fishermen's Bastion. Pest is famous for its shops, government buildings and banks. It wasn't until 1873 that the two halves merged.

Angela and I stood at one end of the Chain Bridge (on the Pest side), staring at the pair of lions guarding the entrance. Later that night, hundreds of lights would illuminate the bridge, but for now, it looked almost ethereal in the mist of the cold morning. It was hard to believe that the Germans had destroyed it during World War II. We took the bridge's footpath to Buda.

The Royal Palace dominated Buda's skyline. After taking the funicular railway up to it, we walked around the impressive grounds, stopping at a statue of a fine and dandy gentleman called Prince Eugene of Savoy. Apparently, he was one of Europe's most successful military commanders.

We walked over to a platform to view the city beneath us. Low-lying translucent clouds blanketed most of Pest, but we could still make out the bell towers of Saint Stephen's, the third tallest building in Hungary. And despite the cold and mist, I couldn't suppress a wry smile. I was in the fifth country of the quest! We walked towards a large fairy-tale castle complex of pointy turrets and white walls called the Fisherman's Bastion.

5

The Fisherman's Bastion was so-called because of 18th century fishermen who had once defended the castle walls. People were crawling all over the white battlements, posing in alcoves, or wandering the many trails up and around it.

"Will you stop saying it like a swear word," said Angela as I rolled the word bastion off my tongue for the tenth time. "And besides, what is a bastion anyway?"

"I think it's the part of a fortress that sticks out," I answered. "Stupid bastion."

Just behind the bastion was the Mátyás Church, a 13th century structure that possessed a great big spire and a nice colourful roof. The Ottomans turned it into a mosque when they'd been in charge. They also whitewashed the frescos and ripped out all the furnishings.

In a small square outside the church was a statue of Saint Stephen, the first King of Hungary.

King Stephen had been an unhappy man in the last years of his life. A fierce boar had killed his only son, and in his search for an heir, Stephen soon realised there were no real contenders among his relatives. A few people wanted the job, of course, but with

King Stephen thinking them all incapable, things were at a stalemate. Enter the evil villain.

Duke Vazul was King Stephen's cousin, and believed himself to be a candidate for the job because even his name sounded evil. Stephen didn't like him though, and so to break the deadlock, Vazul did what any wicked scoundrel would do: he conspired to assassinate the king.

Unfortunately, someone foiled the plot, and King Stephen had the duke arrested. After being tortured in the royal dungeon for a while, Vazul admitted to masterminding the conspiracy, and was sentenced to death. Guards killed him by gouging out his eyes and then pouring molten lead into his ears.

King Stephen died soon afterwards anyway, and one of his cousins took the crown. 45 years later, Stephen was canonized by the Pope and became the patron saint of Hungary.

Below Saint Stephen's statue, two men were dressed in traditional costume. Each had a large bird of prey sitting on their arm. After a small crowd had gathered, the men put on a show, primarily involving the birds catching pieces of meat on the end of some string.

"Come on," I said to Angela. "It's time to find some goulash."

6

Italy has pizza, Japan has sushi, France has frog legs, but Hungary has goulash! We found a nice little eatery in the old town just along from the Fishermen's bastion and ordered a bowl each.

The name 'goulash' literally translates as 'herdsman.' It was named after the people originally responsible for cooking up the delicious paprika-tinged meat stew. In their day, cooks had used iron kettles hung over open fires, but by the 19th century, Hungarian nobles had acquired a taste for the dish, and it was prepared in pots. By the mid-20th century, goulash was the most popular meal in the country.

A young waitress brought two bowls of hot goulash to our table, and it smelt good. I wasted no time tucking in, scooping up a potato with some stew. It tasted delicious, and I could understand why it had become so popular. Just a hint of spice with a juicy piece of beef.

"Why haven't you cooked me this in England?" I asked, after slurping down another mouthful.

"Get lost! You never asked me to!"

"By the way, I wonder if you can answer this question. Which 'G' is the national dish of Hungary?" It was a question I'd heard on the *Weakest Link* TV show.

"Duh! Goulash."

"Exactly. But do you know what the contestant said?"

"Go on…?"

"Goats."

7

After crossing over the Chain Bridge again, Angela and I continued up Andrassy Street until we came to number 60. It was the House of Terror. The large building had been the Nazi headquarters during the war, and then afterwards, the home of the communist secret police. Nowadays, the building hosts a museum.

Several floors made up the House of Terror Museum. Angela and I started on the second floor, walking through rooms displaying different periods of dark history. Videos of people who had lived through the oppression were stark, frank, and often shocking.

In one room, set aside for life under Nazi rule, we noticed an elderly couple pause to watch a video. After just a few moments, the woman covered her eyes and moved away, her husband quickly following. When we got to the TV screen, the grainy footage showed tractors shovelling bodies out of a gas chamber. It was horrible to look at, and I couldn't blame the woman for not wanting to watch. We both wondered whether they had known anyone who had died during Jewish oppression.

Other photos and information placards offered more morsels of misery. Towards the latter stages of the Second World War, Arrow Cross members (Hungary's Nazi Party) carried on persecuting Budapest's Jews even though the Germans had left. Sometimes they killed people individually, but on some occasions, they would tie several Jews together and shoot one of them. Then they would throw everyone into the Danube to drown.

On the first floor, among more bleak rooms, was a courtroom. A few people were already sitting on wooden benches staring at a TV screen. A black-and-white documentary showed the trial of Imre Nagy, the leader of the 1956 rebellion. Angela and I sat down to watch it, a stark piece of footage from one of Hungary's darkest periods.

Down on the ground level, the most striking display was of a large Soviet tank, and behind it, a large memorial to all the people who had died inside the building, their black and white portraits stretching from floor to ceiling. Atmospheric lighting and eerie music added to the effect, creating a chilling and depressing mood.

We came to the basement floor, easily the worst section of the museum. Tiny prison cells, torture rooms (including one room where a prisoner had to sit constantly in water), and the gallows room were the grim sights on offer. Both Angela and I felt the same feelings of horror that we'd experienced inside the Genocide Museum in Vilnius.

Just before we left the House of Terror, we walked through a section called the Walls of Victimizers. Photos of Hungarian nationals who had either been members of the Arrow Cross Party or the AVO, the local version of the KGB, hung on the wall. As we looked at the faces and dates, we realised some of them would still be alive, possibly even living in Budapest.

I turned to Angela. "I wonder what their children or grandchildren think of this museum. I wonder if they've ever been here. I wonder if they even know."

The exit to the museum was a clever thing. In direct contrast to the depressing exhibits in the main sections, it showed colourful photos and smiling faces. Joyous scenes from Hungary's independence celebrations presented a country upbeat and certainly not broken by half a century of occupation. They helped raise our sombre mood.

Hungary's road to independence began in May 1989 with a peculiar event. The barbed-wire fence it shared with Austria was removed. Thousands of Czechs and East Germans on holiday in Hungary began illegally crossing through. The world wondered what Moscow would do. The last time Hungary had showed any discord, they'd sent in the tanks, but this time Gorbachev sat back and did nothing. Soon after, the communist government of Hungary allowed free elections. The People's Republic of Hungary became the Republic of Hungary.

8

"I want to try some Hungarian cake!" Angela announced as we headed back towards the centre of Pest. We'd read that Gerbeaud's Patisserie was famous for its coffees and cakes, and twenty minutes later, we were eating a delicious slice of cake each, in the surrounds of 19th century opulence.

Emil Gerbeaud, the founder of Gerbeaud's Patisserie, was from a Swiss confectionary family. He'd made his name in Paris, whipping up scrumptious butter creams, shortcakes and crèmes. Gerbeaud's cakes and fancies took the confectionary world by storm. He became so famous that he received the *Legion of Honour* in Paris.

In 1882, a Hungarian confectioner called Henrik Kugler found out about Gerbeaud. Kugler offered him a job in Budapest, which he accepted. When Kugler died, Gerbeaud took over the business, and the patisserie took on his name.

"This is delicious," said Angela, sampling a tiny piece of Royal Chocolate Cake, created from only the highest quality and freshest ingredients. With tall chandeliers and old-fashioned furniture, it was easy to image 19th century ladies of leisure stopping by for an afternoon strudel or baked cheesecake. "And with that goulash we had earlier, I think Hungary might be about the best place for food yet."

Afterwards, satisfied with our cakes and coffee, we headed outside to take a late afternoon stroll to Market Hall, the largest food market in Budapest.

9

European markets are always great fun, and this one was no different. Long sausages of every description hung from stalls, presided over by men in white overalls and bushy moustaches. Pigs' trotters, huge lolling tongues, and unrecognisable slabs of white stuff that we assumed was animal fat, were on display in the extensive market hall.

"Did you know Zsa Zsa Gabor was born in Budapest?" I remarked as we perused another stall, this one offering a range of cheeses. "And so was the man who invented the Biro pen." Angela nodded, faintly interested in my recall of facts about Budapest. "And that's not all, Erno Rubik, inventor of the Rubik Cube, was born here as well."

"Was he? Please shut up."

We left Market Hall as night began to fall over the city. Across the river, we could see the statue of Saint Gellert, his vast monument perched high upon the hillside. It was a tribute to Bishop Gellért, an eleventh century figure supposedly murdered on the site. Mad pagans had put him inside a spiked barrel and then rolled him down the hill to the Danube. But at least he had a good statue. The bishop was standing in front of a curving colonnade holding a crucifix. It looked impressive with its nighttime illuminations. We called it a day and headed back to the hotel.

10

The next morning, our last day in Budapest, we decided to see two things we'd missed. First was the Parliament building, Hungary's largest structure. During Soviet times, a red star had adorned its gigantic dome. It reminded us a little of London's Houses of Parliament due to its spiky gothic architecture.

Next to the huge building, on a small piece of greenery, was a small statue of a man sitting down. Droplets of water hung from his nose, making his forlorn face seem even more miserable. His name was Attila Jozsef, a famous Hungarian poet. His story is one of tragedy.

Born in 1905, to a factory worker father and a peasant mother, Attila didn't stand much of a chance. Dad absconded when he was three-years-old, leaving his mother to provide for him and his two elder sisters. Times were hard, and his mother couldn't afford to feed them all. She put Attila up for fostering.

Things deteriorated quickly, because Attila's new guardians treated him cruelly. Things got so bad that young Attila escaped. He returned to his mother, who reluctantly accepted him back, but she died soon after.

In his adulthood, he tried supporting himself by selling poetry, but started displaying signs of schizophrenia. Never marrying, but often falling in love with the women treating him for his condition, things continued to spiral out of control for Attila. On the 3rd December 1937, aged just 32, he laid himself across a railway track until a passing train killed him.

"Well that was a nice story," said Angela after I'd told it to her. "That's cheered me up no end. Thanks."

We caught a taxi up to Gellért Hill to visit the Citadel. During the Middle Ages, witches celebrated their Sabbath on the hill, but today, the area contains residential houses belonging to the affluent of Buda.

The Citadel is a major tourist draw, mainly due to the gigantic Soviet monument on the top. The Liberation Monument is one of the few survivors of the statue cull following independence.

Constructed by the Russians as a tribute to troops who had died fighting the Germans, the forty-metre tall woman (the same length as a Boeing 737) stood proud and mighty, holding a gigantic palm leaf of victory. At her base, two equally proud-looking statues represented good and evil. We stared up, taking in the sheer Sovietness of the monument. But it was soon time to leave.

"Right, Angela, that's it," I said as we traipsed back down the path leading to some waiting taxis. "Time to go home. So what did you think of Budapest?"

"I enjoyed it," said Angela. "A bit overcast for my liking, but much better than I thought it was going to be. And I loved the food. I didn't expect that."

"Yeah, I'm looking forward to some goulash back home."

We walked in quiet contemplation until we reached a taxi. After climbing in, I decided to question Angela about where to go next. I wanted to get in early before any talk of Italy came around again. "I know we've not even left Budapest, but—"

"I think we should go to Moscow."

I thought I misheard Angela. Had she actually said she wanted to go to Moscow? As in the capital of Russia?

"Chloe at work was telling me about it," continued Angela. "She and her husband went there last month and really enjoyed it. She asked whether we'd been, and when I said no, she told me we had to go. So I quite fancy it. What do you think?"

I nodded like a galoot. My mind began to swim with the possibility of visiting the capital of Russia, the motherlode of the former Soviet Union! I almost whooped for joy.

"I thought you'd be pleased."

As we drove through the centre of Budapest, I couldn't stop smiling. The Red Quest was about to enter a new level. *Moscow!*

6. Mother Russia

Interesting fact: Moscow has more billionaires than any other city.

Phil put his drink down and stared at me closely. "Tell me something. Are you planning to visit every former Soviet Republic? Because it looks that way to me."

"Maybe," I said tentatively. I didn't want to tell Phil, *yes,* in case saying it aloud jinxed things somehow.

"*I knew it!* I was telling Julie you were trying to get to all these weird countries, and she didn't believe me."

"They're not weird, they're just different."

"They're weird, trust me. But forgetting that for now, after Russia, how many countries will you have been to?"

"Six," I answered.

Phil took a large slurp of his beer and then gave the satisfied burp of the seasoned beer drinker. "Out of how many?"

"Thirteen."

Phil's eyes widened a fraction. "Thirteen? There's more than that, isn't there?"

"Yeah, but I've decided to concentrate on just the ones in Europe. The countries in Asia, like Kazakhstan and Uzbekistan, are too far."

"Kazakhstan?" Phil said, grinning. "That's where Borat's from, isn't it?" He had a devious look about him. "You've got to go to Kazakhstan!"

"I'd love to," I answered truthfully. "But it would cost a fortune."

"But if your plan is to visit all these old Soviet countries, then you've got to go! You can't be half-arsed, Jason. Think about it, anyone can go to the ones in Europe – they're easy – even I've been to a few - but only someone with dedication can go the extra mile and fly to Kazakhstan."

I laughed and shook my head. Apart from anything, what would Angela think? *Hello, love, pack your bikini, we're off to Kazakhstan.* No, I had to be practical about things. Flights to Asia were hellishly expensive, and besides, some countries over that part of the world sounded a bit dangerous.

Tajikistan, for instance. Being the country north of Afghanistan, it was a major transit route for heroin. Angela wouldn't want to go there, and I wasn't sure whether I did, either. Even places like Armenia and Azerbaijan sounded like they had an edge to them. Wasn't there a ceasefire in place or something? How would Angela react if we got shot? Not well, I suspected.

Phil was still smiling. "If you don't go to Kazakhstan, then it seems a bit of a cop out to me, that's all I'm saying."

I sat back and brooded.

2

Getting to Russia was not as straightforward as the other places Angela and I had been to. For a start, we had to obtain visas before travel, which meant sending our passports to the Russian Embassy in London.

"They want a letter of invitation," I told Angela after I'd checked the embassy's website. "From someone in Russia."

In the end, I managed to persuade our hotel in Moscow to write me this invitation letter, but only after I'd agreed to pay them for the service. That sorted, I filled in the onerous application form, wrote out a postal order for the fees, and then sent it all off to London.

A week later, our passports returned containing newly minted Russian visas. They took up a whole page. I was intrigued when I discovered the embassy had printed our names in Cyrillic, and so spent the next few days learning the strange alphabet.

H meant 'n', P meant 'r', C meant 's', a backwards N meant 'i', and a backwards R made a 'ya' sound. Restaurant was spelt РЕСТОРАН, and Russia was spelt РОССИЯ.

3

Without Moscow, none of the countries on my list would have existed in their present form. For decades, Moscow was the epicentre of the communist world with its tentacle-like influence affecting the lives of millions.

Endless spy stories originated from the Soviet Union, and most of them were set against a grainy and wintry Moscow, with shadowy figures in fur hats and thick-collared overcoats furtively searching for microfilm.

After negotiating passport control at Domodedovo Airport, I could feel my excitement growing. We negotiated the signs (with me reading Cyrillic) and managed to board a train. Forty minutes later, we arrived at Paveletsky Station, where we came face to face with the city's infamous taxi drivers. Hordes of them were waiting in the arrival hall chasing down stray passengers. With a determined glint in our eyes, we passed them and headed outside into the searing heat.

It was like being in a furnace, bone dry and scorching. The sun was sizzling any exposed areas of skin. No wonder vagabonds were throwing themselves into fountains. We could even taste the heat, a searing flavour of car fumes and bubbling concrete.

We spotted a lone taxi. A moustached man sat inside reading a newspaper. He looked up as we approached, a cigarette dangling from his lip. Then another man arrived on the scene.

Ignoring the newcomer, I handed the taxi driver a piece of paper with our hotel address written in Cyrillic. Almost immediately, the other man tried to grab it. An intense argument broke out in thick Russian, forcing Angela and me to wait in total confusion.

Pulling and froing of my piece of paper ensued, but a minute later it died down and the victorious taxi driver ushered us into the back seat of his prized vehicle. The other man walked away, shaking his head. Feeling slightly uneasy, we climbed inside the battered old Lada.

"What was that about?" whispered Angela as she searched for her seatbelt.

"God only knows," I replied, noting without surprise that seatbelts were not included. And then we were off, driven by a maniac with no regard for any other person on the road.

Insane swerving, lunatic speeding, and then some screeching of brakes happened within seconds of setting off. The car threw us sideways and then a split second later, thrust us backwards into our seat as the driver jostled for position on the Moscow highway. At one point, I thought I caught a glimpse of Saint Basil's Cathedral, but before I could get my bearings, the car screeched to a sudden halt, narrowly missing the vehicle in front. We lunged forward in terror. Twenty hellish minutes later, we arrived at the hotel. Breathing a sigh of relief, I paid the man his precious roubles. We had arrived in Moscow!

4

The next morning, Angela and I left the hotel and walked down the road to the famous Bolshoi Theatre. Built in the 1850s, it was the place where Tchaikovsky had premiered *Swan Lake*. But we didn't really care about the theatre – we had bigger fish to fry, namely Red Square.

Just the name conjured up images of Sovietness. We'd both seen it on TV countless times growing up, and now we were about to enter the famous place ourselves.

"How do we get in?" asked Angela, breaking my feelings of childish glee.

I shook my head. There didn't seem to be any obvious entry point to the square, and so we ended up walking around for a bit until we spotted a queue. A man in uniform, wearing a huge dinner-plate cap, was in charge. We joined the back of the line and every few minutes the man allowed a few people in. Soon it was our turn.

We quickly realised we were not heading into Red Square, but to Lenin's Mausoleum. A guard shepherded us into the entrance of the small brown building. Darkness engulfed our senses as soon as we stepped inside. After a moment, our eyes adjusted, and we could see another guard directing us down some steps. At the bottom, we found ourselves walking single-file around the edge of a dimly lit room. In the middle was the tomb of Lenin.

All chattering ceased and everyone stared at the embalmed body of a man who had died in 1924. The chamber was cold, which was actually quite nice after roasting in the sun outside, but there was still an undeniable air of eeriness. As we shuffled past Lenin, I couldn't quite shake off the notion I was staring at a waxwork and not the actual body of a real man. And then we were out, back into the heat. We'd been inside for perhaps two minutes.

5

Finally, we found the entrance to Red Square, but instead of military parades, the square was full of tourist hordes. They were everywhere, except for the roped-off areas guarded by unsmiling police officers.

Just past the entrance were a trio of babushkas peddling flowers and dolls. More stout ladies staffed some toilets, looking every inch the proper Russian matriarchs we'd imagined. "I bet they won't let you stare at their turnips!" said Angela.

The babushkas were in direct contrast to young Russian women, because one word described them: gorgeous. They reminded me of

Anna Kournikova, the tennis player. All were dressed as if they were about to hit the nightclubs, even though it was only midday.

"Jesus, this temperature is insane." I said, as we headed into a shaded part of the square. Yet despite the heat and crowds, we couldn't help but be impressed. Everywhere we looked were grandiose buildings, impressive towers and colourful churches. Along the square's eastern edge was the massive GUM department store, the only outlet not to suffer from shortages during the Soviet Era. We walked past it towards Red Square's most famous cathedral.

6

Saint Basil's Cathedral was as iconic in the flesh as it was in pictures and film. It was a remarkable building, easily the most popular tourist attraction in Moscow. Its onion domes caught a person's eye first, the striped candy design offering a kaleidoscope of mesmerising colours. If ever an image deserved to epitomise Russia, then surely Saint Basil's was it.

"It's the most beautiful building I've ever seen," I said, as we stood staring at the construction before us. Angela nodded, unable to tear her eyes away from the thing.

Black Mercedes lined the streets of downtown Moscow or else sped past with a screech of rubber. The young and trendy sat about in parks or cafes soaking up the sun. But on the periphery of the affluence were the unfortunates.

We relocated to a bench to enjoy the view of the towers and walls surrounding Red Square. Angela and I watched an old man shuffle over to a litterbin. After rooting around, he grabbed a McDonald's cola carton and pulled off its plastic lid. After smelling the contents, he deemed it okay and noisily sucked the remnants through the straw. Then he wandered off, a plastic bag his only companion. We watched him go, shuffling past a trio of young women. To them, he was invisible.

"I think," I said with a grin, "It's time to see the Kremlin."

7

The Kremlin was another name that could conjure up old-Soviet imagery. Instead of being the haunt of secret service agents though, the largest medieval fortress in the world was actually a complex full of beautiful palaces, golden cathedrals, and the official residence of the Russian President.

The imposing Kremlin Walls and Towers surrounded it. Inside, strategically placed guards were making sure tourists never strayed off the official tour line. But the sights were gorgeous, and it was hard to believe that when Napoleon had occupied the Kremlin for a week in 1812, he'd wanted to blow the place up. In the end though, the rain extinguished most of the fuses placed by his departing troops.

Angela and I stared up at the Grand Kremlin Palace, formerly the Czar's residence. As its name suggested, it was massive and grand, with an expansive green roof.

The Kremlin was also the place that saw the final lowering of the Soviet flag. This historic event took place on Christmas Day 1991, but the breakup of the Soviet Union actually began in the late 1980s when Mikhail Gorbachev became the General Secretary of the Communist Party.

Gorbachev's policy of openness, known as *Glasnost,* quickly ended up having unintended repercussions, especially with regard to the media. Newspapers and TV could report on all sorts of things, including poor housing, alcoholism, crimes committed by Stalin, and even the mishandling of the 1986 Chernobyl disaster.

In 1988, Gorbachev became president, and things got worse. As well as the press creating havoc, the countries of the Warsaw Pact were causing problems by holding democratic elections. But Gorbachev sat back and allowed them! The West could hardly believe it, and nor could large sections of Gorbachev's government. By the end of 1989, Poland, Hungary, Romania, Bulgaria, East Germany and the Czech Republic were independent.

Then the first independence protests broke out in some of the actual Soviet republics. At first Gorbachev opposed these movements, but as they gathered in strength, he sat back and did nothing again, as dictated by his policy.

To many, Gorbachev had lost the plot, especially when Latvia, Estonia and Lithuania actually declared themselves independent. How many more republics would go before the rot stopped? Why wasn't Gorbachev stepping in to save the Empire? Like a story from a Tom Clancy novel, a shady conspiracy began.

8

The Chairman of the KGB led the plot, quickly recruiting other high-ranking communists into his fiendish scheme.

In August 1991, while Gorbachev was on holiday in the Crimea, the plotters met. Then they flew to the Crimea and boldly asked Gorbachev to resign. He refused, and so the conspirators ordered guards to hold him under house arrest while they flew back to the Kremlin.

Once there, the plotters declared a State of Emergency in Moscow. It was a coup d'état! They banned all newspapers (except state-sanctioned publications), stating that the 'Dignity of the Soviet Man must be restored.' The next day, tanks and paratroopers rolled into Red Square.

The citizens of Moscow were wondering what was going on. Hoping to allay people's concerns, one of the coup leaders gave a press conference. He lied and said that Gorbachev was resting.

Meanwhile tanks moved towards the Parliament Building (full of Gorbachev's supporters), and in the early hours of 21 August 1991, they attacked it. Three people died. Worried at these events, the conspirators ordered the troops to pull out of Moscow immediately. They also told the guards holding Gorbachev to let him go.

Gorbachev returned to the Kremlin, and one of the first things he did was reopen the media. Then he recognised the independence of the three Baltic Nations. He also arrested all the conspirators, except for one man called Boris Pugo, who had committed suicide the moment the coup d'état had failed.

But Gorbachev couldn't stem the tide of other republics declaring independence. Three months after the failed coup, all but four Soviet Republics were independent, with the rest about to follow. Under this backdrop, Gorbachev formally resigned as President of the Soviet Union. It was Christmas Day 1991. While I'd probably been having a glass of Bailey's, or perhaps enjoying a turkey sandwich, the Hammer and Sickle lowered for the final time over Moscow. The unthinkable had happened: the Soviet Union dissolved. Boris Yeltsin became the first president of a democratic Russia. A new era began.

<h1 style="text-align:center">9</h1>

During the couple of hours we spent inside the Kremlin, Angela and I visited all the famous attractions: the golden-domed cathedrals, the Tsar Cannon (one of the biggest cannons ever produced) and the Czar Bell (with its missing chunk). We had a wander past the famous Bell Tower and goggled at all the glinting gold. We eventually left and headed into the famous Moscow Underground.

After buying a ticket for a few roubles, we entered the barriers and descended a long escalator into the bowels of Moscow. The station we were in was called Revolution Square, just off Red Square. As we reached the bottom, we could hear the whoosh of trains as they sped along the platforms.

The Moscow Underground is famous for its subterranean artwork. It began appearing during Stalin's rule when he ordered architects to incorporate designs representing Soviet brilliance. Soon, metro stations were full of reflective marble walls and spectacular chandeliers, often with statues and other bombastic artwork.

Red and yellow marble arches graced Revolution Square station, together with 76 sculptures, including soldiers, athletes, farmers and children - all industrious citizens of the Soviet Union. But the most famous sculpture was of a guard and his dog. Rubbing the dog's nose was supposed to bring good luck and judging by the shine on the mutt's snout, plenty of people had already done this.

A large portrait of Stalin had once graced the station. In most of Moscow's metro stations, paintings of Stalin heavily featured, always high up on the walls, encouraging the casual observer to gaze upwards, subconsciously viewing Stalin as a God. After a good look around, and a spot of nose rubbing ourselves, we boarded a train bound for Lubyanka Square, home of the former KGB Headquarters.

10

The massive golden-bricked building that had once housed the dreaded KGB headquarters dominated Lubyanka Square. Inside it, secret service agents monitored the movements and activities of all its citizens (and of course, any visitors to Moscow).

It was a great block of a building, originally used as an insurance office, but after the Bolshevik Revolution of 1917, it began its more sinister life. Angela and I gazed up at the third floor, the home of secret police chiefs, including men like Yuri Andropov. Andropov had championed sending tanks to crush the Hungarian Uprising of 1956. Following that particular deed, he'd gained promotion to Chairman of the KGB.

The lower floor had been the KGB prison. One famous inmate was the man to inspire James Bond. His name was Sidney Reilly, otherwise known as the *Ace of Spies*.

11

Possibly born in Odessa (Ukraine) in 1873, something happened in his early twenties that caused Reilly to fake his own death. Afterwards, he sought illegal passage to Brazil, where he began to call himself Pedro.

After taking up a few menial jobs, he then landed himself a comfortable position as a cook, working for some British Intelligence officers who were conducting an expedition through the jungle. During this adventure, some natives attacked the party, but Reilly/Pedro saved the day by fighting them off. As a reward, he was given a British passport, 1500 pounds, and a free ticket to England. He set sail almost immediately, and when he arrived, Pedro became Sidney Rosenblum.

Living in London, Sidney made a living by selling miracle cures, but also gained extra cash from being an informant to the British Secret Service. Described as well-manicured, preferring good suits, and having neat black hair, he probably cut a dashing figure in downtown London. Other descriptions weren't so kind, however, noting his cruel expression and droopy bottom lip. Despite this, he still managed to find himself a wife and changed his name again, this time to Sidney Reilly. It was around this time that Sidney became a spy.

Using his British passport, he travelled to Russia, taking note of oil deposits for his British bosses. After a spot of espionage in Paris, he relocated to Germany, where he managed to steal a prototype engine part from an aircraft. He did this in a most cunning way: he attended an air show and waited for the plane in question to crash, as they inevitably did in those days. Somehow passing himself off as a pilot, he managed to remove the engine part from the wreckage without anyone noticing, and replaced it with a similar-looking part. After detailed drawings had been made, Reilly infiltrated the hangar and switched it back again.

His next mission sent him to a Baltic port in Germany. This was an even more audacious scheme. Disguised as a local ship worker, Reilly got a job as a welder. As part of this ruse, Reilly learned to weld. His real job though was to gather intelligence of weapon manufacture. A foreman heard him rummaging one day and went to investigate. Reilly strangled the man and escaped with the plans.

Next, he upped the ante even further by plotting to assassinate Lenin. Despite careful planning, the scheme failed, and Reilly was identified as the leader. He fled the country as fast as he could via Finland and arrived safely back in London.

In Moscow, there was a media storm. The Soviets stated that if Reilly ever stepped foot on their soil again, he would be executed. Despite this, Reilly carried on spying in the Soviet Union, and even managed to seduce a Soviet minister's wife to obtain information about weapons.

Sadly, Reilly's luck ran out when undercover agents captured him at the Soviet Border in 1925. They bundled him straight to Lubyanka Prison to face interrogation and torture. After he had 'confessed,' the KGB took Reilly to a secluded forest and shot him.

His legacy has proven compelling. With his fondness for gambling, his linguistic ability, and his immense skill at seducing women, it was no wonder Ian Fleming decided to create a character based upon the Ace of Spies.

12

Though our hotel was quite upmarket, mainly catering for businessmen, it still seemed to encourage prostitution. As soon as Angela and I entered the hotel bar, we spotted a trio of ladies working the room.

As we sipped our drinks, the women tried catching the eye of any stray men. At one point, one of the girls, an attractive blond, wearing a clingy white cocktail dress, stood up and strutted a few steps. When she was sure she had some male attention, she bent over, made a show of adjusting her high-heels, and wriggled as much as she could. My eyes swivelled back to Angela, who was shaking her head.

"Pervert," she said.

13

The next morning we caught the train to the airport for our flight home. In the check-in queue, we got talking to a man in his late-fifties who was standing behind us. The man had wild hair and a scraggly beard.

"You're the first English people I've spoken to in six months!" he boomed, shaking our hands. "I work in Siberia!"

"Siberia?" Angela asked incredulously. At least it explained his unkempt hairstyle and huge backpack.

"Yeah. I work as an English language teacher in a place called Chita. It's about six hundred miles east of Irkutsk. It's the best thing I've done in my life. I used to be an antiques auctioneer in Kent, but got sick of that. I got a teaching qualification and flew to Siberia!"

I smiled. "Wow! But why Siberia?"

The man laughed. "A lot of people ask me that, and when I first arrived I wondered why myself. But I love it. In fact, I'm going back in a few months to start the new term."

14

On the flight back to the UK, our route took us over the eastern fringes of Belarus. I peered downward, pondering my progress in the quest so far.

As it stood, it had taken me fourteen months to notch up six countries. Therefore, at the current pace, it would take at least another year and a half to visit the other nations in Europe. And that was before I even considered venturing into Asia. If I ever did.

Angela had enjoyed Moscow, but as of yet hadn't mentioned where she would like to go next. I hadn't said anything either, not wishing to upset the apple cart. But with the forests of Belarus passing under us at five hundred miles per hour, I came to the sobering realisation that if I wanted to complete the Red Quest within the next decade, then I had to get a move on. Visiting one country at a time was simply too time-consuming and flight-heavy. The only way forward was to combine stops.

My mind began to sift through the logistics of doing this while keeping things quiet from Angela. If she caught wind of the new shift in operations, she would most likely put a stop to the whole thing. I had to think carefully.

7. The Quest Quickens in Bucharest!

Interesting fact: the British Government once knighted mad dictator, Nicolae Ceausescu.

"How do you fancy going to Bucharest in July?" I asked Angela a fortnight later.

Angela sighed. "We've just got back from Moscow, Jason. And now you want to go somewhere else."

"But it's meant to be really nice."

I decided it wasn't the time to mention the roving gangs of gypsy children that plagued the city, most of them waiting to rob tourists. Nor would it be prudent to talk about the packs of feral dogs that patrolled the streets at night, searching out and then hospitalising eight people a day. No, I wouldn't mention that. And I certainly wouldn't talk about the fact that Romania was only the first stop on the trip I'd planned. Bucharest was the easy bit. I also wanted to go to Moldova and Ukraine. My proposed trip would cover three capital cities in one week.

"So how about it?" I asked.

"No, I'm sorry. I don't really want to go somewhere like that for a while. Maybe later, but not yet. Can't you get one of your mates to go with you?"

2

In the pub, a few days later, I met Michael, who in Bratislava had ended up with some stripper's knickers hanging from his glasses. Phil was also there, and I relayed my proposal to them, outlining the itinerary and some basic costs.

Phil's reaction was expected; in fact, he laughed, but Michael seemed a little more amenable. Out of any of my friends, I knew Michael was the most likely to go with me.

"And three countries can be done in a week?" he asked.

Phil sniggered. "Michael, you're not seriously thinking of going are you? Cos if you are, you need your head examining. You know he calls it the Red Quest?"

Michael smiled.

Phil turned to me. "You've had your fun. You've been to a few weird places. Some of them have been quite good, I know, but Romania and Moldova. Why do you want to go to Moldova?"

I took a sip of my lager. Michael was looking at me too. "Because nobody ever goes there. Everyone goes to Paris or Rome, but no one goes to Moldova."

Phil laughed. "There's a reason for that. It's shit."

Michael decided to speak up. "Actually, I agree with Jason. I think going to places that nobody else visits is exciting. And Romania and Ukraine are places I've always fancied. I'm not too sure about Moldova. But do you know what? I'm happy to give it a go. Just let me see if I can get some time off work, and then you can count me in."

Phil said nothing. He simply sat back shaking his head. I didn't care though. The quest was on!

We decided to have a game of pool. After Phil had taken his shot, he passed me the cue. "Have you had any more thoughts about Kazakhstan?" he asked.

I put some chalk on the tip. "Do you know what Phil? I think it might be on the list. I don't know how I'll get there though."

"Well you're insane."

I smiled. "But it was you who said I should go there in the first place!"

"But I wasn't being serious, for God's sake."

3

Michael and I were sitting in a Bucharest airport taxi at the start of our weeklong trip through Eastern Europe. Angela had been fine about me venturing off with Michael, secretly hoping, I suspected, that the trip would quell my need for visiting far-flung places. Michael's girlfriend had given him the all clear too.

Our first impressions of the Romanian capital were favourable, but this may have been due to the July sunshine bathing the otherwise drab buildings in a healthy glow. As Michael and I headed through the city centre, we could see grand buildings with streets full of eager faces going about their business. In and among the concrete were ornate little churches, and as we passed one, our driver made the sign of the cross repeatedly (with one hand still on the wheel), until it disappeared from sight.

Thirty minutes later, Michael and I found ourselves wandering through an impressive area of greenery called Parcul Carol. As well as having an ambling promenade, it had some lakes and statues, and a couple of soldiers standing to attention beneath a huge arched monument.

"Well," I said, sipping some freshly made lemonade I'd bought from a nearby stall, "I think I like Bucharest. I think it's time we sealed the deal and found a bar."

There were plenty to choose from, but before we sat down in one, we passed the Palace of the Parliament, the second biggest building in the world. It was perhaps the most iconic of Nicolae Ceausescu's mad ideas of communist grandeur. But it did look impressive, sat at the end of a long boulevard that had been built on top of a destroyed suburb. It was the sort of building every megalomaniac deserved.

4

Michael and I were sat in a central Bucharest cafe, a chic looking place that had been the headquarters of the dreaded Communist Securitate. On the wall was a large black-and-white photo showing a scene from the 1989 revolution. A phalanx of tanks was parked in front of the building we were now sitting in.

"I was a baby when this happen," said a waiter who appeared at our table. He had obviously noticed us looking at the photo. "And do you know something? Maybe they shouldn't have shot him. I know my parents would disagree, but I'm beginning to think that executing Ceausescu was a bad idea."

I regarded the waiter, who couldn't have been more than twenty-five. The man looked serious.

"His death was meant to signify great change and prosperity," the young man explained. "But nothing has changed in Romania. The government is just as bad. At least when Ceausescu was in charge, everybody had a job and some money to spend."

5

Nicolae Ceausescu had been a dictator with all the necessary traits required for the job.

Do you have a brutal regime? Tick! *Do you give high-powered jobs to members of your family?* Tick! *Are you unaware of what your citizens really think of you?* Tick! *Can you come up with mad ideas that no sane person would ever entertain?* Tick! *Do you force people to look happy on your birthday? Tick! Will you send them to prison if they don't?* Tick! Yes, Ceausescu (or Genius of the Carpathians as he liked to call himself) was more than qualified for the job.

Born into a peasant family, young Nicolae's parents sent him to work in the factories of Bucharest aged only eleven. Three years later he joined the Romanian Communist Party and ended up in prison a few times, once for fighting and other times for political agitation. Even back then, he was a hothead.

When the Soviets took over the country, they rewarded Ceausescu handsomely, and he quickly rose through their ranks, becoming Minister for Agriculture, Minister for the Armed Forces, and then a member of the Politburo. But in 1965, he hit the jackpot and became the leader of Romania.

Initially he was popular, with even the West appreciating his forward-thinking ways, but then, bit by bit, he became power-crazed. One of his decrees was that women should have numerous babies. Mothers having ten or more children were declared heroine mothers. When the population began to swell, this policy caused another problem: child abandonment.

When he fell out of favour with the Soviets, he borrowed thirteen billion dollars from the West to fund development projects. When the bailiffs came knocking, Ceausescu began sending most of Romania's agricultural and industrial output abroad. It was the only way to pay off the debts. The result was that Romania ended up on the brink. Power cuts became the norm, and food rationing began.

To quell unrest, Ceausescu banned radio and controlled the TV. One of the few permitted TV programs was usually dedicated to the president himself, often showing Ceausescu visiting well-stocked stores full of food, showing his people that all was well. Little did they know it was plastic food. It was during these harsh times that he decided to build his palace.

To clear room for the gigantic building, Ceausescu ordered that huge swathes of Bucharest's historical area be demolished. Bulldozers destroyed 21 churches, six synagogues and 30,000 homes. In replacement, 3500 tons of crystal, a million cubic metres of marble, and masses of gold, silver, and velvet, together with the finest embroideries, were all brought in.

By 1989, the people of Romania could take no more, especially since Ceausescu had re-elected himself for another five years. A crowd assembled in front of the Communist Party Building. They started shouting and booing. Ceausescu seemed clueless as to why his citizens were unhappy. He stepped out onto the balcony to give what he hoped would be a rousing speech.

Immediately, the crowd heckled him. Ceausescu appeared shocked. As the booing continued, he decided to offer all Romanian workers an immediate pay rise. Unfortunately this didn't cut the mustard, and so he went back inside for the rest of the day to sulk. Outside, the mob grew, and the tipping point was when the army joined them, turning against their president.

The next day, just a few days short of Christmas, Ceausescu appeared at the balcony once more. It was to be his final speech. Unsurprisingly, the crowd was in no mood to hear him, and began pelting him with stones. The president fled back inside. This spurred the mob into action, and they stormed the building, overpowering Ceausescu's bodyguards. Realising the game was up, Ceausescu and his wife escaped by helicopter. They didn't get far though because the army intercepted them. A firing squad executed the Ceausescus on Christmas Day 1989. Free elections soon followed, and Romania joined the other Warsaw Pact nations to become an independent country.

6

The next morning was hot and sunny. Once again, it surprised me how much better Bucharest seemed to be in the flesh, as opposed to in print. Sure, some of the buildings looked like they needed a good old scrub, or in some cases total demolition, but overall the city looked just fine, rather like an old piece of jewellery that had lost some of its lustre, but still possessed much of its charm.

Most of the people passing us on the street looked affluent and content. Perhaps the waiter had been wrong about Bucharest, I thought. Yes, we could see a few stray dogs slinking about in the bushes, and a few cracks in the pavements, but we hadn't come across any gangs of children in operation. No, to us, Bucharest seemed to be a city on the up and up.

Suddenly Michael spotted a supermarket and insisted we go inside.

"Why?" I asked.

"To look at plastic bottles. Come on."

Sighing, I went inside the store and followed Michael to the drinks' aisle. Within seconds of eyeing up the bottles of fizzy liquids on offer, Michael grew excited. One of them featured a design he'd never seen.

"Interesting," he said as he turned the bottle around in his hands. "Interesting. Hold it a second while I take a photo."

Sighing again, I did as requested, hoping no one was watching. To me, the bottle looked like any other.

Michael's unhealthy interest in plastic bottles was due to his job. To some, he had one of the coolest jobs in the world, but those people were usually ten-year-olds.

He worked in a soft drinks factory, and one part of his job was to taste new flavours of fizzy drinks. I remember one day turning up at his house to find an array of brown bottles in his kitchen. All of them had white stickers scrawled with untidy handwriting. One read: *Strawberry Cream and Marshmallow.* Another read: *Chocolate and Orange Sundae.* It was like being in Willy Wonka's private laboratory.

"Oh ignore them," said Michael. "They're just testers?"

"Testers?"

"Yeah, new flavours I need to try out. Most of them will be horrible and won't ever make it to production. Try one if you want. They're safe."

I picked the Strawberry Cream and Marshmallow, opening the screw top to have a sniff. Bubbles rose to the surface, and it smelt faintly of fruit. I took a swig and almost gagged. It was terrible, nothing at all like strawberries or marshmallows.

Michael laughed. "Yeah I thought the same thing too. That one is definitely crossed off the list."

But sometimes Michael's expertise was required in the bottling department. If a new prototype bottle ever arrived at his factory, it was Michael's job to test its capabilities. This explained why I was standing in a Romanian supermarket with a bottle in my hand while Michael zoomed in to take a photo.

8

The Romanian version of the Arc de Triomphe was located to the north of the city. Like its French counterpart, it was a roundabout with traffic charging around it at a hundred miles an hour. But it did have a great big Romanian flag dangling in the middle.

"Let's visit the Museum of the Romanian Peasant," said Michael, as we walked past the giant edifice. "It's not far from here."

My face grimaced. It was the moment I'd been dreading. Michael and his museums. I didn't mind ones dedicated to torture (like in Bratislava), or Soviet oppression (like in Vilnius and Budapest), but one dedicated to Romanian peasants...

"It was voted the best museum in Europe in 1996," Michael said, trying to sweeten the deal.

"Was it?" I whispered under my breath. "Sounds great."

Fifteen minutes later, Michael cheered me up by announcing that we had somehow passed the museum, and so spent the next few moments looking at his map and scratching his bald patch. I kept walking, making it clear I was not going to double back on myself. He caught up and told me it was still ahead of us.

Drat and double drat, I thought, coining the phrase made famous by Dick Dastardly. Now I could only take solace in two measly thoughts – one, that the museum might be closed, and two, even if it was open, it would be small, consisting of a single room with one exhibit.

I was wrong on both counts.

The museum was open and had three floors! *Three!* Virtually as soon as we entered, I left Michael in my wake as I sped around, pausing only to take a photo of some pots.

"No photo!" screeched the harridan who had followed me from behind.

I ended up lasting twenty minutes inside the peasant museum, and in that time, I saw manikins dressed in peasant clothes. I walked past reconstructed peasant homes. I perused peasant pots, and I stared at lots of painted eggs, presumably painted by piss-poor peasants. In the entrance foyer, I found a place to sit and wait for Michael.

He took over an hour and a half.

9

Later that evening, we were sat in a bar enjoying a cold bottle of Romanian lager. As a football match played out on a large screen, Michael asked me something. "What are you going to do if Angela finds out about the Red Quest?"

I picked up my pint of Ursus and took a sip. Its cooling taste was a perfect way to enjoy a summer's evening in Bucharest.

"I don't know," I answered truthfully. "I just hope she never does."

Michael nodded. "But you'll have to tell her eventually. I mean, how are you going to get to places like Uzbekistan? It's one thing going for a week in Europe, but to spend thousands of pounds getting to Central Asia...what will she think of that?"

"You could always go with me?"

Michael shook his head. "You know there's no way I could do that. Sarah would have a heart attack. Plus, we don't have enough spare cash."

I sat back and felt a wave of despair wash over me. Michael had put into words the dark thoughts I'd been having for some time. There was no way Angela would allow me to go to Central Asia, and now that Michael had admitted he couldn't go with me, the Red Quest suddenly seemed like a ridiculous idea, the schoolboy fantasy of a grown-up man who should know better.

But dwelling over Central Asia could wait for another day, I decided. I picked up my drink and made a toast. "Anyway, here's to Romania," I said. Michael and I clinked glasses and looked at the TV.

On the way back to the hotel, we could hear the baying sound of hounds. Their shrill barks and yaps reverberated around the dark alleyway we were taking a shortcut through. At night I knew they tended to form packs. Thankfully we got back to the hotel unharmed.

10

The next morning, our last in Romania, was overcast but warm. With a few hours left before our flight to Moldova, Michael and I began to wander the streets of Bucharest aimlessly. We noticed that old women selling flowers tended to congregate on street intersections, and turnips did indeed seem the vegetable of choice in Romania's capital.

Eventually we found ourselves in Revolution Square, home of the former Communist Party Building. It was where Ceausescu had given his final speech.

Michael and I looked up at the balcony where history had been made. We were actually standing in the area where the mob had assembled. It all looked so normal and nice.

11

Our final stop in Bucharest was the Count Dracula Club, a low budget, horror-themed restaurant with a large metal bat hanging over its doorway.

"Please enter the abode of Dracula," said the pallid young man who opened the door for us. He led us into the darkened lobby and then showed us around various small rooms (featuring impaled heads, reaching hands and red atmospheric lighting) before taking us down into the dank-smelling basement.

"Please be seated," he said theatrically. "And do not be afraid of the vampire hordes. I will get you the menu."

Michael ordered the Black Cock Salad, which I thought was brave of him. I went for the rather mundane-sounding Grandma's Chicken.

"Well there are no cocks in it as far as I can tell," quipped Michael twenty minutes later, as he tucked into a mouthful of normal-looking chicken salad. "And for that I'm thankful."

Soon we were in a taxi to the airport for stage two of our adventure.

"I can't believe we're going to Moldova!" I said as we sped through the outskirts of Bucharest.

"I know," agreed Michael. "I'm glad you convinced me to go. Phil is missing a treat."

8. The Poorest Country in Europe

Interesting fact: In 2010, Chisinau was the least visited capital city in Europe.

The Romanian Airlines night flight from Bucharest to Chisinau (pronounced Kish-i-now) only took one hour. Soon after, Michael and I were sat in a taxi bumping along the uneven road towards the hotel. Outside, it was almost pitch black. As far as I could tell, there were no streetlights.

"Just how poor is Moldova?" I whispered to Michael.

"Very," he answered. "I think a quarter of the population live on less than two dollars a day."

"Jesus."

Surprisingly quickly, we arrived at the Hotel Cosmos, an establishment that had seen better days. It was an ugly grey tower block with a large reception area and a dingy bar at one end. Men sat around drinking beer and smoking cigarettes and after depositing our suitcases, we joined them, delighted to discover that the local brew, Beer Chisinau, only cost 60p.

"Cheers!" I said to Michael as I took a slurp of the fine tasting ale. "Welcome to Moldova!"

2

Moldova, an almost unknown country in Eastern Europe, was somewhere I'd wanted to visit for a long time. Perhaps it was to do with a book I'd read by British author, Tony Hawks, entitled *Playing the Moldovans at Tennis*. In it, Hawks had visited Moldova to play each member of the national football team in a game of tennis, and as I followed his quest, I became intrigued by the country, especially because as a tourist destination it was well and truly off the map.

Finishing our first beers, Michael and I looked around at our fellow drinkers. All were hard-looking men, and none seemed particularly happy. We wondered whether they were guests of the hotel, or merely boozers knocking back a few to ease the pain of living in Moldova. One man, wearing an old grey suit was slugging back vodkas like there was no tomorrow. No one spoke to each other. The room was thick with cigarette smoke.

"I'm hungry," I said, eyeing the bar and wondering whether it sold sandwiches.

"Yeah, me too. Let's have a three-course meal," quipped Michael. "I'm sure the Hotel Cosmos can cater to our needs."

I told Michael to sit tight while I headed for the bar.

The bartender was sitting at one end watching a small TV. He eyed me sullenly as I approached. Eventually he stood up and came over.

"Do you sell any food?" I asked.

The man nodded.

I eyed the bar looking for any sign of sustenance, but couldn't see anything edible, not even crisps or nuts. I looked back at the man. "What sort of food do you have?"

"I have no food."

I was confused. Did the bar sell food or not? It seemed a straightforward question, and I wanted to know the answer.

"Do you sell food?" I repeated.

The man nodded. "Yes."

"Can I buy some please?"

"No. Food is from restaurant but is closed now. You wait until morning. You have Beer Chisinau if you like? Yes?"

In the end, we bought and consumed another few bottles of beer and retired to our rooms hungry.

3

The next morning, we rushed down for breakfast like men possessed and chomped away on bread with lashings of cheese. Actually, we both agreed, the hotel was not as bad as we'd originally thought, and it exuded a certain charm. In fact, it seemed as if we were back in the 1970s, and I quite liked that. No pretentiousness at the Hotel Cosmos. You got what you saw.

Our guidebook said there were only a few tourist attractions in Chisinau and so with an overcast day beckoning, we left the Cosmos and stepped into the gloom.

Not far was a large statue of Grigory Kotovsky, a Moldovan military leader. As usual with this type of monument, the great man was sitting on a mighty steed. We stared up at him for a moment, pondering where to go.

Suddenly it started to rain which made us cease our upwards gaze. We looked around to get our bearings and in the distance, could see a blue church with some golden onion domes.

"That looks like an Orthodox Church," Michael said. "That's tourist attraction number one. Come on." We strode through some puddles towards it.

4

Nowhere looks good in the rain, except perhaps the Sahara, and Chisinau was no exception. Downcast people with their collars pulled tight were standing around waiting for trolley buses, or dancing around puddles on their way to somewhere else. Cars and buses splashed along potholed roads, while stray dogs looked furtive and fearful, slinking out of sight if anyone drew too near. Compared to Bucharest, Moldova's capital looked down at heel and in need of repair. In fact, it was the most Eastern Bloc city I'd been to on the quest.

Michael and I crossed a road and came to an area specialising in casinos and moneychangers. These two businesses were doing a roaring trade in Chisinau; ominous signs, I thought. Even though it was only ten in the morning, plenty of people were entering the casinos. To me, that smelt of people having too much time on their hands. Secondly, the abundance of moneychangers in a city with an almost total absence of tourists could mean only one thing: the citizens of Chisinau did not have much trust in the Moldovan lei. They were changing it into hard Western currency.

The Orthodox Church, when we eventually arrived, wasn't big and looked like it needed a lick of paint. Around the back was a small graveyard, mainly consisting of simple crosses made of metal bars. Weeds were everywhere. "This bloody rain," I said. "I can feel it sliding down my back. Come on, let's find a café. I need to dry out."

5

We found a cafe near a small park and ordered a coffee each. They cost 20p. We were the only patrons. Rain was spattering the windows, and everything outside looked dull and dark.

"What do you think of Chisinau?" Michael asked, peering out. The park was empty, I noted, except for an unusually high concentration of green benches.

I shrugged. "Not as nice as I expected. But it is early days. Everything's cheap though, and if we want to get dry later, there are plenty of casinos to choose from."

Half an hour later, with the rain still coming down, Michael and I trudged our way towards the centre of town. Rain dripped from lampposts and tree branches, occasionally catching us unawares as thick droplets hit our ears and necks.

Chisinau had no old town as such because of World War II. First of all, the Red Army had occupied the city, and then, a few months later, an earthquake had struck, demolishing huge swathes of it. As if this wasn't bad enough, the Germans then began a campaign of aerial bombardment to get rid of the Soviets. It worked, and then the Germans ransacked the place. They also rounded up ten thousand Jews, took them to the outskirts of the city, and shot them all.

Eventually the Soviets fought back and after a hellish five-month battle, they retook Chisinau. By the time the dust had settled, three-quarters of the city lay in ruins, and the old town was gone.

The Cathedral of Christ's Nativity, a large white building with a huge grey dome, was the main tourist attraction in the city. Nearby was its restored bell tower that some local communists had blown up in the 1960s. Partly to escape the rain, we went inside the cathedral.

"Wow!" I whispered. The Cathedral's interior was gold, red, and sparkly. There were quite a few people inside with us, but all of them were praying or touching the icons. Most had looks of pure awe etched on their faces.

I was just about to have a closer look at an ornately decorated statue when Michael nudged me and gestured that we should leave. "I don't feel comfortable looking around here," he whispered. "Not while people are praying."

6

The rain had eased, and so we headed northeast to another of the city's prime sights - the Holy Gates, better known as Chisinau's Arc de Triomphe. Built in 1846, it had four sturdy pylon legs and a great big clock on the side. Just beyond it was the gigantic Government House, which had a large Moldovan flag on top. The flag was identical to the Romanian one, except for the Moldovan coat of arms in the middle. We walked onwards, avoiding the puddles littering our way, towards a great-looking statue of King Stephen.

Stephen the Great featured heavily on the front of the Moldovan lei. He had an impressive beard and large sword too. Stephen had ruled in the fifteenth century and was famous for winning 44 of the

48 battles he fought. In one of them, he successfully fought off some Muslim Ottomans, which won him the Pope's approval. That's how he became a saint.

"If I was a king, I'd want a name like his," I said.

Michael nodded and thought for a moment. "How about Jason the Jubilant?"

"Not bad," I said. It sounded promising, even if it was a little alliterative. "But I reckon Jason the Unmerciful is better. You wouldn't want to mess with a king like that, would you?

"Probably not. But he sounds like a baddie from *Flash Gordon.*"

The statue of Stephen the Great had been the focal point for the Moldovan independence movement in the late 1980s. Aware of what was happening in other Soviet Republics, the citizens of Chisinau had gathered around the statue, demanding freedom of speech, a return of the Moldovan language, and an acknowledgment of Moldovan traditions. The Soviets agreed to the terms. By March the following year, anti-Soviet candidates were in power, and by August 1991, Moldova was an independent country, albeit with a couple of breakaway states in tow.

7

That evening Michael and I ventured out to find a bar to watch some football. The rain had long since stopped, and the sun was bathing the city in a pleasant golden glow. It really was incredible what a bit of sun could do to a city, because Chisinau now looked agreeable and inviting, and its people walked with quicker steps in their toes.

We passed the Holy Gates again, but instead of dour locals huddled underneath trying to keep dry, it now featured teenagers laughing and joking. Chisinau had transformed itself.

We found a bar close to the centre of town. It was full of TV screens showing a football match. While Michael went to get some drinks, I sat down, looking forward to another bottle of Beer Chisinau. Five minutes later, Michael came back empty-handed.

"They don't sell it by the bottle," grinned Michael. "Only by the vat! Someone will bring it over in a minute."

A waiter deposited the huge container with its own pump on our table. Three litres of Beer Chisinau sat waiting inside. I poured myself a glass and asked Michael how much it had cost.

"Seventy two lei, about £3.50! Bargain!"

The other patrons in the bar were mainly men, cheering when either side scored a goal. On a nearby table was a group of teenage boys who didn't look much older than thirteen. They too had a vat of ale, and all were chain-smoking cigarettes. Just then a man in his forties approached us. "Are you lads English?" he asked in a cockney accent. "Cos if you are, come and join us."

Brad told us he was an ex-military helicopter pilot who, after leaving the RAF, had decided to travel around Europe. He'd been all over Eastern Europe, but eventually settled in Chisinau, where he'd met a beautiful Moldovan girl who was now his wife.

"And if you're ever looking for a wife," he told us with a wink, "it would take about two days. And she would be bloody gorgeous! There are few eligible men in Moldova."

I pointed at the young boys drinking on the next table. Brad nodded. "I don't think there's a legal limit for drinking alcohol here. If you have the money, then you can do what you like."

I mentioned to Brad that my only knowledge of Moldova had come from the book by Tony Hawks. Brad nodded and smiled. "I know Tony. I've met him a few times at the Embassy. He's making a film over here. He's a really nice guy, and even better than that, he's putting Moldova on the map."

Brad was with three other men, all ex-pats. One was from Denmark, another from New Zealand (who also had a Moldovan wife), and the third was a fellow Brit, who worked at the Embassy. They all seemed a good bunch, and at one point after the bar decided to offer free vodka to anyone watching the match, the evening quickly turned into an alcoholic oblivion.

8

The next morning, nursing hangovers from hell, Michael's phone rang. Through a blur of alcohol fever, I heard him muttering to someone. I tried to go back to sleep, but he jumped up, causing a racket in the process.

"Bloody hell!" he said. "Madhia's waiting downstairs!"

"...Who...? My head was killing me, and I wanted to close my eyes for at least four more hours.

"Madhia! Brad's wife. She's sat in the lobby!"

"....Uh?"

And then it all came back to me. Somehow, in the midst of the previous night's vodka and Beer Chisinau frenzy, the topic of Transnistria, Moldova's breakaway republic, came up. And at the time, it sounded like a good idea.

"Shit!" I said to Michael as he scurried about searching for a t-shirt. I was now fully awake. "You mean we're actually going to a breakaway republic? Are we insured?"

9. A Day Trip to a Breakaway Soviet Republic

Interesting fact: Transnistria declared itself independent in 1990, but no country recognises it (not even Russia).

I couldn't believe we were on our way to Transnistria, or the Pridnestrovskaya Moldavskaya Republic, to give it its catchier title. The UK Foreign Office website stated: *We advise caution if considering travelling to the Transnistria region. It is outside of the control of the Moldovan authorities, and British services may be limited in their ability to help.*

Michael and I had our passports at the ready but had left our wits back in Chisinau.

We sat in the back of a car with a driver called Christian, who couldn't speak English, and Madhia, who could. Brad was working in Chisinau and so had left us in the capable hands of his wife.

"Let me tell you a Russian joke," Madhia said, trying to break the ice. "It is about a man with a fifty centimetre dick, who meets a witch..."

I nearly choked, but Madhia continued with the joke, in that sexy accent only women from Eastern Europe can deliver.

"...Because of the size of his dick no woman was willing to marry him, so he decided to see a witch..."

By the time Madhia had finished telling the joke, most of it had been lost in translation. As well as the witch, there had been some frogs, but apart from that, I had no idea what the joke was about.

2

Transnistria, a self-declared communist state on the eastern side of Moldova, had decided in 1990 to align itself with Mother Russia. The majority of its citizens spoke Russian, and since it had no desire to play second fiddle to its Moldovan overlords, it decided to do something about it.

It came up with a flag featuring the hammer and sickle, it called its currency the rouble, and finally declared itself independent from Moldova, sparking a bloody civil war that left both sides bitter and resentful. And I'd only heard of the place because I'd seen it on a BBC program entitled: *Holidays in the Danger Zone!*

Madhia was twenty-eight, with long dark hair and slim features. She was a fairly typical Moldovan beauty. The previous night, Brad had mentioned that his wife worked as a tour guide, and that was how the discussion had turned to Transnistria.

"As well as guide," Madhia said as we drove through the Moldovan countryside. "I am worker in Chisinau casino. But this not pay much money, and so I like to do tour guide sometime."

She suddenly spotted something out of the window and addressed Christian in thick Moldovan. Soon we came to a standstill beside a field. After another exchange, Madhia told us to wait in the car while she and Christian went to get the cucumbers.

"Did she say cucumbers?" Michael asked when they had gone.

I nodded. We stared out as they raced into the field. A minute later, they returned with six cucumbers, three each. Both started chomping away. "You want one?" Madhia inquired after seeing our incredulous faces.

3

Less than an hour later, we approached the makeshift border of Transnistria. Madhia turned to us, a serious expression on her face.

"Please do not take photo," she warned. "The guards will be armed, and they do not like the camera. We will park the car and go to the control hut where guards will check your passport and make you fill in form. In the hut, I will do the talking, and you will just smile nicely. After we get Transnistria visa, we can carry on to Tiraspol. Okay? You understand?"

Both of us nodded.

The Transnistrian border consisted of a set of barriers along the road. Men wearing combat fatigues and wide-brimmed Soviet-style caps stood around waiting for vehicles to approach. It looked like we were about to enter the setting for a spy novel, and I was both excited and apprehensive. Beside me, Michael was peering at the scene ahead.

As promised, Christian parked the car and we all got out. Christian disappeared into a small hut, and we quickly followed him inside.

The interior was a place of utter confusion. A line of hatches was located along one side of the thin room, but only one of them was open. There were two disorganised queues leading to it, and Christian had elected for the one furthest away. Madhia directed Michael and me into the nearer queue and began to fill in some forms she had picked up. "Remember," she said. "Just smile and let me do the talking."

At the head of the queue, people were thrusting pieces of paper and passports towards the grim male official sitting behind the booth. With only one hatch open though, the queuing system wasn't working well. Things turned worse when the hatch suddenly closed, and another opened a bit further along. Understandably, this didn't go down too well with those who suddenly found themselves at the front of a redundant queue. But the most worrying aspect was when an angry scene developed around us.

Two of our fellow queuers were shouting at Madhia after she'd edged us towards the other hatch. We couldn't understand the heated exchange, but from the gist of the pointing, we soon gathered that the men thought we had pushed in front of them. An intense argument quickly broke out, but Michael and I were helpless to join in. All we could do was smile. Christian, our driver, had already left the hut, and while we stood in confusion, a third man piped up. He had a leather jacket on and looked like he could bend steel with his nose. He began yelling at the first two men. This seemed to calm things down.

I turned to Madhia asking if everything was okay, but she shook her head. "No it is not. These men, they all want to fight with you."

Whooah! Hold on just a minute! *A fight?* This wasn't part of the deal! After all, we were standing in a tiny hut without air conditioning, on a border that no country in the world recognised, and surrounding us were agitated people suffering from queue rage. Just as I was wondering what we could do to get out of this tricky situation, another hatch opened, which averted the crisis.

4

Transnistria, when we eventually crossed through, looked just the same as Moldova. The only differences were the car number plates, and the soldiers armed with guns standing at checkpoints. Oh, and the occasional camouflaged tank covered with cargo netting at the side of some roads.

A baton-waving policeman pulled us over and studied our passports. After some discussion with Madhia, he handed them back and waved us through. Fifteen minutes later, we arrived in Tiraspol, the small capital of Transnistria.

One of the first things we saw was a huge billboard with a hammer and sickle on it. Seeing it made me excited. This was the real thing! Even though Transnistria wouldn't count as an actual country, what it did offer was a real taste of former Soviet life. The four of us climbed out of the car, stepping onto communist soil.

The first issue was getting some Transnistrian roubles, which we managed to do at a local moneychanger. I was delighted to find the money looked suitably Soviet, covered in Cyrillic writing and showing a man with a bushy moustache.

The four of us left the money exchange and headed off to buy some brandy - one of the few things that Transnistria was famous for. *Kvint Brandy* was of high quality, according to Madhia, but also incredibly cheap. "It is even cheaper than Moldovan brandy," she told us. "We always buy some when we come here."

5

For a breakaway republic, the streets of Tiraspol seemed mundanely normal. There were no posters of megalomaniacs to speak of, and we could only see one tank.

The day was sunny, and perhaps because of this, people seemed reasonably happy. Soldiers walked in pairs, old women carrying bags of turnips waddled down paths, and cars sped along the streets. Not all of them were Ladas.

"This way," said Madhia. "We have a lot to do before visa runs out."

I didn't want to think about what would happen if our 'visas' ran out (the visa consisted of a stamped piece of card), and so we followed Madhia along a main street towards a splendid church.

"It was built in 1999," Madhia told us. "And you can take photo if you please. Taking photo in Tiraspol is okay. Just no photo of the soldier or policeman."

Michael and I stood staring at the cathedral, especially at its beautiful golden onion domes that were shimmering in the sun. And even though we appeared to be the only tourists in Tiraspol, nobody seemed bothered by our presence. A few people looked at what we were taking photos of, but then quickly lost interest.

As we walked away I asked Madhia if she liked visiting Transnistria, and her reply was a curt and definite no.

"But I don't like England either," she added. "When I lived there with my husband, I got a cleaning job with a Ukrainian woman. Brad said the work would be easy because I could speak Russian with her." Madhia paused and scowled. "Well let me tell you something! The work was not easy! The woman only speak to give orders! I clean ceiling, floor and everything! But I think to myself, if I work hard, then she might pay extra. But at end of two hour all I get is fifteen pounds. I was so angry I went straight to bar and bought drink and packet of cigarettes, even though I stop smoking years ago! After buying these things, nearly all my money was gone! Just like that! So that is why I do not like England."

6

Just along from the cathedral was a flea market. It was brimming with fruit and vegetables, supervised by women wearing headscarves who also guarded ancient-looking scales. Inside a large building were piles of meat, perhaps the most meat I'd seen in a single place ever. Hunks and slabs of mutton, beef, and pork, together with rolls of white fat, were everywhere. Dogs wandered the aisles, as did old ladies in flowery dresses.

"The market in Chisinau is better than this," commented Madhia, turning up her nose. "It is cleaner with no animals allowed where the meat is. Come, I'll show you second-hand market, it not far from here."

She was right, because it was just across the road. Old clothes, rusty tools and random electrical components made up much of the wares on offer, everything laid out on the ground with the owners sat nearby. We quickly passed it and arrived at a statue of a man on a horse cast in a suitably heroic pose. It was Alexander Suvorov, the Russian general who had founded Tiraspol.

"You can climb it if you want," suggested Madhia.

Michael and I wandered over to the statue's base, quickly deciding against such foolhardy action. Instead we posed underneath the huge monument while Madhia took a photo. We barely reached the pedestal.

"It's not quite the police state I was expecting," said Michael after he'd said *cheese*. "In fact, it all feels fairly normal."

We walked back over to Madhia.

7

Our next stop was the Presidential Palace. It was a commanding building with a billowing green and red flag on the top. I was surprised to see an absence of guards in front, but was pleased that it did have a huge statue of Lenin, once again confirming the allegiance of Transnistria.

Across the road was a memorial to those who had died in 1992, during the War of Transnistria with Moldova. Etched into a wall was a long list of names. After posing by an old Soviet tank, we went to get a drink at a riverside bar.

"So what do you both think of Tiraspol?" asked Madhia when our drinks arrived.

The view from the bar included a bridge, a river, and a small sandy beach. I was surprised about the beach. People were actually sunbathing on the small slither of sand.

I answered the question first. "It's not bad, actually. The church was great, and I liked the statue and tank. But I don't think we'd have come here if it was just part of Moldova."

"It is part of Moldova," said Madhia curtly. "It is just that the people here do not agree. But I know what you mean. Tiraspol is not special place. Chisinau is much better."

Michael nodded. "It's been a pleasant day. But it's not the - step back in time - place I was expecting."

When Madhia got up to visit the toilet, Michael turned to me. "I'll tell you something I can't get my head around, though: why did Transnistria decide to break away from the poorest country in Europe to form an even poorer country? I just don't get it."

Ten minutes later, we finished our drinks and headed back to the car. Our day trip into the danger zone had been great fun. An hour later, safely through the border, we arrived back in Chisinau.

8

That evening, Michael and I were having a Beer Chisinau in the hotel bar when my phone beeped. It was a text message from Phil.

He was asking where we were. When I replied that we were in Moldova, but had just returned from Transnistria, he replied with a simple '?'

Michael texted him back, explaining about Transnistria's status and then my phone started ringing.

"You're honestly telling me that you've been to a breakaway country? As in a country that doesn't exist?" Phil sounded incredulous. "I thought you were mad before, but that takes the biscuit. You could've been kidnapped, and no one would've known!"

"I know!" I said. Next to me, Michael was grinning. He could obviously hear the conversation I was having. "That's what made it exciting!"

"Exciting?" said Phil. "That's not exciting...it's...bloody dangerous."

"And we almost got into a fight with some men in a border hut. That was exciting."

Phil didn't speak for a few seconds. When he did, he asked where we were going next.

"Kiev," I told him.

"Well at least it's back to civilisation, sort of. But look, Jason, this quest is getting a bit stupid now, isn't it? Going to Riga or Budapest is one thing, but driving to a breakaway country? Most sane people wouldn't even think about it. And getting Michael to go along with you...pass me over to him please..."

I gave my phone to Michael and took a slurp of Beer Chisinau. Phil was wrong, I thought. Going to Transnistria had been a tad foolhardy, but hardly reckless. Madhia was the perfect tour guide, and kept us well within the bounds of safety. Plus, it *had* been exciting. Surely that was one of the requirements for visiting a new place - to get the blood pumping and to experience something new.

By my side, Michael was telling Phil that he was enjoying himself, and that he wasn't insane. "Look Phil," Michael said. "We have to pack so we'll see you when we get back. If we make it alive! See you soon." He closed the conversation and passed the phone back to me.

"He just doesn't get it," I said.

"No, but most people wouldn't get it either. We are the minority here. Anyway, here's to Moldova and Transnistria!" We clinked bottles, thinking ahead to Kiev, capital of Ukraine, the final stop on our tour.

10. Chased by the Hounds of Kiev

Interesting fact: At 107m, Kiev has the deepest metro station in the world.

The plane from Chisinau to Kiev belonged to the almost unpronounceable Dniproavia Airways, but it got us there in under an hour.

Driving towards the city, Michael and I passed areas of pure primeval forest, occasionally broken by billboards splashed with Cyrillic. Then we reached the outskirts of Kiev, and the concrete tower blocks appeared, always a feature of ex-Soviet cities.

Kiev was big. It made Chisinau seem like a village. It stretched in all directions, both outwards and upwards. The centre of town was much nicer than the outskirts, but full of hills. Our hotel was located in a prime spot for sightseeing, and after dumping our things, we were out, hitting the early evening streets of Ukraine's capital.

2

"I can't believe the mullet lives on in Kiev!" I said, as we walked past a man sporting a particularly fine specimen. His was one of many.

"It's like being back in the '80s," answered Michael with a smile. "I just hope none of them visit Iran. They've banned the mullet over there."

Both of us were starving, and entered the first restaurant we saw. We weren't surprised to find the menus were in Cyrillic, and the waitresses didn't speak English.

"Well there's only one thing to do," said Michael, turning to a random page in the menu. "It's got to be pot luck."

When the waitress reappeared, Michael pointed at something on the undecipherable menu, and I did the same. The waitress nodded and disappeared, leaving us to wonder what we had ordered.

A boiled fish, complete with head, tail and skin, arrived in front of Michael, and a grilled piece of white fish with some fried cucumber, arrived in front of me.

"Not bad for a wild stab in the Cyrillic dark," Michael said prodding his fish. "But so much for your so-called ability to read Russian."

I sighed because we had been through this before. "Look," I answered, picking up a forkful of cucumber. "Reading Cyrillic is easy. But that doesn't necessarily mean I can understand it. How was I supposed to know that *reeba* meant fish? So shut up and munch on your reeba head."

3

The beauty of Kiev's churches was astounding, most of them in fetching royal colours, topped with distinctive onion domes. The sun helped too, pouring a warming glow over the city. As Michael and I walked towards Saint Michael's Monastery, one of the largest cathedrals in the city, things got even better. It was white and pastel blue, with a staggering amount of golden domes. Both of us stared agog at the architectural masterpiece.

A platoon of fierce babushkas rattled tins when anyone passed through its entrance, and so we waited until a group of Japanese tourists entered and slipped in among them.

Inside, we spied black-robed Orthodox priests and then heard some singing from the cathedral's interior. We decided to investigate. Other people were heading inside too, but we managed to slip to the front to see a line of priests singing a haunting tune. A smell of incense filled the air as we stood watching.

"Do you know what I'm getting sick of?" said Michael a few minutes later. We had left the singing priests, and were now making our way out of the complex. The babushkas were rattling their tins, but were focussed on a woman walking with a young child. "It's folding this tourist map we picked up at the airport, and finding a load of tits hanging out the edge. It doesn't feel right looking at an advertisement for a massage parlour as you step out from a church."

4

The guidebook stated that Andrew's Descent was a must-see sight. Wondering what was special about it, we arrived at the top of a steep, winding cobblestone path lined with stalls. They sold everything, from Russian dolls, fur hats, and framed art, to traditional Ukrainian handicrafts. The guidebook was correct; Andrew's Descent was deliciously pretty.

Its name came from the quite stunning Saint Andrew's Church that stood at the top of the descent. It was one of the few buildings in Kiev to escape serious damage during the Second World War. It got my vote as the best cathedral in town, which was no mean feat. I was especially impressed with its domes that seemed covered in green velvet and finished with glittering gold. It looked like a crown.

An hour later, we were in Independence Square, staring up at a huge statue of a woman stood on top of a massive white column. The square surrounding her was clearly a meeting place for the teenagers of Kiev. They sat about chatting, or making a splash in the nearby fountain. It was different from Kiev ninety years previously.

When the Soviets had taken over Ukraine in the 1920s, they inherited a country shattered by famine, homelessness, and 1.5 million dead. But they couldn't complain, because they had been the cause of it with their civil war.

Perhaps out of guilt, the Soviets allowed Ukraine a bit of leeway, even encouraging Ukrainian art and literature. Health care, housing, and education improved, and the Soviets created plenty of jobs. All of which brought about a massive turnaround for the country. Output and productivity increased, and Ukraine became the powerhouse of Soviet industrialization.

Then things started to unravel. It started with Stalin and the Ukrainian peasants.

5

In the 1930s, Stalin decided to put a stop to Ukrainian freedom. His main issue was with peasant farmers. He felt they were doing a bad job of farming the land and so collectivised it, effectively putting it under government control.

Suddenly peasants had increased quotas to meet. If they failed to reach them, they couldn't have any more seeds. The plan was to make the peasants work harder, but it had a devastating effect. With no surplus produce, people began to starve.

The quotas came on regardless and those that tried to question them were either tortured or sent to Siberian gulags. Anyone caught hiding food was killed and their stock taken anyway. Because of this policy, between 1932 and 1933, millions of peasants starved to death, something Ukraine's parliament would later class as genocide.

In the years following World War II much of Ukraine was in ruins, but then something significant happened – Josef Stalin died and the Soviet regime began to tolerate Ukrainian nationalism again. Industrial output expanded almost immediately, and during the 1950s and 60s, Ukraine became renowned for its technical research and weapons production.

By 1990, with some Soviet states dallying with independence, Ukraine wondered what to do, especially since relations with the Soviets were generally okay. In the end, they decided to establish the *principle* of an independent state, a rather woolly way of testing the water. Even so, the Soviets didn't like this move and waded in to sort things out. But then, with impeccably bad timing, there was the attempted coup in Moscow. In the confusion, Ukraine declared independence, and that was that.

6

In a bar close to Andrew's Descent, Michael and I hatched a cunning plan. It involved a set of Russian dolls and an engagement ring.

Michael had been toying with the idea of proposing to his girlfriend for some time, and we both agreed that finding a ring in a tiny wooden doll would be an extremely romantic gesture. That decided, we headed to a stall at the top of the descent.

"Good evening," said the man in charge of the stall. "Please take time to choose right set."

All around him were dolls of every size and colour. Some were huge, capable of containing over twenty individual pieces; others consisted of just three dolls. These were usually the cheapest.

Barak Obama, Joseph Stalin, Saddam Hussein, and David Beckham featured heavily on some of the dolls, but Michael steered clear of these and pondered over some exquisitely painted dolls that contained about eight individuals.

"I'll have those," he said eventually, picking out a nice set, the smallest of which would just be about capable of holding a ring. After he'd paid, Michael turned to me. "I'm getting nervous already."

7

That evening we found a bar in an area surrounded by concrete tower blocks. A table away from us, an extended Ukrainian family sat talking animatedly, with an occasional argument thrown in for good measure. Most of the family were hardened drinkers, interspersing shots of vodka with pints of lager. And the men were just as bad. We watched a football match on the TV whilst keeping a wary eye on our neighbours.

After a few beers, Michael and I began playing a silly gaming that involved thinking up ridiculous names for pornographic films. The name had to be based on a fairy tale.

"Rumpleforeskin," Michael said, after pondering for a short while. We both laughed causing the Ukrainian family to look over.

I countered with the quite obvious Pussy in Boots. A lame effort. Michael thought so too. One nil to him.

Michael thought for a minute, and then said, "Big Willy Goes Rough."

"What?"

"Big Willy Goes Rough. Three Billy Goats Gruff."

I shook my head. "Rubbish. Doesn't even work."

Eventually, after coming up with even sillier ones, it was my turn, and so I took time to come up with a good one.

"Pornochio!" I croaked, sniggering to myself. "And its tag line is: When he tells lies, it's not his nose that gets bigger!"

We both doubled up laughing.

"And the co-star is...wait for it...Jiminy Cockit!" added Michael.

The Ukrainian family looked over again, causing us to quieten down sharpish.

8

"What was that?" I asked Michael as we walked back to the hotel along an almost deserted street. We seemed to be heading away from the centre for some inexplicable reason. The graffiti scrawled on walls looked ugly, and I wondered whether Michael's internal GPS had failed him, possibly due to the number of alcoholic beverages he had consumed. We were lost, and it was almost pitch black.

We stopped to listen, and there it was again: a definite scuffling sound, like something was in the bushes, watching and waiting to pounce. It was probably a cat. At least, that's what we hoped.

We carried on for a few metres and then came to a dead end. The only thing in front of us was uneven ground hidden in shadows. Wasteland.

"Where are we?" I whispered, peering into the blackness. I was actually getting pissed off. All I wanted to do was get back to the hotel, so I could get some sleep. None of the buildings around us had any lights on. Perhaps their owners had abandoned them.

Just then, a black thing rushed from a dark place and then swiftly bolted into some shadows. Then another did the same, and another. Dogs.

Without a word, both of us turned and walked in the opposite direction. Behind us, we could hear the scampering of feet, but neither of us dared to look. "Well done, Michael," I whispered through gritted teeth. "Leading us down some deserted dead end full of rabid dogs. We'll probably get eaten, and no one will find us for years."

"Shut up and keep walking. Don't let them know you're scared. They'll sense it."

Just then, there was a whimper and a bark, and so I looked over my shoulder. I couldn't believe it; there were about six or seven dogs, two of them large. They seemed to be following us. As I looked, even more dogs furtively rushed in and out from the undergrowth by the side of the road. It was a pack! It was like being in a horror film. I felt like vomiting.

"They're after us," I said. "And they look hungry."

"Just keep walking."

This wasn't easy, especially with a flock of hellhounds on our tail. I could hear more scampering of claws on the road, and imagined drool dribbling from their mouths, bloodlust in their brains. Beside me, Michael steeled a quick glance at them, and I registered the look of shock on his face too. But then Michael did something even more shocking. He stopped dead in his tracks and turned fully around. I did too, involuntarily covering my throat in case one suddenly attacked. But thankfully the pack had stopped some distance away. We stared at them, and they stared at us.

Without warning, Michael clapped his hands and charged towards the beasts, screaming and yelling like a maniac. Instead of eating him, they scattered in all directions, disappearing into the shadows from whence they came. Michael walked back to me. He seemed to be shaking.

"You mental bastard!" I said, beginning to laugh. "You scared me shitless!"

We hurried off towards some heart-warming streetlights up ahead. A few moments later, we could hear the reassuring sound of a car engine. I decided to turn around just one more time and saw that the dogs were back!

"Run!" I screeched. And we did, right up until we arrived at the main road, panting, but grateful we'd survived.

9

The next day was a sightseeing extravaganza beset by humid heat and foot blisters. Instead of jumping in a taxi (which is what I'd have preferred), Michael persuaded me that we needed to save some cash, and so we ended up getting a mixture of buses and metro trains, followed by a hellish five mile walk to the Museum of the Great Patriotic War. When we arrived, I was sweating like a person made entirely from sweat.

The gigantic Motherland Statue was worth the hike though, towering above everything and gleaming in the sunlight with her titanium sword and shield held aloft. Nearby were a few tanks, a missile, some Migs, and plenty of artillery. The main museum however was actually inside the Motherland Statue, but was closed. Instead, we headed to Caves Monastery.

Caves Monastery was another prime tourist spot in Kiev, and was a huge complex of magnificent cathedrals. It reminded me a little of the Kremlin in Moscow. Women had to wear headscarves before entering, and it was interesting to see young women who had covered their hair displaying copious amounts of flesh below their hot pants. Orthodox priests were everywhere inside the complex, all black robes, long beards and huge silver crosses.

"Now that's an interesting monument," said Michael, pointing at a sphere made of painted wooden eggs. We circled it, admiring the work that had gone into it. The sculpture featured 3000 eggs and looked amazing. A woman holding a toddler's hand walked over to it. The child was beaming.

The caves were the most popular part of the complex though, a narrow system of underground corridors that contained chapels and burial chambers. One of the most famous chambers supposedly contained the relics of Ilya Muromets, a possibly fictitious knight from the 12th century. His story made for interesting reading.

Born into a farming village, Ilya suffered a childhood accident that left him unable to walk. However, when he was 33, a couple of passing pilgrims miraculously healed him, enabling him not only to walk, but also to run, dance and caper. As amazing as this was, what happened next was even better.

While Ilya was out rambling one day, testing his newfound mobility, he stumbled upon a dying knight. After tending to him for a short while, the knight died, but not before he'd given Ilya an unexpected gift. It wasn't a bag of gold or even the key to his castle; it was the power of super-human strength!

Unlike many people in his position, Ilya decided to use his superpower for the good of the people, and the first thing he did was to liberate Kiev. That done, Ilya thought it was time to tackle a monster.

The monster he chose was the quite terrifying, Nightingale the Robber. It was half human and half bird, and lived in a nest near the edge of a great forest. The Nightingale's modus operandi was to sit and wait for passing strangers, and then whistle. But this was no ordinary whistle; it was a deadly whistle capable of murder! And it could kill at a thousand paces.

The whistle didn't faze Ilya though, and he calmly strode into the forest and found the thing lurking up in the trees. Before the monster could react, Ilya fired off a couple of arrows that landed in its eyes. Horribly wounded, the creature fell to the ground, but not before it emitted a half-hearted whistle that destroyed most of the forest and creatures within.

Ilya, with his handy super-powers, was unhurt, and dragged the monster to Kiev so that Vladimir the Great could see it.

"Make it whistle!" demanded Vladimir. "I want to hear the beast's terrible whistle!"

Ilya prodded the swine until it came awake. He ordered it to sing, but Nightingale refused. "I am too wounded," it croaked. "However a nice glass of wine might help. It may heal my wounds, and then perhaps I might be able to whistle."

This should have sent alarm bells ringing, because after all, the creature's whistle was its weapon, but someone summoned the wine anyway. Soon Nightingale the Robber was sipping on a nice glass of claret, and then, as it had predicted, its wounds began to heal. When it was strong enough, it put the glass down and whistled a most terrible of whistles. The sound destroyed most of the palace and killed hundreds.

Standing amidst the carnage and destruction, Ilya said, "Right, that's enough. You and your bloody whistle! I'm going to finish you once and for all."

He dragged the brute into a field and chopped its head off. No wonder they'd made him a saint.

11

The next morning was another hot and clammy day. For our final sight in Kiev, Michael insisted we visit the Chernobyl Museum, a memorial to the nuclear accident that occurred a hundred kilometres north of the city.

Inside were lots of photos and displays showing what had happened. Both of us stopped at a glass case containing a dead puppy. Its head looked okay, but the poor creature's body was a twisted and deformed mess. Its deformities were a direct result of its mother's radiation poisoning.

One room looked like something out of a nightmare. Atmospheric lights shone over manikins dressed in radiation suits and gas masks; the only thing spoiling the effect were a couple of babushkas who constantly hounded us about taking photos. Even so, we both agreed the museum had been worth a visit.

"Right then," I said an hour later. "Back to the airport. Which place was your favourite?"

Michael thought for a few seconds. "Bucharest I think. Kiev came a close second, though. If it wasn't for the hills and how much things cost, it might have come out on top."

Kiev *had* been expensive, especially after cheap and cheerful Chisinau. But I'd enjoyed each place, even the eventful side-trip into Transnistria. And even better than that, I'd crossed nine countries off the list. The Red Quest was coming along nicely, thank you very much.

"And everything went according to plan," I said. "No missed flights, no lost luggage, no arrests or muggings, and best of all, no dog attacks. I still can't believe you did that."

Michael laughed. "Nor me. I've never done anything like it before in my life. It worked though."

"Thank God."

"But now, all I can think about is when to give Sarah the Russian dolls. That's scarier than facing a pack of hounds."

"Good luck for that."

12

A week later, while Michael's girlfriend was having breakfast in their kitchen, he handed her the Russian dolls. After opening each individual piece, Sarah finally came to the last doll.

She said yes.

11. Sofia: Capital of Bulgaria

Interesting fact: In Bulgaria, a nod means no and sideways waggle means yes.

The woman operating border control at Sofia Airport certainly looked striking. Thick, dark eye make-up and a shock of orange hair greeted us as we approached her booth. She said nothing as she scanned our passports. After a cursory glance, she waved us through. Bulgaria was now part of the EU.

"Did you see that woman's eyelashes?" I said to Angela.

"I know! How much mascara must she get through?"

I was glad to see Angela smiling. It had taken some hard convincing to get her to visit Sofia, especially since it had only been three weeks since I'd returned from Kiev with Michael. But the way I had done it had been a masterstroke. As well as crossing Bulgaria off the list, we were also going to the Czech Republic. By chance, we had a five-hour layover in Prague on the way back from Sofia. And even though I'd already been to the Czech capital, I knew Angela had always wanted to go there. Five hours would be ample time to flavour the highlights of the city. This multiple country lark was working a treat.

2

Driving into the centre of Sofia on a hot August afternoon involved passing block after block of Soviet-style apartment buildings. Most were in a state of major disrepair, with graffiti everywhere. Cyrillic lettering on road signs and billboards made everything look distinctly Russian too, but what took up most of our attention was the taxi meter. It was running hell bent for leather.

Avoiding the touts in the arrivals hall of the airport, Angela and I had stepped outside and quickly spotted a waiting taxi. I handed the driver the address of our hotel, and while he rang someone, presumably to find out a price, a young man approached.

"Zis not official taxi," he said. "Watch out for zis man. He will rip you off! Official taxi over there - look."

The yellow taxi was parked by itself. I grabbed our piece of paper and thanked the young man. We headed across the road where the new driver got out, already opening the boot for our luggage.

"How much to this hotel?" I asked the driver, passing him the piece of paper.

The man shrugged. "I not sure. I not do zis trip before."

Alarm bells started ringing, but I ignored them. Besides, Angela was already loading the bags into the back.

"Can you give me a rough price though?" I pressed.

The driver smiled. "Sorry, no! But it will be on meter. Please, get in. Come."

We did, and as soon as we set off, the meter began going up like the clappers, finally stopping on sixty lev as we pulled up outside our hotel. It was four times the normal price. We had been stitched up good and proper!

3

Sofia is not on most people's list for a city break in Europe, and if people do venture to Bulgaria, it's usually to the Sunny Beach resorts in the east of the country. The sheer lack of tourists as we wandered along a main city street confirmed this.

Like the airport lady, the women of Sofia seemed to favour long eyelashes and strange hair shades. The men seemed almost Greek looking, but the strangest people were the Orthodox Priests. Occasionally we'd see one wandering about wearing a black robe and long Father Christmas beard.

"Look at that woman's melons!" said Angela. My eyes widened as I spotted the blonde girl in question. She most certainly did have a fine pair of melons. They looked succulent and ripe. In the poster, the model was holding one in her hand, the other lay on a tray. We wandered past the poster advertising the fruit, trying our best to keep in the shade.

From a sightseeing point of view, Sofia turned out to be compact, with all the major areas of interest congregated within walking distance of each other. We walked past one such sight, the notorious Party House, once the headquarters of the Communist Party.

The area surrounding the Party House was where the militaristic might of the communist regime once paraded itself. It was also the focal point for Bulgaria's path to independence. Once the Berlin Wall had fallen, anti-communist groups in Sofia had decided to get in on the action. When they realised the Kremlin wasn't going to march in, they got braver and demanded that the Soviet-backed leaders of Bulgaria stand down. Astonishingly, they did, and by November 1990, Bulgarian democracy was a mere stone's throw away. The final act that sealed the deal was the removal of the communist symbol from the national flag. Bulgaria did it. It gained independence without any fuss whatsoever.

4

Angela and I found a posh café just up the road from the Party House. Inside was decoratively furnished, but empty of patrons. We sat down and ordered a hot drink and a cake each.

"So what are your first impressions of Sofia?" I asked.

Angela looked outside. "It's a bit tatty in places, and I think they need to empty the bins a bit more, but overall, it's not bad. Seen better, seen worse."

I pointed at the menu. "It's cheap though. Maybe the cheapest place I've been to, apart from Moldova."

Our tray of goodies arrived, and Angela wasted no time in tucking into her apple pie, which she deemed delicious. My tiramisu was scrumptious too, but when I took a gulp of my hot chocolate, I was in for a shock. Instead of being the milky liquid I'd expected, it was a gloopy mass of chocolaty hotness that slid, lava-like, down the back of my throat.

"Ahhhhhh..." I gurgled. "Hot!...Burn!...Urghhh!" I held a hand to my throat as tears escaped from my eyes, possibly turning to steam as they did so.

Angela couldn't control her laughter as the lump made its hellishly slow way down my gullet, searing the lining of my throat with its progress.

"You're a nugget!" Angela said, unsympathetic to my plight.

And then, thankfully, the pain subsided, leaving only a mild burning sensation. I pushed the mug of hot chocolate away, wondering if it was, literally, *hot* chocolate.

"Last time I order hot chocolate in Sofia."

5

At the end of the First World War, the fantastically named Boris III became Tsar of Bulgaria. While Europe cleaned up the mess and formed new alliances, Boris steered his country towards neutrality. However, with the approach of World War II, this neutral stance ended up being tested. Boris reluctantly agreed to become an ally of Germany and Italy.

Despite this move, it was clear to everyone that Boris didn't really want his nation involved in any fighting. He refused to declare war on the Soviet Union, and then only half-heartedly declared war on the United Kingdom and USA. Tsar Boris hoped the Allies would not notice, but they did. They started bombing Sofia.

Things got worse. With German troops allowed free reign inside Bulgaria, Jewish deportations to the death camps were a daily occurrence until Boris stepped in. He made a stand and refused to hand over the 50,000 Jews remaining. In doing this,

Bulgaria became the only European country to save its Jewish population from extermination, and Tsar Boris the only leader to openly defy Hitler.

In the face of these refusals, Hitler summoned Boris to a meeting in Germany. Boris went, but refused to be swayed, and returned to Sofia. Two weeks later, he died of heart failure in suspicious circumstances. Boris received the Medal of the Legion of Honour from the Jewish community, the first time a non-Jew had received such a prestigious award.

A year later, Bulgaria decided to leave the Axis Powers alliance and declared war on Germany. They allowed Red Army troops into their country, and the Kremlin repaid this noble gesture by taking over the country. Bulgaria was now poised to be a puppet state of the Soviet Union.

6

The Banya Bashi Mosque was Sofia's only remaining Islamic place of worship. Around the back of it was a pleasant area with a fountain at the centre. Angela and I sat on a bench there, taking in the sun.

There were a few homeless people nearby, some walking with dogs, most by themselves. One lady sat on a bench with her bags by her side. After wiping her brow, she rooted around, retrieved a packet of crisps, and began munching on them.

A massive church was just a short walk away. The Alexander Nevsky Memorial Church was capable of holding ten thousand people, making it one of the largest Eastern Orthodox churches in the world. It was the prime tourist attraction of the city.

Alexander Nevsky had been a 13th century Russian military commander who, as well as having a grandfather with the spectacularly excellent name of Vsevovod the Big Nest, had once defended Russia's borders from some Swedish hordes. His famous catchphrase was 'Whoever will come to us with a sword, from a sword will perish.'

Just before his death in the early thirteenth century, he became a monk, which no doubt helped him achieve sainthood two hundred years later. A 2008 television poll voted Alexander Nevsky as the greatest Russian in history.

Angela and I found an outdoor bar to get some food. Women with orange hair were wandering past, and almost every man was smoking. The sun was out, and my mood was high. I was in the tenth country of the quest. Almost half way there!

7

The next day, Angela and I were in a park near Sofia University. In the middle of the park was the Soviet Army Monument. It was a 111ft statue depicting a soldier, a woman and a child standing above a selection of friezes.

Built in 1954, when Bulgaria was under the firm control of Moscow, it was gloriously Soviet in its design. Proud gestures, valiant poses and courageous gazes from all three individuals. The carvings around the base were more of the same, portraying the Soviet army as brave and respectful soldiers, ready to take arms against any threat to their freedom.

The only thing spoiling it was the ugly graffiti around the lower pedestal. But it wasn't as bad as what had happened to the monument prior to our visit.

In the dead of night, unknown people entered the park armed with brushes and colourful paint. Then they set to work. After they had finished, instead of being heroes of battle, the friezes depicted heroes of the comic world. Batman, Robin and even Wonder Woman were now carrying rifles or throwing grenades. Santa Claus and Ronald McDonald were also there, as was Superman, who seemed to be in charge of the colourful assault. Three days later, the sculpture was returned to its normal state of affairs.

8

The next morning, we caught a taxi back the airport.

"I'm looking forward to Prague," said Angela as we rushed through the tired-looking outskirts of Sofia. "People have told me how nice it is. In fact, I think we should've just gone there in the first place."

"What? And missed out Sofia?"

"Yeah. Don't get me wrong, I've enjoyed Sofia, but it wasn't exactly the prettiest place we've been to, was it? Tallinn beat it hands down. So did Riga."

Angela was right, of course. Sofia could never compete with the Baltic capitals. But the Bulgarian capital had something that a lot of other places didn't - it had exclusivity. I turned to face my wife. She was waiting for my reaction.

"I know what you mean," I said. "But hardly anyone goes to Sofia, that's what makes it exciting."

Angela frowned. "You keep saying that. *Hardly anyone goes there.*" She glanced outside at the grey buildings. "Look, Sofia was all right, but nothing special. In fact, it seemed a bit of a waste of money to tell you the truth. Like I said, I'd have rather gone straight to Prague. Or even just gone to Paris. That's all I'm saying."

I kept quiet and stared outside too, alarm bells rattling in my stomach. Was that it, then? Was the Red Quest finally coming to end? What chance did I have of getting Angela to visit Asia if she didn't want to go to any more countries in Eastern Europe? The euphoria I'd experienced in the bar the previous day came crashing down to zero.

We spent the rest of the journey in silence.

12. Turning Point in the Czech Republic

Interesting fact: In 2010, the Czechs were the biggest beer drinkers per capita in the world.

If ever there was a former Soviet buffer zone country to shake of its communist past, then the Czech Republic was it. More or less as soon as it gained independence in 1989, it turned itself around economically, and in the process became the third most peaceful country in Europe (number one and two were Iceland and Denmark).

When budget airlines began flying into Prague, the Czech capital saw its annual visitor numbers rise to almost four million, making it the sixth-most visited city in Europe.

That was the great thing about Prague: not only was it so damned pretty, it was also cheap and easy to visit. Just hop on a plane, arrive and see the sights. The bad thing about the Czech capital was all the above. With the likes of Ryanair and Easyjet offering flights for next to nothing, and with large amounts of cheap beer flowing, Prague quickly established itself as the Stag Capital of Europe.

2

I'd been to Prague once before, for Phil's birthday, in fact. A whole troop of us flew to the Czech Republic in the late 90s to sample some of its famous nightlife. This was before I became a discerning tourist, and long before I'd ever thought of my quest. And all I can really remember about the trip was the girl.

We were walking home after a night on the beers when a gorgeous young lady approached us. As we staggered in a weaving line of drunkenness, I heard her saying something to me. Before I knew it, her arms were wrapped around me.

"Hello, good-looking boy," she said in a suggestive voice.

"…Uh?…What…?" I stammered, carrying on walking.

She smiled and walked on with me for a few feet, trying to kiss my neck. "Yeah, I think I really like *you*!"

Even in my drunken state, I knew something was amiss. After all, why would a beautiful young woman approach a set of pissed-up British lads she'd never met before and drape her arms around one of them? Besides, I had a girlfriend back home.

"C'mon," she whispered in my ear. "You must like me a little bit?" And then she moved one of her hands down the front of my body.

"Get off!" I mumbled and brushed away at her. But then her other hand was doing the same thing, and so I twisted my body away, staggering from her grasp. "Leave me alone!"

She stood still for a moment and then turned tail, walking calmly away. It was only the next morning that I realised she had stolen my phone.

3

More than a decade on, I was back in Prague with Angela. The sun was out, the weather pleasantly warm, but my mood was less than glowing due to the conversation we'd had back in Sofia.

But what could I do, apart from face the fact that the quest was almost certainly over? I might be able to persuade Michael to go on a few trips with me, but I could kiss good-bye to the nations over in Asia, that much was certain. As I brooded upon this, I realised I had to think positively. I'd had a good run; I was in my eleventh country (twelfth if I counted Poland, which Angela and I had visited a few years previously) which was not a bad figure to end with. Plus, Angela might be right; Paris would be a nice city to visit. And think of the cash we would save. I decided that the best course of action was to cheer up and be grateful for what I'd already achieved.

The taxi dropped us off at Prague Castle, the largest castle complex in the world.

"Wow," said Angela, surveying the gorgeous surrounding. "Prague *is* pretty. Much better than Sofia." She shot me a glance, assessing my mood. I nodded at her observation. Prague was remarkably beautiful. Grand buildings, stately statues and sweeping gargoyles were everywhere around us. I'd not noticed its beauty the last time I'd been there.

Just opposite us was a guard in a pale blue uniform. He was standing to attention inside a small booth. We walked past him towards Mathias Gate, and then wandered into a huge courtyard where the twin spires of Saint Vitus Cathedral towered above us. Inside the cathedral were the relics of Good King Wenceslas.

Despite his name, King Wenceslas had never been a king. Instead, he'd been Duke of Bohemia (now present day Czech Republic). But he had been responsible for many good deeds in his day (including giving alms to the poor) until his younger brother murdered him in 935. But with a name like Boleslav the Cruel, you could hardly blame the younger sibling.

How amazing that both these characters were from the same family. One man was the inspiration behind a charming Christmas Carol, the other in possession of the most evil name in Czech history.

We left the castle and headed towards the River Vltava.

4

Tourists were everywhere, all of them ambling, pointing, gawping, or blocking the cobbled pathways. Angela and I merged into the thronging mass that slowly headed downhill to the magnificent Charles Bridge, named after the fourteenth-century king who had commissioned it.

In its time, battles and floods had damaged the bridge, and once, after a revolt in the 17th century, the severed heads of 27 riot leaders were put on display along it. Nowadays, the Charles Bridge, though undeniably pretty, was a tourist trap.

Photos of the Charles Bridge depict the gothic-tinged crossing as a serene place, perhaps an area for quiet contemplation, or somewhere to take a leisurely afternoon stroll. In the evening, it could also be the setting for microfilm exchanging. It wasn't like that when Angela and I tried to cross. The Charles Bridge was a jumble of humanity.

There were stalls and accordion players. There were men with puppets, and ladies flogging tacky trinkets. Tourists gawped in all directions with digital cameras recording their progress behind a sea of people's heads. Children in pushchairs, grandmothers with sticks, teenagers with ice-creams, and beggars lying on all fours added to the mayhem.

The view was good, mind you, offering a panorama of the old town, full of quant old medieval buildings and gothic church spires. Prague had been nicknamed The City of a Thousand Spires, and it was easy to see why from the Charles Bridge.

"Come on, lads," yelled a beefy young man coming towards us. He was wearing a T-shirt emblazed with MEATHEAD'S STAG DO. His accent was unmistakably Geordie and he had a troop of similarly dressed men just behind him. "It's beer o'clock and the alarm's gannin' off in me head."

The crowd pushed us along until we came to the other side of the bridge. Here the crowds were even worse, reducing us to a shuffling pace. But then we came to the central square, an area so expansive that we were finally able to stand in our own space. We marvelled at the view before us. It was a medieval fairytale land. No wonder people from all over the world rushed to Prague.

5

People were sitting eating elaborate ice-creams or drinking pints of beer in the bars and cafes around the edge of the square. Angela and I sat in one bar and watched a large crowd gather around the famous Astronomical Clock, the oldest one in the world that was still working apparently. A tourist train snaked its way around the square, disappearing off along a side street.

"What is an astronomical clock?" asked Angela, as she dug a spoon into her mound of ice-cream.

"I think it's a clock with special bits showing astronomical information. Things like the location of the moon and zodiac signs."

We stared at the one in front of us. The top bit was blue and orange, and extremely intricate, the bottom bit all gold and sparkly. It was on the side of the Town Hall, a building so pretty that if snow had covered its pointy spire and zigzag roof, it would've guaranteed it a place on a Christmas card.

"What are they waiting for?" Angela asked, as another crowd of people congregated near the clock.

Just then, there was a surge in the crowd, and I decided to investigate by standing on my chair. Angela did the same, and soon other people were following our lead. As the clock struck the hour, a set of small, carved figures emerged from the Astronomical Clock, and began moving in rhythmic motion. The crowd oohed and ahhed in admiration, but I was a bit disappointed and so was Angela.

"Was that it?" I said, climbing off my chair. "A bit of a let down." Angela nodded, but it seemed we were in the minority. Most other people were smiling as they dispersed.

6

The press had dubbed the Czech Republic's road to independence a Velvet Revolution. Velvet always sounds nice and a bit special, and the revolution in Czechoslovakia was exactly that.

Events started on 17 November 1989 when heavy-handed riot police put down a small-scale student protest. This sparked other rallies that ballooned into citywide protests. Four days later, half a million people gathered in Prague, and in the face of these mass demonstrations, the Communist Party of Czechoslovakia announced it would allow free and democratic elections. This was only eleven days after the initial protest. The bigwigs in Moscow gave their consent to these events.

By December, a non-communist government was in power, and Czechoslovakia was free of the Soviet Union. Three years later, Czechoslovakia went through the Velvet Divorce when it split from its neighbour, Slovakia. It became the Czech Republic. Again, it was all peaceful and amicable, leaving both countries on friendly terms with one another. How very refreshing.

7

For our final hour in Prague, we found a nice side cafe and bought ourselves some drinks. Czech lager really was a cut above the rest, I mused, as I took a cooling mouthful of the amber liquid. However, I almost spat it back out a few seconds later.

"Right," Angela said, "Tell me about the quest."

My mind went into overload. How did she know about the quest? Was this what had been on her mind in Sofia? How should I handle this? Eventually I stammered, "What quest?"

"The one where you're trying to visit all the countries that used to be in Russia or something. The one that has cost us a fortune, and has meant not going to places like Rome or New York for a year. Does that jog your memory about the quest, or shall I give you some more clues? "

I shook my head and remained silent.

"And if you're wondering how I know, Julie told me."

Julie was Phil's wife. Sometimes the four of us went out together. *Bloody Phil!* I'd told him not to tell Julie. I looked at Angela, trying to work out if she was angry. Her eyes were unreadable.

"So tell me about this silly quest of yours."

I took another sip of beer to dampen my bone-dry mouth and decided to tell her the truth. What did I have to lose anyway? It wasn't as if the quest was continuing or anything. I told Angela it had started with our visit to Latvia and had snowballed ever since.

"Look," I said. "I never thought I'd get near to finishing it, but somehow I have. There are only nine more countries to go."

Angela digested this piece of information. "Nine? Which ones?"

I began to count them off on my fingers. "Belarus, Kazakhstan, Tajikistan, Uzbeki—"

"Okay, that'll do. Nine more to go and then that's it? Your schoolboy quest will be finished?"

I nodded uncertainly. This seemed to be going better than expected. Maybe she'd had a rethink on the flight over from Sofia. I picked up my drink again, allowing my pulse to calm down.

"Okay, Jason," Angela said. "And listen to what I'm going to say carefully."

I looked at my wife.

"I don't know why you're obsessed with these Russian countries, but I'll give you one more year from today to finish your quest. You can pay for everything out of your own money. And if you haven't finished it in twelve months from now, then that's too bad. No more."

"Really?" My mind couldn't comprehend that Angela had given the Red Quest a new lease of life.

"Yes. One year from today."

I tried to calculate the logistics of visiting nine countries in one year, especially since most of them were in Asia. But twelve months was twelve months. That meant I had until the end of August, the following year to complete my quest.

"So you'll come to Kazakhstan and places like that with me?"

Angela shook her head and rolled her eyes. "No. That's not what I said. I said *you* have twelve months to go to these places. I'm not going to any of them."

I felt a stab in my stomach. "But who'll go with me?"

"That's your problem."

I stared at my drink, half of me euphorically happy, the other half full of dread.

"Do we have a deal?"

I stared at Angela. "Deal," I croaked. "One year from now to finish my quest."

13. Going Solo in the Caucuses

Interesting fact: Armenia was the first country in the world to adopt Christianity as its official religion.

I spent the next few months planning. And saving up. Christmas came and went, and the deadline was now only six and half months away.

For my first foray into Asia, I quickly narrowed my options down to Armenia and Georgia. Both countries were close together, both had easy entry requirements, and flights would be relatively simple. Furthermore, from what I'd read, both capitals were distinctly European in flavour, meaning that I wouldn't stand out like a sore thumb. All I needed to do was persuade Angela to go with me.

"No," she said.

We were having a nice meal, and even though it was the answer I'd expected, it still made me wince.

"And I can't believe you even asked," she added.

"But no one else will go with me! Michael can't get time off work, Jon has no money, and I'm not even going to ask Phil because he'll tell me to piss off."

"I don't care. I'm not going to Armenia. I told you that in Prague."

I put my glass down and stared across the table at Angela. All my planning had been in vain if she wouldn't go with me.

Angela looked back at me, clearly seeing self-pity etched across my brow. "Here's an interesting idea: why don't you go by yourself?"

The idea seemed ludicrous.

"Yes. If you're that bothered about going to Armenia, then go by yourself."

I sat back and considered this ridiculous proposal. To board an aeroplane and fly to some strange destination without anyone to accompany me - how scary would that be? What if something went wrong? What if I got lost? What would I do at mealtimes? What if someone arrested me? What if? What if?

"I think it's the only way you'll finish this quest of yours," said Angela. "So it's up to you."

2

On the flight to Armenia, I settled down thinking about my solo adventure to the Caucasus region. For my February half-term break, I'd be spending two nights in Yerevan, before driving north to Tbilisi, Georgia. I'd be all alone except for my camera and guidebook.

As we flew eastwards, my mood flickered between apprehension and excitement. Phil had thought me even more deranged than before, and perhaps he was right. I closed my eyes.

I'd always thought that people who travelled alone were incredibly brave, or incredibly stupid. Brave for doing it in the first place, but stupid for wanting to do it. Where was the joy in going on holiday when no one was around to share the experience? Yet here I was, heading to Yerevan doing precisely that. My trip to the Caucuses would be a test case for me, an experiment at seeing whether I could stomach doing it alone. If, at the end of the trip, I decided I couldn't, then the Red Quest would die a sudden death.

3

The plane began its descent into wintry Yerevan. Outside looked desolate and cold; a grim reminder that February in the Caucasus was not a journey for the faint hearted. In fact, just the previous week, the nighttime temperature in Yerevan had been a blood freezing minus eleven degrees Celsius, possibly explaining the lack of passengers on the flight. Thankfully my arrival coincided with a relative heat wave, with the temperature hovering around zero. As the aircraft began its final approach towards Zvarnots International Airport, I sat back thinking about Armenia.

Most people I'd talked to before my trip didn't really know where Armenia was, and so I told them it was at the crossroads of Western Asia and Eastern Europe, straddling the sometimes difficult line between the Islamic south (Iran and Turkey) and the Christian North (Russia and Georgia).

When the Soviets annexed Armenia in the 1930s (along with neighbouring Georgia and Azerbaijan), the people of Armenia had experienced a time of relative prosperity. After long years of Ottoman rule, the chance to get decent medicine and food from Moscow was a welcome development. But then Stalin came to power, and the good times ended. He had thousands of Armenians killed or sent to Gulags during his great purge. He also created a future problem when he gave a region of Armenia called Nagorno-Karabakh to Azerbaijan. Both countries would end up at war over this disputed area.

When Stalin died in 1953, things improved for Armenia. The Soviets tolerated religion, and Armenians began to enjoy an acceptable standard of living again. Things were looking up for the people of this small republic. At least for now.

4

A long line of people was in front of me at passport control, and being the only tourist in town, I had plenty of time to regard them as we shuffled along.

Older men sported flat caps and thick jackets that gave them a vague thuggish-look. If I were casting extras to star in a Cold War movie, I knew where I'd come to get them. Older women were generally on the stouter side, preferring fur hats and thick scarves. Younger women were all dark-haired and beautiful. The customs official stamped me in, and I was on my way.

Yerevan looked harsh and grainy from my seat in the taxi; the perfect backdrop for my Cold War movie. In the distance, I could make out Mount Ararat, the supposed resting place of Noah's Ark.

Ladas were everywhere, zipping about in the light traffic or parked by the side of the road with flat tyres and dirty windscreens. Most of the communist-style apartment blocks I was passing looked well past their sell-by date, as indeed did most buildings. The only exceptions were the casinos - they seemed brand new. A whole line of them stood glittering, and adding colour, in an otherwise listless street.

Road signs and shop lettering were in the strange Armenian script that looked like a random set of curls and loops to me. Consisting of a mind-boggling 38 letters, the alphabet bore no relation to English, or even Russian, and it was pointless trying to decipher it.

"Why you in Erevan?" asked the taxi driver, using the pronunciation that the local population favoured.

"Just visiting," I answered.

The man harrumphed. "You come for a holiday in February? You are mental patient!"

5

My hotel was located smack in the centre of the city, one of the reasons I'd chosen it. After depositing my things, I was out in the cold, searching for an ATM, but none accepted my card.

This was a worrying, but not an unexpected, development. Prepared for such an eventuality, I found a moneychanger and swapped some US dollars into the local currency, dram, and that done, I visited a supermarket and bought some bread and beer: surely the staple food of any traveller. If I'd been with Angela, we would have gone for a nice meal, and that thought made me feel slightly depressed. I was alone in a city, thousands of miles from home.

When night fell, I ventured outside again, this time towards Republic Square. It was large and well lit, giving the surrounding buildings a pleasing glow. The Soviets had called it Lenin Square, but nowadays Lenin's statue was long gone, replaced by the Marriot Hotel and the National Art Gallery. Zipping my coat tighter, I had a wander around the large square until weariness took over, and I retired back to the hotel. I'd survived my first night alone.

6

The next morning was drizzly and overcast, not really the weather for sightseeing, but with only one full day in Yerevan, I wrapped up warm and stepped outside. My first stop was close by. It was Saint Gregory the Illuminator Cathedral.

It was large and beige, standing proud and quite magical in the dim light of morning. Only finished in 2001, the cathedral contained the relics of Saint Gregory.

Gregory was born in the year 257. Just prior to his birth, Gregory's father was executed for assassinating a local king. Thus, things did not bode well for baby Gregory, especially with pitch forked peasants wanting to kill him too.

Luckily, Gregory's nannies managed to save him, and whisked the infant away to a secret location where they raised the child as their own. A few years later, they sent Gregory to a church to be educated in the ways of Christianity. He eventually grew up, got married and had some children of his own.

When the king found out that Gregory was living the high life, he had his guards arrest him. After all, Gregory was the son of the man who had assassinated his father. The guards delivered Gregory to the palace. The king sentenced him to life imprisonment inside a pit.

For the next few years, nothing much happened, except for Gregory's hair and beard getting longer, but then, quite unexpectedly, the king went mad. This turned out to be great news for Gregory because the king believed, for some reason, that his old nemesis was the only person who could help him.

Guards pulled Gregory from his pit and ordered him to cure the king of his insanity. Being a committed Christian, Gregory decided that, even though the king had separated him from his family, leaving him to languish inside a smelly pit for years, he would still help. He did so by baptising the king. And by God, it worked! And soon everyone in the royal household was being baptised. The king was so impressed that he ordered Gregory to baptise everyone in the country. Soon the whole of Armenia had converted to Christianity, and Gregory had secured his passage to Sainthood.

7

On a busy street beyond the cathedral, Lada taxis sped past and trolley buses trundled along. Small, rotund old ladies were shuffling by, often with plastic bags filled with produce. Just then, I spotted a lady wearing the most hideous fur coat ever. She had the monstrosity draped over her shoulders, with flaps of fur dangling everywhere. But the worst thing was the head. It was still attached. It looked like a fox. Younger people were more fashionable. Their features looking like a cross between the people of Eastern Europe and the people of Turkey.

Armenia seemed a nation of dog lovers. As I made my way through a city centre park, I noticed one dog not on its leash. As soon as it spotted me, it charged, chops slobbering in meaty anticipation. It was large and black, perhaps a Rottweiler, and my heart raced immediately. As it galloped closer, I recalled the dogs of Kiev and wondered whether to charge it like Michael had done.

By now, the dog's owner was shouting for it to return, or perhaps ordering it to attack, I couldn't tell, and a second later, it sped past me to sniff another dog. It then returned to the shouting man.

I exhaled deeply and carried on with my quest of sightseeing. Where was Michael when I needed him? Actually I knew exactly where he was because he was in England planning his upcoming wedding.

8

"Damn," I exclaimed under my breath.

It was thirty minutes later, and I'd just trailed up a long road. As usual, my map had led me to the general location of where I wanted to be, but had fallen well short of actually taking me there. Stuffing it into my pocket I looked this way and that, but could see no sign of the Zorovar Church.

After wandering aimlessly for a while, I spotted a man wielding a saw. He was trimming some branches of an overgrown tree. I showed him the map and pointed at the church, but like many people in Yerevan, he didn't understand English. Luckily I remembered I had a picture of the church and so fished it out of my bag. It immediately brought a smile from the man, and he pointed along a tiny street I'd never have found by myself. I thanked him, plodding off.

The Zorovar Church, one of the oldest in Yerevan, was small, but it still had plenty of people around it. Most were purchasing thin candles from a small stall before going inside. By peering through an almost iced-up side window, I could see lots of lit candles with people kneeling down. Feeling guilty to be intruding upon their prayers, I headed away. A minute later my phone rang. It was Angela.

"How is Armenia?" she asked.

"Not bad," I answered truthfully, finding a shop alcove to stand in. "There's quite a lot to see, but it's cold."

"And what's it like being by yourself?"

"Strange. It was scary at first as well. The worst thing was being on the plane over here. That felt really odd. But I think I'm getting used to things now. It helps that no one is staring at me. In fact, I reckon I fit in quite well. But I'd still prefer you to be here."

Angela wished me well for the rest of the trip and said she'd ring me later.

9

I caught a taxi to an Armenian Genocide museum. During World War I, Ottoman forces killed 600,000 Armenians (other estimates put this figure at 1.5 million). Mass burnings, drowning of children, morphine injections, and starvation were some of the methods used by the Turks.

On one occasion, Ottoman troops herded schoolchildren into a school hall and gassed them to death. Elsewhere, troops forced people to go on marches to Syria across the scorching desert. Most died. Theodore Roosevelt later said that the Armenian Genocide had been the greatest crime of the First World War.

The Soviets built the genocide monument in 1966. It featured a huge stone spike with an eternal flame. The wind-chill factor on the hill was rather high, and so I sought refuge inside the museum.

Some of the photos were harrowing. I stopped by a set taken during the death marches to Syria. They showed bedraggled individuals staggering with whatever possessions they could carry. They also showed dried corpses of people who had collapsed during the march.

Another set of photos was even worse. They showed dead children wrapped in rags who had starved to death. Then I came so a set of images showing Armenians being hanged. To me, hanging was one of the worst ways to go. To know that you're about to die in one of the most painful and public ways possible had always deeply scared me. The photo I was staring at showed a set of gallows with four people already dead. Another gruesome photo showed a set of decapitated heads that had been impaled on poles. It was unbearable to look at, and I felt sick.

"They are not nice photos are they?" said a voice behind me. I turned to see a young man who introduced himself as Abgar, a museum guide.

I shook my head. "They're horrible."

Abgar nodded and pointed at another photo, this one showing a boat at the edge of a lake. "These boats were filled with children and then taken to the deep water. Soldiers threw the children overboard. And this photo here shows the remains of burning victims. One Ottoman army officer said it was the most efficient way to dispose of women and children."

"I didn't know any of this had happened."

The young man smiled. "A lot of people say that. But it did happen. And it is something we Armenians will never forget."

10

Another issue that Armenians will never forget about is the disputed region of Nagorno-Karabakh. At the end of the 1980s, when Armenia began to grow vocal about independence, the problem of Nagorno-Karabakh reared its ugly head, a problem rooted in a decision made by Stalin over half a century earlier.

The issue was the amount of Armenians living in Nagorno-Karabakh under supposed Azerbaijani control. Armenians living there wanted to join up with the rest of Armenia, but Azerbaijan refused to entertain this idea. When Armenia declared its independence in August 1990, a brutal war broke out between Nagorno-Karabakh (with support from Armenia) and Azerbaijan. Both sides lost thousands of men, and the issue continues to this day. And all because of a poorly made decision from the 1930s.

Today, there is a tense ceasefire in place, but rather like Transnistria in Moldova, Nagorno-Karabakh acts as a de-facto independent republic, even though no other state recognises it, apart from, ironically enough, Transnistria. With one breakaway republic already crossed off the list, I decided to steer well clear of

Nagorno-Karabakh. Georgia to the north also had a pair of breakaway republics, namely Abkhazia and South Ossetia. I'd be missing those out too.

11

The most imposing building in the northern part of Yerevan was the mammoth Opera House. Cafes and a large outdoor ice rink surrounded it. I headed past it, towards the base of the Cascade, a never-ending series of steps commemorating the 50th anniversary of Soviet Armenia. At the top was a large monument I wanted to see. Sighing in resignation, I accepted my fate and began the climb.

A canoodling couple sat on one of the ledges of the staircase, and as I passed them, I tried to keep my breathing under control, but as soon as I was out of earshot, I let loose a ghastly exhalation of air. Finding a ledge of my own, I decided to take a rest. The views were really quite impressive even if my breathing wasn't. I looked out over the frost-covered roofs of the city, which was interspersed with ugly tower blocks.

Fifteen minutes later, I arrived at a metal fence blocking any further travel. I was about three-quarters of the way up and couldn't believe my bad luck. The monument at the top was annoyingly close.

I found another bench and sat down. The young couple had gone, I noticed, but just then, some people caught my eye by coming down some hidden steps further up. So the path did continue! I got up and headed onwards, eventually reaching the base of the huge monument. My muscles were searing, and my pulse rate was in the danger zone. But I didn't care - I had made it!

It was then that I found out I could have caught an elevator to the top. No matter, I thought bitterly, I was at the top now and so swivelled my head to look at the monument. It was really good actually, consisting of a huge gold leaf mounted on top of a tall pedestal. But there was an even better monument nearby. Crossing a busy hill top road, I headed towards Mother Armenia.

12

Like the Mother Kiev Statue in Ukraine, Yerevan's prime statue was a giant metal lady. Mother Armenia wasn't hard to spot because she was so big. I found myself staring up at the statue, and couldn't help but marvel at the 23-metre high statue of a woman holding an impressive sword. She had replaced a statue of Lenin, who had stood on the pedestal until the 1960s.

Speaking of the pedestal, it was also mammoth, so large, in fact, that it contained a military museum. The surrounding square also displayed some impressive hardware, including a few tanks, a Mig fighter jet, some armoured vehicles and a huge missile. Children accompanied by their grandparents were wandering around the square, mostly looking at the tanks. But I loved the statue. So imposing and so dramatic.

Just next to Mother Armenia was a fairground. Everything was closed because it was out of season, giving the place an almost sinister feel. The young couple I'd seen earlier were sitting in one of the vacant Ferris wheel compartments, once again kissing. We were the only people there. Half an hour later I was back at the bottom of the Cascade.

13

After a bite to eat, I began to wander aimlessly through the shopping district of Yerevan. This part of town looked like any other city, full of clothes shops and the odd KFC thrown in for good measure. Parked police cars were all over the place, with uniformed men standing about, mostly just chatting to each other. I passed a tiny medieval church and crossed a road towards it. Like the church I'd visited earlier, this one had a fair smattering of people hanging around outside or praying within. Not that many could fit inside though, the Katoghike Church was the tiniest I'd ever seen.

Later that night I decided to avoid the fast-food joints and elected to visit a restaurant near the hotel. This was the worst part of travelling alone, I was quickly discovering, meal times. It wasn't so bad in places like KFC (where I'd had lunch) when you were in and out fairly quickly, but in a restaurant you had to wait.

I opened the door, and even though it was almost seven thirty, the place was empty. I sat down anyway, thankful that the menu had an English section. I quickly ordered steak, cooked medium.

Ten minutes later a huge piece of meat arrived on my table, and I wasted no time in cutting into it. But when I'd said medium, I didn't realise the chef would cook it with a medium-sized match. About two millimetres of the outside was cooked and the rest was raw. Blood seeped from the bulk of quivering flesh on my plate. I forked some into my mouth, immediately tasting blood. For the next five minutes, I scraped off the cooked bits and ate them with the potatoes. Afterwards there was a large mass of red jelly lying on my plate. I finished my beer and left.

The next morning a minibus picked me up from my hotel at the start of a long drive to Tbilisi, Georgia. The next country of the quest was beckoning.

14. Road to Tbilisi

Interesting fact: Georgia still has wild populations of bears, wolves and lynxes.

My original plan was to fly to Tbilisi. However, that was before Armavia (the national airline of Armenia) had cancelled their short 45-minute hop from Yerevan. They sent me an email telling me this, of course, but it did throw my plans into disarray. In the end, I used the refund to pay for a private minibus and driver.

Jivan was in his mid-fifties and picked me up from my hotel in Yerevan. We were soon on our way, climbing through the outskirts of the city into the hills, as the morning rain turned into a sheet of snow.

Twenty minutes later, the blizzard was really coming down. It was adding a fresh layer to the already deep carpet of white. As we snaked our way upwards, I caught sight of red taillights ahead. If it hadn't been for the lorry, I wouldn't have even known we were on a road. It was a total whiteout.

"Good yah?" boomed Jivan, skilfully recovering from a skid. "You like snowstorm?"

I looked at him and shook my head.

"You not like?"

"It's a bit scary."

And then we saw our first accident - three smashed cars by the side of the road. Thankfully, nobody seemed injured and we soon passed them. I watched them disappear into the whiteness.

Despite speaking only the barest smattering of English, Jivan still managed to tell me that he'd driven the Yerevan to Tbilisi run many times. "On normal day it take five hours, but with snow, longer. More fun, yah!"

The storm suddenly grew worse, reducing visibility to maybe twenty metres. With nothing to see apart from white, I sat back, leaving things in the capable hands of my driver.

An hour later, the blizzard stopped, and Jivan pulled over for a cigarette. I joined him outside. We seemed to be traversing an alpine valley. I mimed that it looked good for skiing. "Yes, is good for that!" Jivan said, striking a match. It flared briefly to add a tear of colour against the white surroundings.

Five minutes later, we were back on the slippery road, occasionally passing through small villages. Men wearing black jackets and woolly hats were shovelling snow from cars. Further on, Jivan slowed down. A large truck was coming in the opposite direction, with a couple of men standing in the back. Both were tossing something over the side. I strained to see and realised they were gritting the road. The men had done a good job, because the next stretch of the road was largely free of ice, allowing our wheels good purchase on a road overlooking sheer cliff faces.

"Two kilometres to border," Jivan told me. "You have the passport?"

I nodded and fished it out from my pocket, excited as ever at the prospect of crossing into a new country.

Georgia had a great flag, I soon discovered. It looked like England's, only better. It consisted of a large red cross on a white background, but with the bonus of some extra red crosses in each corner. My first sighting of one was at the Armenia-Georgia road border.

Formalities were painless, and the beautiful border guard working there soon stamped me in. No visa, no hassle, just as it should have been.

An hour later, we arrived in the outskirts of Tbilisi, after a seven-hour journey of snow-filled fun. Rain took over from the snow as we descended into the lower parts of the city, and further in, the standard-issue Soviet apartment blocks came into view, as did a huge landfill site near the river. In the gloom and drizzle, Tbilisi looked grim.

Georgia's route to independence did not run smoothly. In 1988, cracks began to appear in the Georgian Communist Party when the people of Tbilisi held strikes and demonstrations. Events culminated with thousands of Georgians demonstrating outside the Government House.

At first, everything was peaceful, but after four days of constant protest, Soviet troops arrived at the scene. With tension growing, a local priest tried to calm things down, asking everyone to leave before things got out of hand. The protesters refused to budge.

That night, Soviet troops surrounded the whole area. In response, the protestors began to pick up things they could use as weapons in case of an attack. Then the order came for Soviet troops to clear the protesters by any means necessary.

And this they did.

At one point, troops chased a sixteen-year-old girl until she fell by the steps of the Government House. There, they beat her to death with shovels while her mother watched on helplessly. Across the street, in an upstairs balcony, someone filmed this attack. It caused outrage when it surfaced in the resulting investigation.

In the ensuing stampede, nineteen more people were killed, most of them women. The Soviets claimed they had died because of the pandemonium created by the protesters, the Georgians claimed otherwise, saying the Red Army had launched CS gas at them. Whatever the reason, the effect was devastating for the Soviets because the next day, Georgian protestors showed the bodies of the dead women on TV. The citizens of Tbilisi declared forty days of mourning, and the country went into shutdown.

With world reaction aghast, the communist government resigned, and less than a year later, Georgia was an independent republic. The tragedy become known as the Tbilisi Massacre, and 8 April would eventually become a public holiday.

4

My hotel was up a steep street that specialised in fruit and vegetable shops. After I'd dropped my suitcase off, I walked down the hill until I came to a busy street.

It was late evening, and people were heading home after a day's work. Police cars patrolled the road, I noted, periodically stopping cars with their flashing lights and tinny sirens.

Tbilisi seemed okay, I thought now. Even in the drizzle, it exuded a certain charm, and I was looking forward to seeing more of it the next day. After grabbing a bite to eat, I headed back to the hotel, along the way passing a moment of slapstick comedy.

The man was struggling to raise the bonnet of his Lada. As I approached, he finally got the thing up and proceeded to pull the latch down. Satisfied that he'd done this, he bent to inspect the engine, just as the bonnet came crashing on his head. Shouting and cursing, the man removed his head and slammed the bonnet with such force that I could hear the metallic clang reverberating off the buildings around me.

5

The next morning I was getting the full Georgian works for breakfast. Being the only person in the dining room meant the waiter could give me his complete and undivided attention. As I tucked into some thick slices of bread and cheese, the young waiter brought me a triangular piece of baked bread.

"This iz traditional Georgian recipe," he said beaming. "We call it Georgian Pizza. The cook has made especially for you!"

I could see the cook, a woman aged about sixty, toiling away inside a small kitchen. I finished my sandwich and took a bite of the new thing. It tasted like bread with warm cheese in the middle. As I munched away, the waiter brought something else. "This iz also traditional food of Georgia. It has been deep-fried and I'm sure you will enjoy!"

Bloody hell, I thought, this was a banquet, and I wasn't even hungry. In fact the only reason I'd come down for breakfast was because someone had rung my room asking what time I'd be eating. With the waiter hovering nearby, I picked up one of the fried bread pieces and took a bite. I now had three plates of bread, a bowl of pickled vegetables and a yoghurt. With my stomach already full, the waiter approached once again. "Please, sir, how would you like your eggs cooked?"

6

With a swirling stomach, I finally stepped outside into a cold Tbilisi morning. Once again I passed the small shops peddling carrots, turnips and potatoes, also noticing a few other shops specialising in strange cheeses.

With my coat zipped tight, I looked up at the sky, hoping the rain would keep at bay. There was already a mist in the hills obscuring the snow-covered peaks. On one piece of high ground, I could see an almost ethereal Ferris wheel and a massive TV Tower. Both flickered into view before disappearing again. Later that evening, both structures would be lit up like fireworks, offering the strange spectacle of a light show high in the hills.

All around me, the people of Tbilisi were rushing into metro stops or else buying cooked pastries from the many stalls. I stopped near the Parliament Building, thinking of that poor girl who had died on the steps. The fact I could walk so freely down this street had been due to people like her.

Freedom Square seemed to be the heart of Tbilisi and featured an amazing monument smack in the middle. It was a huge column with a golden statue of Saint George slaying a dragon. There was even a golden spear sticking into the beast's mouth. Around the square was a set of fine buildings, including Tbilisi City Hall and

The Bank of Georgia. After a warming latte in the Marriott Hotel, I was off once more, heading towards the river.

The almost unpronounceable Mtkvari River was a grey strip of water favoured by fishermen with long poles. On the other side was the Presidential Palace, a large building that looked standard issue, except for the strange blue dome in its centre. It looked like the abode of a James Bond villain. It was at this point that I realised I was enjoying myself. To be able to do what I wanted, and when I wanted, was something quite liberating.

7

Now that I was used to the idea of being by myself, it actually simplified things. For instance, I could avoid all form of clothes and shoe shops. I could cross a road and take a photo of a building, all without fear of Angela getting bored. I could have KFC for lunch and a McDonald's for dinner if the desire took me. I was a free agent!

As I ambled along the river, Tbilisi seemed perfectly safe for a tourist. The only dangers were the slippery cobbles beneath my feet, and the odd political protest. The British Foreign Office (a website I always checked diligently before any trip) claimed that protests were common in the Georgian capital, and often violent. Well, so far, I hadn't seen anything like that.

In the distance, I could see a huge golden-domed cathedral and wondered whether I could be bothered trailing to it. In the end, I decided to go for it, and was glad because it turned out to be great.

The Holy Trinity Cathedral was the third tallest Orthodox Cathedral in the world, and stood in an area full of other churches. Georgian flags and ornately designed lampposts surrounded it, and I was the only person there apart from a flea-bitten mutt sniffing the ground.

The cathedral *was* tall; the top of its golden dome was almost obscured by the low-level clouds hanging over the city. I looked back at the dog who had slumped down on a path. It looked towards me briefly, but seemed more interested in a couple of ducks it had spotted in a fenced-off pond. I decided to head back down the hill towards the river. It was time for lunch.

8

While waiting for my food to arrive, I read the Lonely Planet guide to Tbilisi from cover to cover, and then read it again. After I'd eaten, I decided to visit a statue of a falcon. It was next to Tbilisi's famous sulphur baths, a group of brick domes with steam escaping from them.

The statue was a memorial to King Vakhtang's falcon. According to legend, the king had been hunting with his falcon when it had caught a pheasant. Then a surprising thing happened: the falcon fell to the ground and died. Upon investigation, the king discovered steam emanating from a spring, and quickly ordered building work to commence. This resulted in the birth of Tbilisi.

The statue of the falcon was rather small, but showed the bird in the full throes of life, pheasant grasped in its talons.

Close to the statue was the only remaining mosque in the city. Although quite striking in blues and yellows, it looked a bit haphazard. The main section was at ground level, but its main minaret was on the side of a nearby hill, tucked in between some residential dwellings. Higher still though were two of Tbilisi's prime sights: the Narikala Fortress and the Mother Georgia Statue. The fortress looked every inch the proper castle – all battlements and towers, and wondering whether I'd make it to the top without passing out, I began the climb.

9

The Narikala Fortress dates from the 4th century, but a builder called Dave added an extension in the eleventh century. I knew this because the guidebook told me so.

Born in 1073, of royal stock, and raised during a period of Georgian history known as the Great Turkish Onslaught, King David took the throne at the tender age of sixteen. Deciding that he needed to teach the nasty Ottomans a lesson, he declared war on them. In turn, the Turks declared a Holy War on him, and soon gathered a huge army that outnumbered David's troops ten to one. Against the odds though, the Georgians won, and King David II (also known as David the Builder), became the greatest king in Georgian history. He had once lived in the fortress I was huffing and puffing towards.

Clambering up some slippery cobbles, I came to some metal steps that led almost vertically upwards. After only two minutes, I was panting like a sex fiend but still climbed onwards. I could have done with a set of grappling ropes, I thought, or perhaps a helicopter. Then, after scaling close to a million steps, I came to a dead end.

"Bugger!" I shouted into the cold, wintry sky, knowing nobody could hear my exclamations. "Bloody steps!"

Which maniac had built a set of steps that led to a dead end? With wobbling thigh muscles, I climbed back, down pondering how I would ever get to the top. The answer turned out to be a narrow winding path that I'd seen earlier but stupidly ignored in favour of the more direct route.

When I eventually reached the top, I had the whole fortress to myself. I climbed upon old battlements that afforded me a fantastic view of Tbilisi below, all red roofs and church spires. It reminded me a little of Prague, only a slightly grimier version. I peeped over turrets, pretending I was repelling Ottoman invaders, and even the wind whipping across my face couldn't dampen my spirits.

Not far from the fortress was the Mother Georgia statue. Made of aluminium and twenty metres tall, I could only stare in wonder at the huge monument. Erected in 1958, the metal lady (with impressive metallic boobs) held a bowl of wine in one hand (to welcome guests) and a sword (to fight off enemies) in the other.

She could be seen all over the city. At her base, someone had spray-painted: *Lala loves Eda.* To me, Mother Georgia was easily the best sight in Tbilisi – so big, so drastic, so Soviet. I headed back down the hill into the centre of Tbilisi. Early the next morning I was due to leave for England.

10

That evening, as I was packing my bags, I decided to check on the US dollars I had hidden away. They were gone, about a hundred pounds worth, and so were some Armenian Dram and Georgian lari. Thinking that they had perhaps dropped out of their hiding place, I searched the suitcase but found nothing. I searched all over the room, including under the bed and behind the desk, but still failed to locate the missing money. I emptied the suitcase and searched through everything a second time. Nothing. After another look in every nook and cranny of the room, I had to face facts, someone had been in the room, most probably a cleaner, and had helped themselves.

Steeling myself, I went down to reception. The young woman there listened to my story and immediately looked worried. Next the manager appeared and soon he was looking shocked too. "This is first time in fifteen years we have had anything like this," he told me. "Please sit down and wait, sir."

Next an older woman came into the room, the same friendly woman who had cooked my breakfast that morning. She didn't speak English, but when she heard my story, via the manager, she looked stunned. Mentally berating myself for even coming down in the first place, I waited for whatever was going to happen.

After informing me that the woman doubled up as the hotel cleaner, the manager wanted my assurances that I had definitely left the cash in my suitcase.

"Yes," I said. "Like I said, I left it there when I arrived. But now it's gone."

We all trooped up to my room, with the older woman looking highly stressed. A new search began, but no money turned up.

"We will reduce your bill," said the manager eventually. "That is all we can do. But in the meantime could you please do another search of the room, just in case."

I told him I would.

11

When they had gone, I shook my head. The cleaner didn't seem the type to steal money, but I certainly couldn't see the other two doing it either.

Thinking that I'd never see the money again, I emptied my suitcase for a third time, and this time found the cash, hidden between some folds of a T-shirt.

Oh my God, I thought in horror, thinking of the mayhem I'd caused. A hotel's reputation is built on the promise of honesty and security, and I'd basically accused them of theft. Feeling about as guilty as I'd ever felt before, I slunk back to reception and told the girl and the manager I'd found my money. Apologising profusely, I asked where the other lady was.

The manager took me to another room, and the woman in question came out. Through translation, I told her I was sorry and handed her twenty dollars as compensation, a trifling amount for the pain I'd caused her. Finally I returned to my room, feeling like a cad of the highest order.

12

Sitting in the departure lounge of Tbilisi International Airport, after I'd rung Angela telling her I'd be on my way back home soon, I pondered my first solo trip. At the outset, on the flight to Yerevan, I knew it would be a test case for the Red Quest. If I couldn't handle being alone, then the quest would fail: simple as that. But travelling solo had proven to be a revelation. I had found I could sit in a bar or restaurant by myself and feel more or less okay. I could walk around by myself and not feel pathetic. No one had stared at me, and no one had given me any cause for concern. And as Angela had pointed out, doing it by myself was the only option if I ever wanted to finish the quest. There was no other way.

While I waited for my flight to arrive, I thought about the countries that remained in the quest and how, if ever, I'd get to them in the six and a half months still available.

All five 'Stans remained, a block of Central Asian republics shrouded in relative mystery, and cloaked in visa application hassles. Getting to places like Kazakhstan and Tajikistan was not going to be cheap and would require careful planning.

The third Caucuses country, Azerbaijan, remained obstinate too. If I'd had more time on this trip, I might've squeezed it in, but as it stood, Azerbaijan would just have to wait. Hopefully I could tag it onto the end of my trip to the 'Stans. And that left Belarus, the hardest country in Europe to visit. I'd only briefly looked at the entry requirements for Belarus, and even that made my head ache. Belarus, I felt, would have to wait until the end.

Outside snow was falling but I could see a plane landing, hopefully mine. Six and half months left, I pondered. Six and a half months to visit the seven most difficult countries of the quest. A tall order by anyone's reckoning.

15. Borat Land!

Interesting fact: Kazakhstan is the largest land-locked country in the world that still has a navy!

"You are mental if you are seriously thinking of going to Kazakhstan!" said Phil. "And how the hell are you affording these stupid trips? I mean, your savings must be gone by now."

Phil was correct; my latest jaunt was going to cost a fortune. Most of my savings had gone funding my trip to Armenia and Georgia, and now, with the most expensive countries still ahead of me, I was relying on the flexible little friend in my wallet to help me out. But the quest was like a maddening thing in my brain: it simply wouldn't let go.

It had been the same when I was ten-years-old. I'd religiously collected football stickers to put in my Panini album. Every penny of my pocket money was spent buying packs of five stickers from the local newsagent. And the urge to complete the collection had continued unabated until I had each one of the spaces filled. And now a new worm had burrowed into my mind, with the sole purpose of making me visit every former Soviet republic, regardless of the cost. The only thing that could curtail it was Angela's deadline. It was April, and the deadline was now five months away.

"Why don't you come with me?" I asked, picking up my pint.

Phil laughed aloud; such was his mirth. "To Borat Land? No thanks. I'd rather put my testicles in a turnip masher."

"You'll miss out on a real treat. Almaty is supposed to be really nice."

"No it's not. Kazakhstan's full of peasants and inbreeds. They eat turnips for breakfast, lunch and dinner. They probably shag them over there. Why would I pay a shed load of money to go there? Even Michael thinks you're mad about this one."

"Actually they prefer apples to turnips," I corrected, but Phil had already gone to the bar.

2

Since arriving back from Georgia, it had taken endless amounts of effort and time to organise my mammoth four country extravaganza of Kazakhstan, Uzbekistan, Turkmenistan and Azerbaijan: The other two 'Stans, Tajikistan and Kyrgyzstan, I'd worry about later; there simply wasn't enough time to get to them during my Easter holiday trip.

All four countries turned into a visa headache of epic proportions. Letters of Invitation and pieces of paperwork written in Cyrillic passed back and forth via email. It was a bureaucratic nightmare brewed in hell. In the end, I made contact with a company called Stan Tours, whose website stated they specialised in travel to the 'Stans. After a few emails explaining my trip, they soon got to work. A week later, they sent me a whole stack of forms to fill out and a message explaining the next steps. They also put my itinerary into some sort of logical order. Things were starting to make sense.

By April, I was ready to rock with a set of visas in my passport and a dollop of excitement in my brain. First stop was Almaty, Kazakhstan.

3

Kazakhstan, the ninth-biggest country in the world, is definitely at odds with the nation depicted by Borat, because it is actually an oil-rich Central Asian republic doing well for itself. Skyscrapers are shooting up all over Almaty, and Westerners on the scent of a dollar are arriving in droves.

Landing early morning at Almaty Airport, the outside scene was decidedly alpine, with conifers and jagged, snow-capped mountains dominating the horizon. As the aircraft taxied in though, it became clear we were not in Switzerland. The amount of Antonovs, Ilyushins, and Tupolevs parked around the place, most looking as if they had not flown in a long while, were good indicators I was in a former Soviet republic. Some large red Cyrillic lettering spelling out Almaty Airport on the front of the terminal building strengthened this notion, and cementing it further were the customs officials wearing sombre uniforms and gigantic dinner-plate hats. The caps were so huge and cumbersome that I wondered whether they ever got caught in doorways.

4

"You have visa?" asked the unsmiling border official. I nodded and passed him my passport. He opened it and flicked through until he found the page in question. After studying it for a few moments, he turned to the front of my passport and began turning through each page in turn, scrutinising every stamp and visa.

"Where you go after Kazakhstan?" he finally asked me.

"Uzbekistan," I answered.

The man shook his head. "You have no visa for Uzbekistan."

Stan Tours mentioned that this might happen and told me to explain that I'd get the visa on arrival in Uzbekistan.

With a hefty queue shuffling their feet behind me, the man stared at me for a few seconds and stamped my visa. "I hope you are correct."

Wondering what I'd let myself in for, I entered the arrivals hall where a man with my name written on a placard was waiting for me. He doubled up as my driver into the city centre.

5

"You have come at right time," he told me as we set off, his accent sounding noticeably Russian despite his almost Chinese appearance. "Two days ago there was snow blizzard and frozen street. But is okay now. Spring has come to Almaty for you!"

Stunt drivers of doom populated the three-lane highway. Swerving was always at the last second, and the only time the madness ceased was whenever a pedestrian stepped into the road. Brakes were jammed on with such haste that I could hear squeals of rubber over the din of the radio. Evidently running down a pedestrian was a big no-no in Kazakhstan.

The airport road resembled others in former Soviet cities: well maintained and flanked by high-rise apartment blocks. The ugly buildings gave the city a slightly grim look. Locals stood at bus stops, huddled in small groups or else chatting into phones. We suddenly screeched to a halt to allow a pedestrian to cross.

"This highway follows old Silk Road," mentioned my driver as we set off again. "And not far is Chinese border. You know Silk Road?"

I nodded, staring at a gang of women armed with huge brushes who were splashing white paint onto the bases of trees. The Silk Road had once stretched from Europe to China, and Almaty had been an important trading stop along the way. I asked the man whether anything remained of it.

"No," the driver answered sadly. "Nothing apart from the city itself."

My hotel offered horse on its restaurant menu. It tempted me to be honest, especially since it was a meat I'd never sampled, but after such little sleep, I elected to give it a miss. Instead I opted for a beef sandwich. For the remainder of the day, I recovered from my long flight, thinking of what lay ahead on the Red Quest.

6

The next morning, my first impression of Almaty was that it seemed distinctly European. Wide boulevards, tall concrete office blocks, advertising billboards, and trams and trolley buses made me feel as if I was in Bulgaria or Ukraine and not the middle of Asia.

Kazakhstan was the first Islamic nation of the Red Quest. Three-quarters of the population were Muslim, meaning there were a fair few mosques dotted around the city. Near the Central Mosque, a grand building with a huge golden dome, I had a sneaky glance at the people on the street. Like in Yerevan and Tbilisi, I was pleased to find that no one was paying me any attention. With a large ethnic Russian population living in the city, people probably assumed I was one of them.

Nearby was the Zelyony Bazaar, otherwise known as the Green Market, possibly due to the green lettering emblazoned on its massive roof. I wandered inside, passing clothes, vegetable, and flower stalls until I came to an area specialising in plumbing equipment. Here, broad-shouldered men fingered pieces of piping apparatus, turning them over in their large palms as if inspecting precious pieces of silver.

I wandered onwards to find myself in a cavernous meat hall split into sections according to the animal type for sale. I trotted straight for the horse section.

Women wearing red aprons and colourful headscarves stood about looking faintly bored while they waited for customers. I wasn't bored though because I couldn't stop staring at the dangling horse penis for sale. I really fancied taking a photo but didn't dare. I was getting funny looks as it was. It was only later that I found out it wasn't penis after all, but qazy, a local delicacy made of horse rib meat stuffed inside an intestine.

7

According to my guidebook, upstairs in the Zelyony Bazaar was a café that specialised in steamed mutton. As delicious as that sounded, I was more interested in the fermented mare's milk it sold, a drink known locally as kumis.

I quickly found a stall selling it, and after an initial bit of communication difficulty, I managed to procure myself a glass of the stuff.

It was white and milk-like, and so I spun it in the cup a few times and saw it moving about in a normal fashion. So far so good, I thought. Next I smelled it, and found it had a bit of a nasty aroma, reminding me of cheese that had gone off. Still, that wasn't too bad – I'd certainly had worse.

Finding a secluded corner, I sat down and regarded the beverage. Then before I could back down I raised the cup to my lips and steeled myself. As soon as the cold liquid touched my tongue and splashed over my taste buds, I almost gagged. Fermented mare's milk was hideous, like I'd coughed up a load of milky vomit. I spat it out, deposited the cup on a nearby table and fled.

8

Panfilov Park, a few blocks away, was a large area of green favoured by families with young children. A huge Soviet war memorial dominated one end of the park. It was a typical Soviet sculpture, full of heroic poses and proud gestures, but it was still impressive because it was so bloody big. After a moment staring up at the thing, I walked towards a quite remarkable cathedral.

The Zenkov Cathedral was made entirely of wood, making it one of the tallest wooden buildings in the world. I stared up at the structure, wondering how they had made it so big, because even the nails were made from wood. But it was the colours that were particularly fetching: yellows, reds and blues, giving it an almost toy-like appearance.

Suddenly, I heard a voice behind me. I turned to see a policeman. He was jabbering away at me in a language I couldn't understand. His cap was massive. It was like a flying saucer had landed on his head.

He stopped in front of me, expecting some sort of answer.

"Sorry," I said. "Do you speak English?"

The policeman studied me. He wasn't smiling. A few people in the park stared at us briefly but then carried on with what they were doing. "You American?" he finally asked.

I shook my head. "English."

I'd read that the Kazakh police were sometimes keen on stopping tourists with the hope of extracting bribes. I wondered if this was about to happen to me.

"Engleesh? Give passport."

I told him I didn't have my actual passport but had a photocopy of the relevant pages. My passport was in the hotel safe. I passed my papers to him, wondering how much the going rate for a bribe in Almaty was. I didn't have that much on me. I supposed I could always go to an ATM to get some tenge out.

"Why you in Almaty?" he asked after studying my visa.

I decided to keep my answer as simple and as truthful as possible. I said, "Tourist."

The policeman handed me back my photocopies. "Be careful of pickpocket. There are many in Almaty. You may go."

I did, thanking the man. Perhaps the rumours about corrupt officials were overstated.

9

Although a fairly flat city, Almaty did have a noticeable gradient as I headed towards its southern end. In the far distance, I could see the mountains I'd seen at the airport; large, snow-capped zigzags skirting the clouds and mist. They looked brooding and menacing rising up from the vast pine forests that seemed to surround the city.

By my reckoning, about half the citizens of Almaty were ethnic Kazakhs, displaying faintly Chinese looks about them - the remainder were Russian-looking types, the girls all blond hair and long legs. Also notable was that no one was obese or overweight. Perhaps this was because there were no McDonald's, KFCs or Pizza Huts in the city.

To calm my pounding feet, I stopped in a popular coffee house chain called *Coffeedelia*. Entering it, I found a table and ordered a latte. It came with a heart-shaped froth and a lovely little biscuit. On nearby tables, young Kazakhs sat chatting amiably or typing into laptops, all very modern and civilised. If Phil could see this, I thought, he'd realise how wrong he'd been about Kazakhstan. No turnips for sale in here. I studied my guidebook, wondering where to go next.

10

The Dawn of Liberty Monument was a strange-looking thing. Built in 2006 as a memorial to people killed by communist police in 1986, it was a winged woman holding both arms in the air. She was releasing a bird, heavy in symbolism, light in visitors. Like many attractions in Almaty, I was the only person in attendance.

The protest that the statue commemorated started, as it usually did, with a bunch of students. For some reason, the Kremlin had decided that instead of a local Kazakh man leading the Kazakh Communist Party, it would be better to have their man from Moscow in charge. The students thought this unfair.

On the morning of the 17 December 1986, a whole crowd of them began a march through central Almaty, the then capital of Kazakhstan. As they chanted their way through the streets, other students joined them, until there were thousands of protesters. By evening, things were getting a bit edgy, so the police tried to disperse the crowds. Skirmishes broke out, and by nightfall, cars and shops were being set alight.

The next morning, even more people joined in with the protest, and then on the third day, with no sign of the unrest quieting, the

Kremlin decided to act. They gave the order for police to fire live ammunition.

According to Soviet authorities afterwards, the police killed two people. According to other sources, they killed hundreds. No matter what the true number was, the effect was immediate. The protests ended. The old Soviet method of stamping down on any dissention worked its magic again. Life slowly returned to normal in Almaty, and the Russian man in charge settled down in his job. But beneath the surface, unrest continued to brew.

Less than three years later, another riot broke out, this time in the town of Novy Uzhen. This quickly spread to other towns. A few days later, Gorbachev sacked the Russian leader of the Kazakh Communist Party and replaced him with a Kazakh politician. If only he'd done that in the first place, I thought. The unrest died down immediately.

Just opposite the Dawn of Liberty monument was a building that reeked of sheer and delicious Sovietness. It was massive and rectangular, and covered in grey concrete and glass. Its roof was the best bit, all jagged and severe, with giant icicles of concrete dangling from its awnings. In direct contrast to this stark architecture was the gigantic blue Nurbank advertisement on top. Nurbank was one of the biggest banks in Kazakhstan, and it reminded me I needed to get some tenge out.

11

With a new wedge of Kazakh currency in my wallet, I walked along the road until I came to the former Parliament Building, a structure so immense that it took an eternity just to walk past. Behind it, in a nice little park, was the old presidential residence. When the nation's capital had moved north to Astana in 1997, Kazakh president, Nursultan Nazarbayev, went too, leaving his huge home in his wake.

Nursultan Nazarbayev has ruled Kazakhstan since 1991. Despite looking like a wise old grandfather, allegations of election rigging have dogged his presidency. He's also been accused of dipping his hands into the country's coffers to fund his lavish lifestyle, something he has strenuously denied. Civil rights groups have also claimed that Nazarbayev's government has a history of human rights abuses, an accusation that he also rejects.

Having said that, in many ways, Nazarbayev has done a lot for his country. Through vigorous foreign investment and free-market initiatives, Kazakhstan is thriving, easily the richest of the Central Asian republics. In terms of its GDP, it is above countries such as Argentina and South Africa. Kazakhstan is the world's biggest uranium producer, a top ten in oil production, and somehow Nazarbayev has kept Islamic extremism at bay, something his neighbours haven't quite managed. He even got rid of his country's nuclear weapons (for which he was put forward for receiving a Nobel Peace Prize). His people earn four times as much as those in neighbouring Uzbekistan, and because of this, the president is a hugely popular man within Kazakhstan. As long as the money keeps pouring in, Nazarbayev will probably keep his job.

12

The artfully named Kok-Tobe cable car only took five minutes to reach the top. Plenty of people were up at the hilltop complex, most enjoying the wonderful springtime views of Almaty. Children weren't interested in the views though; they were more interested in the shoot-the duck-type stalls, or the overpriced touristy stuff they could spend their tenge on.

I walked over to a small zoo specialising in goats and chickens from around the world. Bending down to inspect one of the hens closer, I heard something peculiar: it sounded like The Beatles. Intrigued, I headed towards a tucked away part of the complex where I found all four Beatles standing around a bench. Why the authorities had decided to create homage to the fab four I couldn't guess, but I took a photo of their bronze statues while one of their tunes wafted over me.

13

Back in the centre of Almaty, I couldn't help notice that parks were a common feature of the city, often full of families taking strolls, and teenagers canoodling on benches. In the distance, I could see some shiny glass skyscrapers, and it was plainly clear that the Kazakhstan portrayed by the character Borat was at odds with the one I was seeing. I wasn't the only Englishman to realise this.

Vinnie Jones, ex-footballer and now film star, went so far as to ridicule Sacha Baron Cohen's depiction of the Central Asian nation. He'd been in Almaty to star in a Kazakh film entitled *Liquidator*. When casting for the main parts, the Kazakh director had felt local actors would not possess the required menace, and so had hired Jones. Luckily for the British actor, he wasn't required to speak in Kazakh or Russian; his part was that of a mute assassin. But in between filming, Jones managed to sample some horsemeat, something I was toying with the idea of doing myself.

I came across a bar filled with screens showing the Grand Prix. I sat down and picked up the menu, and there it was: horsemeat, as it was on most Kazakh menus. I grimly stared at the words, wondering whether I should go through with it. When the waitress came over, I made up my mind and took the plunge, ordering horse steak and chips. The girl took my order without comment, and I sat back to ponder my choice.

While watching the remaining few laps of the race, I thought about why some countries considered eating horse as taboo. After all, meat was meat, and besides, horsemeat, supposedly tasting of beef, was high in protein and low in fat, and thus the perfect combination. But horses were nice creatures, and that was the problem. Nobody fed sugar cubes to chickens, and hardly anyone rode on the back of cows. Adolescent girls did not cry themselves to sleep over snuffling pigs. And the author of *Black Beauty* did not write about a bullock.

In other countries, it was a different matter of course. In China, Central Asia, and Latin America, horsemeat was most certainly on the menu. China ate close to two million horses a year, while Kazakhstan, the third on the list, put away about 340,000. I sat back and waited for mine to arrive.

14

It looked like an ordinary piece of steak, and if I hadn't known it was horsemeat, I'd have been none the wiser. I picked up a chip and considered the horse. My appetite was still there, but not quite as strong as it had been. I tentatively sniffed the meat and nodded in appreciation. It smelt good. Then I picked up my knife and fork, and cut into it, slicing off a small chunk of the meat. Telling myself it was simply a normal piece of steak, I moved the fork to my mouth and popped it in. Then I chewed. The chef had cooked it to perfection, and it did taste of beef. I chewed a bit more and then swallowed my first piece of horse. It was delicious.

But it was horse! No matter how much I tried to tell myself it was just steak, I couldn't do it. With every passing second my appetite was dissipating and in the end, I managed to eat only about a quarter of the steak. Horsemeat, I decided, was not for me.

15

"How's Kazakhstan?" Angela asked over a Skype call that night. The Internet really was an amazing invention, and my hotel offered it free of charge.

"Good," I said, speaking into my laptop. "A bit nippy, but not too bad. I had horse for my evening meal."

"*Horse?* You didn't!"

"I did. I couldn't eat it all though. It didn't seem right. But it tasted just like a piece of beef."

After I'd told Angela about the hotel, and how safe and dandy Almaty was, she wished me well for my flight to Uzbekistan later that evening. I put the phone down, once again feeling a pang of loneliness. Travelling alone definitely had its merits, but it was still better to travel with someone else.

16

While packing my things, I especially made sure I had all my paperwork for Uzbekistan organised, in particular, the Letter of Invitation (a strange piece of A4 paper filled with writing I couldn't understand with an official stamp on the top). I also made sure I had my visa supporting documents (from Stan Tours) filled in and checked, plus the fifty dollars processing fee. If it all passed inspection, I would get my Uzbek visa on arrival in Tashkent Airport, and only then would I calm down.

Part two of the 'Stan Tour was about to begin.

16. Lost in Uzbekistan

Interesting fact: During the cotton harvest, doctors, nurses and teachers work the fields as unpaid labour.

My first interaction with an Uzbek was on the short Uzbekistan Airways flight to Tashkent. "Hi, where are you from?" asked the beautiful young woman sitting next to me.

When I told her I was from the UK, her eyes widened. "Wow, England! My name Zamira, I'm a student from Tashkent and have just been visiting my sister in Almaty. But one day I will visit London and see Big Ben and do some shopping in Oxford Street!" I had no reason to doubt her either because as we chatted, I found out she was a well-travelled young lady.

"I loved India," she told me. "So colourful! And South Africa was amazing too, especially Cape Town. But Bishkek in Kyrgyzstan was not so nice. It had no good nightclubs."

I nodded, remembering being Zamira's age and thinking that my life revolved around nightclubs too. How things changed.

Soon after landing, I bid farewell to Zamira, and after applying a touch of lipstick she smiled and was off, tottering along the aisle in her impossibly high heels and mini-skirt. I entered the terminal and looked for the place to get my visa.

There wasn't one.

2

Stan Tours told me to enter the terminal and then turn left where I would find a side room to collect my visa from. There was no room on the left, and none on the right. The terminal building simply led to the customs desks in front. I stood still, weighing up my options. Should I join the back of the passport queue, and risk deportation, or should I start crying? Neither sounded like a good plan, but at least the latter would mean I could begin doing something straightaway.

I looked down the line of queuing people, hoping to spot Zamira, but it appeared she had already gone through. Suddenly I thought of my mobile phone and switched it on. As it powered up, I joined the back of the line. If I was to wait somewhere, I reasoned, it might as well be there.

Network Error, the phone said. I felt like throwing it to the floor and stamping on it. *Jesus Bloody Christ,* I thought. I'm stuck in Uzbekistan with no way of calling anyone. Not even my Stan Tours contact in Tashkent. Just as I was about to give up and flop to the ground in a dramatic fashion, a man in uniform appeared and began walking along the line saying something. Everyone seemed to be shaking their heads. Then he came to me.

"Visa?" the man asked.

I could have kissed his shiny feet.

The man took my passport, $50, and all relevant paperwork, and instructed me to wait on a nearby chair. That I did, wondering whether I'd see my passport again. Ten minutes later, the man handed it back with a newly minted Uzbek visa inside. Who-ho! I was in! My papers were in order! Country number fifteen of the quest welcomed me with open arms.

3

My first morning in the Uzbek capital was sunny and warm. I left the hotel and walked along a potholed street towards the main road. My phone suddenly beeped. Finally, it had found a network to use. It was a text message from Angela, wishing me well for the next stage of my adventure.

The people of Tashkent seemed more Middle-Eastern in appearance than the people of Almaty. Young adults were clad in jeans and short skirts, and lots were speaking or texting into phones as they went about their business. Because it was early morning, smartly dressed children were making their way to school, laughing and joking with each other.

In front of me, a little girl wearing a *Bratz* backpack stopped to pick some flowers and then skipped to join her friends, and further on a small boy wearing a white shirt and black waistcoat sat in a tree while his friends tried to shake him out.

Older ladies of Tashkent were generally large and buxom, most wearing colourful dresses, chunky footwear, large headscarves, and strangest of all, gold teeth. And the more I looked, the more I noticed the glinting metal inside people's mouths. I later learned that in many of the Central Asian republics, having gold teeth was considered a symbol of wealth.

4

Needing some local currency, I found a bank and handed over a single $100 bill. The dark-haired woman in the hatch took it without comment and proceeded to open a large safe. After what seemed like an eternity, she handed me a brick of Uzbek som that I transferred to my backpack like a furtive bank robber. The largest note, the 1000 som, was worth just 39p.

Walking down a wide boulevard flanked by apartment blocks, I came across a small booth that sold hot drinks, and so peeled a few Uzbek notes from my wad. "Hi," I said. "A latte please!"

The resulting look of confusion on the young man's face meant I had to try a different tactic. The outside of his booth featured a range of pictures representing, I presumed, what his business sold. One of these pictures was a nice-looking cup of coffee. I gestured towards it. The man poked his neck out from the hatch and, in a strange tortoise-like manoeuvre, he twisted and somehow managed to look at the picture of the coffee. Finally he nodded and set to work.

First he picked up a discarded white plastic cup. After peering inside it, he shook the contents into the sink. Next, the man searched for a spoon and found one under a dirty dishcloth. He gave it a quick rub with his greasy fingers and then dunked it into some white powder that I supposed was whitener. He walked over to a table, added the most miserly amount of instant coffee imaginable, and finally filled the cup with tepid water. After stirring it with the filthy spoon, he passed me my latte, charging me 500 som (20p). Starbucks it was not.

5

At the bottom of the road was the Mirabod Bazaar. I walked under its triple-arched blue entrance.

Inside were crowds of people perusing and prodding produce with a passion. There was a humongous queue of people heading to the back of a large white van. I walked to the head of the line and found a man selling boxes of white eggs. Why everyone had deemed his eggs so special I couldn't guess, but his customers couldn't get enough. One man moved away with a couple of trays full of the things, his golden grin catching the light as he walked past me.

Amir Timur Street was a large multi-laned highway full of Ladas that were swerving around buses. I decided to take a photo when I heard a whistle. I looked and saw a policeman standing against his car waving his arms above his head. To prove his point, he blew his whistle again and gestured that I could not take a photo of the building. I put my camera in my pocket and raised my hands in acquiescence. What was it with the police in these sorts of places? It was as if the Cold War had never ended.

Eventually I arrived at a large and peaceful place that the Soviets had named Karl Marx Square. It was an oasis amid the traffic of Amir Timur Street. I ambled past some well-manicured greenery towards a large statue of a man on horseback. When I inspected it closer, I noticed the guidebook was correct; the stallion's appendage was missing, apparently stolen, leaving only a

large pair of testicles in its wake. I raised my gaze to t̶
the horse. It was Amir Timur, the man they had named the
after.

6

Amir Timur was a highly skilled military tactician, spending most
of his adult life involved in wars and expeditions. All well and
good, but it was his fondness for killing sprees that people took
issue with.

For instance, after capturing the Persian city of Isfahan in 1387,
Timur ordered the mass execution of the city's citizens. It wasn't
until his men had killed 70,000 people that the carnage ceased. The
city was littered with 28 horrific towers, all made from severed
heads.

Perhaps because of his bloodlust, Timur's troops were fiercely
loyal to him. Instead of paying them in actual wages, Timur gave
them permission to plunder to their hearts' content. Anything they
could carry was fair game: money, jewels, and even women.
Towns trembled when Timur had set his sights upon them.

It wasn't all plain sailing however. Timur's army had faced
some unexpected opposition in Delhi. 120 armoured elephants
blocked their path. Timor quickly came up with a plan that was
both terrible and genius. Piling hay onto his camels' backs, he
ordered his men to set it on fire. They then sent the howling herd
of camels towards the elephants, making the tusked beasts panic
and retreat. In the ensuing carnage, the elephants crushed their own
troops, and Timur finally entered Delhi. He ordered the execution
of 100,000 Hindus and left the city in ruins.

Timur's tomb was eventually unearthed in the 1940s, and a
chilling inscription was found inside his casket. 'Whoever opens
my tomb shall unleash an invader more terrible than I.' Two days
later, Nazi Germany invaded the USSR.

ɔek Soviet Socialist Republic had been under hnic Uzbek called Sharof Rashidov. Moscow a degree of free reign, but he soon abused this ... g high-powered jobs to his friends and family. Then came u.. ʲeat Cotton Scandal of the 1980s.

Cotton had always been one of the main exports of Uzbekistan, and the Soviet Union couldn't get enough of it. Rashidov and his government received huge amounts of money from Moscow to fund schemes aimed at improving the cotton harvests. Most of this money went straight into Rashidov's private coffers.

With Moscow believing they were receiving bumper amounts of cotton, Rashidov and his government had no choice but to cook the books. In 1983, things came to a head when Moscow bean counters discovered the truth. Rashidov committed suicide, and most of his government was arrested. A spate of executions and more suicides followed. Ethnic Russians replaced the Uzbek leadership, leading to anger from within the country. To local Uzbeks, Moscow was interfering in Uzbek issues. This resulted in a sudden surge of nationalism. Rashidov, despite his corruption, became a national hero for trying to 'beat the system.'

In 1989, following a series of riots, Moscow finally allowed an ethnic Uzbek to lead the communist party. The new man's name was Islam Karimov.

8

I strolled up a leafy pedestrian-only street until I came to Independence Square. A long silver archway, with some shiny good-luck pelicans on top caught my eye. In the near distance was the huge white Senate Building. That caught my eye too.

Inside the Senate Building was where the government offices of Karimov's regime did their deeds. It looked new and glossy and featured a giant series of columns at its entrance. It was also crawling with guards. Wondering if Islam Karimov was actually inside the edifice, I turned away and walked to a large statue.

The statue of the seated woman holding a baby towered above me. Higher still, on a mighty plinth, sat a giant golden globe. It looked superb, and in Soviet times, a statue of Lenin (the world's largest no less) had stood on the plinth. I shook my head thinking of all the people who bypassed Tashkent in favour of other places in Uzbekistan. They were all missing a real treat, even if a despot did rule the country.

9

In the late 1980s, Islam Karimov brought stability back to the Uzbek Soviet Socialist Republic following the Cotton Scandal. But then Karimov found himself in a strange position. As other Soviet Republics declared themselves independent from Moscow, Karimov wondered what to do. After all, his citizens were not demanding independence, and anyway, relations with Moscow were good.

In the end, after much deliberation, he decided to go for it, but only because everyone else was doing so. On 31 August 1991, Islam Karimov became the first president of Uzbekistan.

Almost immediately, he became a power-crazed maniac. One of the first things he did was breed a regime of anti-Russianness. Why he did this was anyone's guess, but the result was that two million Russians fled the country, leaving huge gaps in the workforce.

The second thing he did was make it difficult for opposition candidates to register themselves against him. Thus, by the time of the next general election in 1995, Karimov was the hot favourite and won.

He completed the hat trick in 2000 when he won again with a massive 92% of the vote. How Karimov achieved this staggering election result belonged in *The Tyrants Guide to Winning an Election.*

During the voting process, the watchful eyes of the authorities were everywhere. So as people pondered their choices, they would have known that the president's loyal (and often brutal) police force was observing them.

If anyone left voting slips blank, these were counted as a *yes* vote for Karimov. Anyone who didn't turn up to vote also counted as a *yes*. To make matters even more unfair, Karimov controlled the opposition candidates.

In the 2000 election, Karimov only allowed one opposition candidate. This man lost, of course, and later admitted that he had voted for Karimov himself. By the time of the next elections in 2007, three opposition candidates stood. All of them began their campaigns by solidly praising Karimov and his leadership. It was no surprise to anyone when Karimov won for a fourth term.

Karimov's regime has also come under criticism for its poor human rights record. The United States describes Uzbekistan as a *Country of Particular Concern* alongside other such notables as North Korea, China, Sudan and Saudi Arabia. To belong in this little list, a nation must do four things: torture its citizens, imprison people for no charge, cause its people to disappear, and finally, deny its citizens media freedom. A bit like Guantanamo Bay then.

Craig Murray, British Ambassador in Tashkent from 2002-04, publicly described Uzbekistan as an affront to human rights. Understandably, Karimov was furious, and so to keep the peace, the British Government removed Murray from office. Well into his seventies, Karimov continues to be President of Uzbekistan.

10

In 1966, a terrible earthquake shook Tashkent, destroying much of the ancient Silk Road city and rendering thousands homeless. After the dust had settled, the Soviets were free to redesign the city, constructing large buildings and wide boulevards. But as a memorial to those who had lost their lives, they also built a monument. I was staring right at it, and like many other Soviet statues, this one was massive and commanding, depicting a man, woman and child, all of them striking valiant gestures. I barely reached their ankles.

A voice addressed me, and I turned to see a policeman. His car was parked by the side of the road, and he was making his way towards me. Like all other policemen in Tashkent, his uniform was dark green, and he had a small cap on his head. He looked to be in his mid-twenties.

"Passport," he barked.

After my incident in Almaty, I had it with me this time and handed it over. The man took it, turning to the information page at the back.

"Not American?"

I shook my head. "English."

The policeman nodded and flicked through my passport until he came to the visa. A woman carrying a baby passed us by, head bowed. There seemed a distinct lack of prams in Uzbekistan, I'd noticed.

After studying the large visa sticker, he looked up at me. "How long stay in Uzbekistan?"

I held up two fingers. "Two days. Then I go to Ashgabat."

"Why you come Uzbekistan?"

Once again, I informed a policeman that I was simply a tourist, just seeing what the city had to offer.

"Tashkent good?"

I nodded because it was true. I'd not expected much from the Uzbek capital, but it had surprised me. "Yes, Tashkent is very good."

The policeman stared at me, as if appraising the truthfulness of my answer. Then he nodded and handed me my passport back. "Enjoy stay in Uzbekistan."

11

After a hefty hike past the InterContinental Hotel, I arrived at the gigantic and spindly TV tower. After paying the entrance fee (and handing my passport over for some unfathomable reason), I was soon in an elevator heading to the viewing platform. The tower was the *highest structure of such type in Middle Asia*, according to the pamphlet I'd received.

At the top, I found a small stall that served drinks and snacks. I ordered a local beer, *Sarbast*, and took up station at one of the large windows. The views, as expected, were impressive, and from my vantage point, I could see just how sprawling (and surprisingly flat) Tashkent was.

The people in charge of the tower had kindly produced scale models of lots of other towers around the world, and it seemed that at 375 metres tall, Tashkent's TV Tower was high up in the world rankings. That said, it still fell well short of Toronto's CN Tower (which came in at an impressive 553m) but easily eclipsed England's Blackpool Tower (or Blekpul, as the tower had spelt it), which only measured a paltry 158m.

12

"Please tell him I want to go to Navoi Park," I instructed the receptionist of my hotel. She had already summoned the taxi driver who was now standing with us in the lobby. He couldn't understand English, and so the young woman was acting as an interpreter. "And when I get there, tell him I want to visit two different places, so I can take some photos. Then he can drive me back here. I need to know how much it will cost, please."

The girl nodded and relayed my request to the driver, a wiry individual with a couple of days' stubble on his chin. He didn't seem impressed with my proposal, but the girl persisted until he looked me up and down and finally came up with a figure. The look of shock that registered on the receptionist's face gave me an indication of how ludicrous his asking price was. She turned and informed me he wanted 25,000 som.

I mentally calculated this to be about ten pounds, which didn't seem that bad to be honest. That said, I didn't want to seem an easy touch, so shook my head. This brought about a new discussion between the girl and driver, none of which I understood. Eventually the girl addressed me again. "He wants to know how much you will pay?"

I thought for a second. 15,000 som (about £6) seemed a fair price. I told her this. She nodded and turned back to the driver, speaking to him in a thick accent. He pulled a face that seemed to suggest he was not going to undertake the lengthy journey for such a pitiful amount. Another conversation ensued before the receptionist finally looked back at me. "He says 10,000 som is the lowest price he'll accept."

Hang on just a cotton-picking second! That was less than I'd offered! What was going on? Plainly something had been lost in translation, but I gleefully accepted and was soon on my way to Navoi Park, Tashkent's largest area of greenery. Fifteen minutes later, we arrived at the northern entrance.

13

My driver got out to chat to a policeman he seemed to know, leaving me to gaze at the enormous Istiklol Palace, a huge concert hall that seemed the focal point of the park. It was quite ugly, I thought, but because it was so large and Soviet looking, I couldn't help but be impressed. In fact, the more I studied the strange concrete awnings and columns, the more the building grew on me.

The area around it was heaving with people. Stalls sold drinks, and a man with a camera and tripod stood waiting for people to pose in front of the large building in return for some cash. Up on the steps of the palace stood a few green-uniformed policemen, all looked faintly bored, some looking at their mobile phones. After snapping off a couple of photos, I was back in the taxi.

The next stop in the park was even uglier. The Wedding Palace was a prime example of bad Soviet Architecture, this one dating from the Khrushchev era. Strangely shaped concrete awnings hung over its rectangular concrete frame with the word *Navroz* mounted on the roof. At least it was set in a peaceful area of greenery. With no weddings going on, if that's what the people of Tashkent even used the building for, I was soon back in the car.

Twenty minutes later, after the taxi driver had dropped me off at the hotel, I paid him his fare and added a couple of thousand som as a tip. He smiled graciously and shook my hand.

14

My final day in Tashkent wasn't as much fun as the first, mainly due to getting lost three times. It was essentially down to the language barrier and abysmal lack of street signs.

The first time I got lost was because of a wrong turn I'd taken. After fifteen minutes of trudging, and wincing at the pain in my shins, I stopped to ponder my options. It was pointless asking anyone for help, because no one could speak English, I'd already tried. There was also no point flagging down a taxi, because I wouldn't be able to explain where I wanted to go. My only choice was to plod onwards, hoping to stumble upon a landmark I recognised.

Twenty-minutes later, I came across a cathedral I'd seen the previous day. Half an hour after that, I was lost again and felt like cursing into the sky. By the third time, I'd had enough, and decided to find a metro station.

Like all other metro stations in Tashkent, a policeman guarded the entrance, and another one guarded the platform. After witnessing my ineptitude at buying a ticket from the booth, the platform plod approached and demanded to see my passport. After flicking through, and studying my visa in particular, he handed it back and waved me through.

The metro was spotlessly clean and featured some fantastic mosaics and marble columns. Unfortunately taking photos was a big no-no, and so I kept my camera in my pocket. The banning of photography was possibly because metro stations in Tashkent doubled up as nuclear bomb shelters. Without any fuss or ado, I jumped on a train and was soon speeding towards the old town of Tashkent.

15

If the Russian population of the city regarded Independence Square as the heart of Tashkent, to ethnic Uzbeks, Chorsu was their centre. Ascending the metro, the scene was of bazaars, women in headscarves, and people with gold teeth. All around me, people were flocking towards the huge Chorsu Bazaar, or else entering the nearby Friday Mosque. It reminded me a little of Istanbul.

Most stalls in the bazaar were selling clothes, fruit, vegetables, and lots of meat. There were also smaller sections peddling spices and nuts, and around one alley, there was an aisle with clucking chickens. Next to it were men selling carpets and skullcaps. Every now and again, a shifty-looking man would sidle up to me, whisper in my ear and wait for my reaction. Not knowing what any of them wanted, I'd brush them away to continue with my wandering.

Just next to the bazaar was the Friday Mosque, a large building with intricately patterned blue minarets. I entered its grounds and found a good viewpoint to observe the market below. Chorsu Bazaar was awash with hustle and bustle, and I gazed at a woman wearing a colourful dress laying some bananas and green leaves on a piece of cloth. After she had arranged them to her liking, she sat down to await customers. Further in, some boys were pushing a cart filled with spices, and at the periphery, taxi drivers were enjoying conversations in the warm sun. This was the real

Tashkent I felt, one at odds with the manufactured Soviet architecture in the centre of the city.

I was soon on the move again, this time heading to the Khast Imom complex. I quickly spotted the enormous minarets of the Hazroti Imom Mosque, the centrepiece of the complex.

I had the huge courtyard to myself, and stood in the middle. The mosque looked stunning, all pastel-blue domes and gigantic arches. Suddenly, from a side building a troop of small children began to walk across the courtyard. With them was a teacher, perhaps showing them the complex as part of a school trip. The children behaved impeccably, and soon disappeared out the other side.

The complex, I read, also contained the oldest Quran in the world, dating from the 7th century. Amir Timur had brought the deerskin-covered book to Tashkent, but the Russians had pilfered it in 1868. Thankfully, Lenin returned it to Uzbekistan in the 1920s, and it had remained ever since.

16

That evening I found a bar that served food with an English translation. After I'd ordered something, I removed the block of money from my bag and placed it on the table. There was no danger of theft, because almost everyone else had similar wads of cash lying around on their own tables. As I began to count how much I had, a waitress appeared with my beer.

"You like the Uzbek currency?" she said in good English, placing my drink next to the pile.

I smiled. "I've never had so much money!"

"Yes. But the Uzbek som is not worth much money. And it will only get worse. Did you know that the bank only introduced the 1000 som note a decade ago, and they have not made larger notes since? By now, we should have the 10,000 som note! That will stop these piles of money I see every day."

I opened an English-language newspaper I'd picked up earlier. It had a section inside dedicated to the Uzbek cotton industry. According to the article, the pressure to meet production quotas was making life hell for Uzbek farmers.

Still using the Soviet system, farmers were required to grow 1.5 tons of cotton per hectare of land. If they failed, they would have to face the consequences. The article didn't say what the consequences were, but they must have been severe because some farmers had committed suicide because of them.

In one example, police arrested and detained a 50-year-old farmer for not meeting his cotton quota. In his cell, the poor man killed himself. His suicide note said he couldn't meet the quota without machinery.

After banning schoolchildren from tending the fields (due to an international outcry), the Uzbek government filled the void by forcing office workers, teachers, nurses, and even doctors, to pick cotton. Every October they started work at 5am, picking cotton by hand without pay. The article claimed that Malvina, a nurse from Tashkent, had been working in a field with a surgeon next to her. She claimed that both had been ordered to pick 60kg of cotton per day, or else buy the shortfall from locals.

After my meal, I headed back to the airport to pack. Later that evening I was flying to my next country of the quest: Turkmenistan. Tashkent had been fun, I decided. However something was to happen that would change my opinion on that.

17

Tashkent International Airport was a nightmare. Never before had I come across an airport bogged down in so much pointless bureaucracy and officialdom.

I queued up for one line, and when I reached the front, the official told me I needed to queue up at another line to get my departure card stamped first. Huffing, I did this, and by the time

I'd received this stamp, the first queue was massive, and I was furious. And possibly because of that, a uniformed official arrived and directed me into a private little room. Inside sat another man with a lot of insignia on his shoulders. In front of him was a small table and chair.

"Please sit…Mr Smart," he said, studying my passport. "I think we need to talk."

18

I sat down on the proffered chair. The last thing I needed was for these men to delay my exit from Uzbekistan.

The officer in charge leaned back and clasped his hands behind his head. "So Mr Smart, what was purpose of visit to Tashkent?"

I told him I was a tourist.

"What was hotel name?"

I told him and the official nodded. "Do you have camera?"

I nodded and pulled it from my bag."

"You take photograph in Tashkent?"

I nodded again, but told him I'd only taken a few, even though I'd taken hundreds. I felt safe with this untruth because I'd already copied most of the photos onto my laptop and then deleted the vast majority of them from my camera; the only ones that remained were a few innocuous snaps.

The officer leaned forward. "Please give camera."

I passed him it, and he asked me to switch it on. He summoned the other guard and they both flicked through the few remaining photos on the camera, mainly of Chorsu Bazaar and the Friday Mosque. Seemingly satisfied with the images, he passed the camera to me. The officer leaned back again. "Where currency declaration card?"

I'd made sure I'd kept it safe in my wallet. On the flight over from Almaty, I'd been handed a card that required me to declare how much foreign currency I was bringing into Uzbekistan. I had to record it all, right down to the last cent. I passed the card to my tormentor, who took it and began studying what I'd written. Eventually he looked up. "You still have this money?"

I nodded. "Except for a hundred dollars I changed into Uzbek som."

"Empty bag and pockets please."

I sighed and shook my head. "Is this really necessary? Can't I just go and catch my flight." I looked at my watch. The officer had already delayed me fifteen minutes. I had forty minutes until boarding.

"Empty bag and pockets. Now."

I stood up and placed the bag on the table. I then made a meal of unzipping every section and depositing what was inside onto the surface. Guidebook, iPod, plasters, sellotape (always comes in useful to fix damaged headphone leads), spare socks (in case my suitcase ever got lost), laptop, matches, cigars (I was a bit partial to the odd cigar), mobile phone, wad of Uzbek som, camera charger, poison-tipped pen and microfilm. Once I'd emptied every nook and cranny, I then set about removing everything from my pockets, including my wallet and boarding card. It took a long time, but both guards waited patiently until I'd finished. Finally I sat back down and folded my arms, staring angrily at the pile of objects. I had nothing to hide and was damned if I was going to pay a bribe to these men.

The officer said something in Uzbek to his underling, and both men sniggered. Totally ignoring the pile of Uzbek som, the officer asked me to open my wallet, so they could add up the money it contained. While I watched, they counted out every US dollar, British pound and Kazakh tenge, checking the amount against my declaration card. Afterwards, I wondered how they were going to angle for the bribe. Would they wait for me to make the first move, or would they open play themselves. No one had ever bribed me before, and I didn't really understand the etiquette of the process.

In the end, I was surprised because none of these things happened. The officer simply smiled and told me I could go.

"Have pleasant flight," he said. I repacked my belongings and left without saying anything.

At last, I approached the now empty desk, and the official allowed me through. Thank Christ for that, I thought as I traipsed past him, entering a long thin corridor. Twenty minutes until boarding. But just when I thought I made it through to departures, a horrendous queue of people confronted me, and when I reached the head of that line, I had to hand over a form that had already been stamped, but had to be re-stamped in order to make progress. With gritted teeth, I moved on to find yet another queue.

What a lunatic system. What sort of a maniac would invent such a time-consuming and totally pointless system for leaving a country? My hands were full of forms, and when I eventually got through to the gate, my flight was boarding. Good-bye Uzbekistan, I said to myself, you have left a bitter taste in my mouth.

17. City of Golden Statues

Interesting fact: When the ex-president of Turkmenistan renamed bread after his mother, anyone caught saying the old name risked arrest.

My fellow passengers on the Uzbekistan Airways flight looked to be mainly businessmen. Most sat in the half-empty cabin reading newspapers or peering outside into the blackness. I looked out too, hoping to see the lights of Ashgabat but saw nothing. Instead I sat back pondering the fact I was about to land in Turkmenistan, a country few people had even heard of.

Turkmenistan, located to the north of Iran and Afghanistan, was 80% desert. Some described its capital, Ashgabat, as a cross between Las Vegas and Pyongyang. All glitz and glamour mixed with a totalitarian police state. Despite this, I couldn't wait to get there. And who could blame me? With every top-end hotel supposedly bugged, I made damned sure I was staying in one. I was literally chomping at the bit to see what Ashgabat had to offer. Two hours after leaving Tashkent, we began our final approach into the Land of the Turkmen.

2

Despite the hell that I imagined at visa HQ, my arrival process went surprisingly smoothly, even if I did have to fill in an eye-watering amount of forms. An entry travel pass, an immigration card, a customs declaration form, and a visa application form (paid for with a hefty fee), were all checked, stamped, and then filed in my bag. Five minutes later, a man wearing a huge cap stamped my visa and I walked through to collect my luggage. I'd done it! I had entered the most difficult of the 'Stans!

"Welcome to Turkmenistan," said the young woman who greeted me in arrivals. "I hope you had a pleasant flight."

Her name was Zarina, an official guide. Having a state-sanctioned guide was the only way to do things in Turkmenistan, and there was no way around this rule. Stan Tours had organised her for me, but luckily, because Ashgabat was my base for the short stay, I'd only need Zarina's services for the airport transfers. We were soon on our way.

3

With it being almost midnight, the airport road was virtually free of traffic, but from what I could gather, it was smooth and pristine. We passed a striking roundabout displaying a large waterfall (all impressively lit) surrounded by sparkling golden statues. I grew even more excited because Turkmenistan was famous for its golden monuments.

And then we were on the main highway. On my right was a massive elongated tubular structure that could only have been a missile production plant. Zarina noticed me looking and told me it was a textile factory.

"You can take photograph if you like," she said. "But you must promise me, Jason, that you will not take photograph of administrative buildings in the city. And if you see anyone in uniform, please keep walking."

I told her I would.

As we sped towards the centre of the city, I decided to check my phone. It still hadn't found a network. As I put it back in my pocket, Zarina spoke again. "Your phone will not work in Turkmenistan."

"Really?"

"Foreign roaming is not allowed. It is possible to buy a local SIM card, but for the two days you are here, I do not think this is worth it. If you are in need of making an international phone call, then the hotel may be able to help. Oh, and one last thing,

Ashgabat has an 11pm curfew. Please do not go out after this time. The police will arrest you."

Wow, I thought. A curfew! I asked why.

"It is just the way things are," answered Zarina.

"But it's past midnight now."

"Yes, this is true, but it is okay because you have just arrived, and we are going straight to your hotel. Even if the police stop us, it will be no problem. Besides, I am official guide. I have all the necessary paperwork."

Eventually we arrived at the hotel without anyone stopping us. Zarina told me to enjoy myself, and said she would see me in a couple of days. Then she left. I was alone in Turkmenistan.

At check in, I handed over my passport, and the man behind the desk explained that the police had to stamp it or something. He told me I would get it back within 24 hours. After changing some US dollars into Turkmen manat, and then emailing Angela on a hotel computer, I retired to my room to search out the bugs. This was real! I had infiltrated a bona fide dictatorship! And they had my passport.

4

The next morning, I nervously left the hotel and stood by the entrance to take in my immediate surroundings. Being quite early, the streets were virtually empty of both traffic and pedestrians. I wondered if the curfew had been lifted because the only people I could see were policemen and road cleaners. The latter were armed with brooms, clearing leaves and other bits of litter - and doing a good job of it, because I couldn't see a single scrap of rubbish anywhere. The policemen looked more sinister in their blue uniforms and large caps. They stood at every street intersection with batons in hand. I could easily picture them walloping me with one.

I wondered what to do. Just then, two businessmen left the lobby and headed off down the street. They rounded the corner; nobody arrested them, and so I set off too.

5

Despite being in the middle of a desert, Ashgabat was fairly cold. I zipped up my coat and rounded the corner to see where the businessmen had gone, but they had already disappeared. The first thing that struck me though was the sheer opulence of the buildings. Most were white marble and finished with gold edging. One of the best examples was the Bank of Turkmenistan, a tall skyscraper featuring a massive gold bar on its front. It looked like a trillionaire had built a monument to show everyone just how rich he was.

I passed a small grocery shop, and out of sheer curiosity, decided to go in. I was hoping to find plastic statues of Turkmenbashi, the old leader, or maybe piles of state-sanctioned literature. Instead I found exactly the same things you would find in any other small store: newspapers, cigarettes, groceries, sweets and crisps. In the fridge, I noticed that the two local beers had first-rate names: *Berk* and *Zip*: possibly the best names I'd seen in my travels.

"You American?" asked the proprietor in neutral tones. Everyone seemed to think I was American. He'd been watching me ever since I'd entered his shop, making me think few tourists came in.

"No. I'm from England."

"Ah Eengland! Gud futball! Wayne Rooney and Manchester United!"

I smiled and passed him the bottle of water I wanted to buy. "Yeah. A good team."

The man gave me my change. "Why you in Ashgabat?"

I shrugged. "I just want to see the city. It seems interesting. I'm here as a tourist."

The shopkeeper raised his eyebrows. "We not get many tourist in Ashgabat. But there is much beauty here. Just be careful of the policemans. They don't like the tourist."

6

A policeman watched my approach with interest, but remained mute as I passed him. I was walking along another street filled with glorious buildings, and I'd toyed with the idea of saying hello to him but decided against it in the end. I didn't really fancy getting a baton whacked across my chops.

At the end of the block was a second policeman, this one standing in front of a grand building. He too watched as I approached, making me feel extremely guilty, even though I'd done nothing wrong. It was then that I spotted my first golden statue of Turkmenbashi, the ex-president.

I quickly surmised I had two choices: sneak off a quick snap and risk arrest, or ask the policeman for permission. I chose the latter, but he rewarded me with a shake of the head.

I gazed at the golden statue as I passed it. It looked like someone had actually carved it from pure gold. I loved it, and couldn't wait to see more of them.

I walked on until I arrived in a park that seemed devoid of policemen. It did however contain a fabulous monument. I stared up at the thing called the Earthquake Monument.

On the 6 October 1948, an earthquake lasting less than one minute demolished Ashgabat and killed 110,000 people. The Earthquake Monument depicted a bronze bull (with impressively sized testicles) balancing a huge globe on its horns. Sat on top of the globe was a woman holding a golden infant - a representation of Turkmenbashi as a baby. His mother died in the earthquake.

Utterly fantastic, I thought, and totally over the top, but that's what I had hoped for in Ashgabat. I took a photo and then another. I checked behind me to make sure there weren't any policemen rushing over, and then took one more.

7

In the 1920s, when the Turkmen Soviet Socialist Republic was under the control of Moscow, the traditional nomadic lifestyle of the Turkmen people had come under threat. A million people fled into neighbouring Iran and Afghanistan and so to bolster the reduced workforce, the Soviets brought in thousands of ethnic Russians. Then the systematic removal of mosques began.

By 1941, only five remained in the country, out of the five hundred that had originally stood. With anti-Islamic sentiment growing, things were looking bleak for the Turkmen SSR, but then an amazing thing happened. Soviet engineers found a massive gas field, and almost overnight, the country was rich. This helped soothe relations.

Then came the fall of the Soviet Union. Caught up in the wave, Turkmenistan declared itself independent in October 1991. The communist leader, Saparmyrat Niyazov, an ethnic Turkman, became the first president, and didn't waste any time in setting himself up as President for Life. The ego had landed.

8

Until his death in 2006, Niyazov managed to create a cult of personality comparable to that of Kim Jong II's of North Korea. Calling himself Turkmenbashi (which meant Leader of the Turkmen) some of his mad schemes included banning beards and gold teeth. He also claimed people who had poor teeth should chew bones instead of capping their gnashers in gold, because as a child, he remembered watching dogs chew bones and their teeth

~ 192 ~

never fell out. Speaking of dogs, he banned them too, saying they had an 'unappealing odour.'

Niyazov also made lip-synching at concerts a punishable offence, and then renamed a town, an airport and even a meteorite after himself.

The airport came under some criticism because in his quest to construct one as quickly as possible, a few mistakes were made. For one thing, the builders put the control tower on the wrong side of the runway. And then there was the problem of the new passenger terminal. It blocked the view for air traffic controllers. When this flaw was pointed out, Turkmenbashi decided to ignore it saying, 'but it looks better this way.'

But his mad schemes didn't end there. He decided to write an autobiography, and when he finished it, he made it compulsory reading for schoolchildren. Then he banned all other books (except the Quran), and made his citizens sit a test based upon it to gain their driving licenses. As a final push for the bestseller lists, he scrubbed the word *September* from the calendar and renamed it after his book. Pure genius!

Niyazov finally died of a heart attack in 2006, and the president who succeeded him has proven not quite as mad. His only real folly is horses. He loves the things. He quickly set up an annual horse beauty contest that included a sideline competition for best 'holiday attire' for a horse.

But not all is bad for the people of Turkmenistan; every car owner gets 120 litres of free fuel per month, which in the UK would be worth over £170. The problem though is that most of the population doesn't own a car.

The government also gives free gas, electricity and water to citizens, but only if they have the pipes and infrastructure to take advantage of the offer. This rules out most of the population living in the countryside.

Turkmenistan: the land of giving, but only if you are rich.

I walked away from the Earthquake Monument towards the greatest monument in the city, the Arch of Neutrality, but found it missing. Engineers had removed it in 2010, I found out later. Cursing my rotten luck, I looked up to where the arch had once stood. At the top had been a giant, golden statue of Turkmenbashi that revolved with the sun, making it fit for a true megalomaniac.

Deflated I left the park and found myself on a grand street filled to the brim with grand buildings. At one intersection was a large billboard that displayed the military might of Turkmenistan past and present. Nearby a platoon of trainee soldiers was trimming branches under the watchful eye of an officer. I moved on, noticing a few people sat inside space-age bus stops. They were the best bus stops I had ever seen, full of electronic gadgetry and blue tinted windows. They looked like they belonged in *Blade Runner*.

The people of Ashgabat had an Iranian look about them, which wasn't that surprising since the Iranian border was only ten kilometres away. The women were either wearing Western-type clothing or else some kind of national dress, which seemed the favoured style. Just then a woman walked past wearing one: a long red dress with a black embroidered waistcoat. Her look was finished off with a patterned hat and plaits.

It was great when places had some sort of national dress, but I'd never been in a country where people actually wore it in public to go about their daily business. In Amsterdam, I'd never seen a person sporting clogs or pointy hats, but in Ashgabat, women in traditional costume were everywhere to see.

I carried on up the street, staring agog at the buildings. Every one of them was large and white, and often framed in gold, especially the Presidential Palace, a huge golden-domed building built in 1997 by order of Turkmenbashi. It was on my right-hand side, guarded by more policemen, and so I didn't even get my camera out. I wasn't that bothered because I'd already managed to get a photo of it from my hotel balcony. But what was strange was the total absence of people entering or leaving any of the buildings. I wondered, not for the first time, whether everything was for show.

Further down the almost-deserted street was perhaps the best roundabout in the world. Its centrepiece was a huge black and gold column topped off with a large globe. I stood staring, mesmerized at the splendour of it all.

Predictably, there was a policeman just across the road from me. He was watching me with interest, and though I may have imagined it, I'm sure I saw his baton hand twitch. I mimed that I wanted to take a snap of the column, but wasn't surprised when I received a shake of the head.

Buggeration, I thought miserably. Why couldn't they allow me to take a nice photo? It wasn't as if I was trying to photograph a nuclear bunker or something; all I wanted was to take a snap of a gorgeous roundabout. While I stared up at the magnificent structure, the policeman shouted for my attention. He gestured that I could take a photo after all. Gleeful and euphoric, I pulled out my camera and snapped away, thanking him.

10

Five minutes later, I came across another policeman. I began to wonder whether the police force was the biggest employer in Turkmenistan. Instead of avoiding him though, I walked straight up to the young man. "Do you know where the statue of Lenin is?" I boldly asked.

"Len-inn?" the policeman answered looking nonplussed.

I nodded. "Yes, Lenin. Vladimir Lenin." I moved into the classic pose of the old Soviet leader and stretched out my arm.

"Ah! Leneen!" smiled the policeman, who couldn't have been more than twenty. In broken English he pointed down a street and gestured left.

Perhaps the police of Ashgabat didn't quite deserve all the bad press they got. Thanking him, I walked away and quickly found the relatively small statue. It was in the middle of a small park standing on an overgrown plinth.

The only other person I could see was a cleaning lady brushing leaves into a small pile. She glanced briefly as I walked up to the statue, but then ignored me. While I angled a shot of the monument, my mind registered a whistle, but paid it no heed. I snapped off a photo and suddenly became aware of movement from behind. Turning, I saw two policemen rushing towards me. I lowered my camera and waited to see what would happen next.

"*PHOTO NYET!*" one of them shouted. He looked flustered, and so did his friend. I wondered if I'd inadvertently taken a photo of a government building behind the statue.

"*DELETE PHOTO!*" he added, gesturing that I should switch my camera on so he could see the photo I'd just taken. I pressed the power button and showed him the innocuous photo. Both policemen nodded excitedly when they saw that it was Lenin.

"*NYET PHOTO! LENEEN!*" the man repeated, pointing his finger at the offending image. "*DELETE! DELETE!*"

Wondering if I was about to cause a diplomatic incident, I pressed the power button on the camera to turn it off, which made the image disappear. Seemingly satisfied that I'd consigned the photo to the ether, both policemen marched away, with the cleaning lady watching from her safe distance. When I was sure they had gone, I pressed the power button again, which brought the image back onto the screen. It was like being in a James Bond film.

11

Ashgabat seemed to have an almost total absence of cafes and bars, and so I was astonished when I stumbled across an establishment called the British Pub. It even had a coat of arms across its entrance. Since it was lunchtime, I decided to go in.

Inside was dim, but I could make out a few pictures of The Beatles on a wall. I seemed to be the only patron, and so sat down and picked up a menu. Who would have thought I could order fish and chips in Turkmenistan!

Just then, three men in their forties entered and sat down a few tables away from me. Two of them were English, and the third was from Scotland. The British Bar was living up to its name. I decided to introduce myself.

The men invited me to sit with them, and I found out they were contractors working in the construction industry. None of them could believe I was in Turkmenistan on holiday.

"You must have more money than sense," laughed John, the Scot.

I asked them if they'd ever had any problems with the Turkmenistan police. It was only half an hour since my altercation near the Lenin statue.

Martin, the youngest of the three answered first. "I've been stopped a few times when driving at night. But mostly they leave me alone when they realise I'm from the UK. By the way, which hotel are you staying at?"

When I told them, all three gave knowing looks to one another. John said, "Aye, it's a decent enough hotel. It's the bar you have to be careful of. Full of ladies of the night, if you know what I mean."

"Yeah," said the third man, whose name I never caught. "But what surprises us, is that the hotel allows it. Prostitution is against the law here. If you are caught walking the streets with a woman who is not your wife, you risk arrest. But in the bar, no problem."

"We might see you there later, said Martin, smiling. "About seven is when things kick off."

12

"This is highest flagpole in world," the taxi driver said as we sped along a modern highway. The mighty Turkmenistan flag in front of us did look huge (and resembled a giant carpet), but I knew it wasn't the highest flagpole in the world. That accolade belonged to the one in Dushanbe, capital of Tajikistan. Nevertheless, it was still impressive, and we soon passed underneath, heading by beautiful, marble apartment blocks totally devoid of human beings.

"This is hospital," the driver announced, pointing at a spectacular spiralling skyscraper that looked like it belonged in Dubai. "And this is concert hall."

I stared at it, wondering whether they allowed lip-synching inside the glorious building, but I had no time to ponder, because we were passing a white building, furnished with gold domes and white columns. I literally couldn't believe my eyes! I shook my head in wonderment, but the fun wasn't about to end. What came next almost astounded me. It was Independence Park.

The guidebook described *The Monument to the Independence of Turkmenistan* as tasteless. To me, it was nothing less than magnificent. Surrounded by large black and gold statues of historical Turkmen, with appropriately positioned flagpoles and waterfalls, the massive marble and gold column was perhaps the greatest monument I'd ever seen in my life.

I couldn't believe I was the only person there - apart from the taxi driver who was waiting in the nearby car park, and a policeman who seemed a bit bored. Even though I could see why the monument had been nicknamed 'The Plunger' (due to its shape resembling a toilet accessory), I still couldn't stop staring at it. It must have cost a fortune. In the lobby of my hotel, there was a picture of the current president walking past it.

"Is photo okay?" I asked the policeman, and was surprised when he nodded. I circled the thing, taking photo after photo. It looked like a giant piece of candy. Just when I thought I couldn't take any more, I spotted two guards, both standing to attention, underneath it. I asked the first policeman (who had followed me from a discreet distance) whether it would be okay to take a photo of the guards, and unbelievably, he nodded again. And then I caught sight of something golden, glinting in the sun. Could it be? Could it...?

I quickly took a photo of the guards and rushed down a path straight towards the gold. *Yes!* It was a golden statue of Turkmenbashi, this one the largest so far. It was mounted on a fantastic plinth surrounded by golden eagles. If this was what megalomaniacs did with their gas reserves, then I could only wish there were more of them.

It suddenly occurred to me that if Turkmenistan were more open to tourism, then people would flock to see things like this. All the city needed to do was to lose its paranoia, build a few more cafes, ease the visa headache, put in some proper street signs, allow foreign mobile calls and Internet, and then sit back and wait for the masses to arrive.

13

Back at the hotel, I decided that despite my weary legs, I simply had to see more of the city. Consulting my map, I learned there was a mosque about 3km west of the hotel. I was soon off again, thinking of how I'd actually considered scrapping Turkmenistan from my trip around Central Asia until a later date. The perceived visa hassles almost put me off. What an error of judgment that would've been.

The mosque was slightly disappointing after the glitz of Independence Park, but it did have an impressive patterned dome. Nearby, troops of soldiers marched this way and that, and as I stood watching, a platoon walked along the road and stood by a bus stop. When a bus eventually pulled up, I wondered whether they were going to arrest someone, but no, the soldiers waited until the regular passengers alighted before climbing aboard. Cheaper than a fleet of armoured personnel carriers, I guessed.

My day in Ashgabat was over, and I had thoroughly (and I mean thoroughly) enjoyed myself. From what I'd seen, I only wanted to see more. For instance, I'd not ascended the Turkmenbashi Cableway, a ride that offered spectacular views of the city, nor had I found time to visit the Tolkuchka Bazaar, apparently one of Central Asia's best sights.

I decided I was too tired to visit the hotel bar, and so, after collecting my passport from reception, and enjoying a solitary meal in the hotel restaurant, I sat on my balcony to watch night fall over Ashgabat. It was quite surreal to watch people scuttling off to wherever they had to go before it got dark. Quickly the streets of Ashgabat became quiet as the lights came on. I retired for the night thinking about Azerbaijan, the final furlong on my trip around Central Asia.

18. Azerbaijan: A Land of Magic Colours

Interesting Fact: According to Azeri folklore, people should not lend money at night.

According to the country's tourist agency, Azerbaijan was the Land of Magic Colours. Fair enough, I thought, but I had a better name for it: Azerbaijan: Land of Insane Visa Rules.

The authorities liked to change their visa rules on a weekly basis. One week you could arrive in Baku and simply get a visa at the airport, but the next week a traveller had to obtain a visa from an embassy *before* travel. Then they might backtrack slightly and allow people to apply online for their visa, which would then be available on arrival at the airport. But then they would change their minds again, the result of which was that nobody really knew what to do except scratch their heads.

As well as this madness, the Azerbaijan Embassy also charged an extortionate amount to issue the visa – so it ended up being the most expensive one of the quest. But at least I had it safely stuck inside my passport as we approached Baku International Airport.

2

My hotel was located smack in the centre of the city, and I was soon out in search of lunch. I quickly arrived at Fountain Square, the pulsing heart of Baku. At one end, a McDonald's loomed, packed with teenagers, but I ignored it and opted for an outdoor café that had a few spare tables. While waiting for my kebabs to arrive, I gazed out at the square and the people passing by.

Like I'd expected, the vast majority of Baku's citizens seemed Turkish, or perhaps Iranian in appearance, but unlike the latter, few of the women were wearing traditional Muslim veils. Instead, they preferred Western-style clothing and free-flowing black hair. It was a world away from Ashgabat, I quickly realised. People looked to be having fun for one thing, and the distinct lack of policemen was another.

The square, as its name suggested, was full of fountains. The most impressive one consisted of silver spheres. Below it, on a bench, a young woman sat applying lipstick. Suddenly, a trio of small boys rushed over to her. While one aimed his camera, the other two sat either side of the poor woman. She wasn't bothered though and stayed totally still. The reason for this was simple: she was made of metal. There were similar statues all over Baku. A bronze girl stood at the entrance to Fountain Square speaking into her mobile phone.

My food arrived and it was delicious, if a little pricey, but with a full stomach, I was off, heading into Baku's old town.

3

"Let me tell you about the Maiden Tower," said the smiling man in a suit. I was standing underneath the twin-towered medieval stone structure, easily Baku's most famous sight. Green cloth cloaked the top section of one cylindrical tower, and scaffolding covered the second, clearly restoration work. I turned to the man, who introduced himself as Natan, a freelance guide of the old city.

I told him I didn't need a guide, but he persisted and offered me his card. It also advertised his service as a taxi driver. I took it, but walked to a nearby booth to buy a ticket for the tower. I was hoping the man would get the message and leave me alone.

"Okay, I understand," said Natan following me, still smiling despite the rebuke. "But let me tell you one thing about the Maiden Tower. Is that okay?"

I bought my ticket and nodded.

"According to Azeri legend, the name - Maiden Tower - came into being because of incest."

"Incest?"

"Yes. A king had fallen in love with his own daughter and wanted to marry her. This disgusted the girl so much that she had to make a plan. She agreed to marry her father but only if he built a tall tower in honour of their marriage."

Natan stared at me for a moment and decided that I was actually listening, and so carried on with his tale. "The King agreed, and ordered his royal builders to work. When it was finished, the tower was taller than any other building in medieval Baku. The girl climbed to the top and threw herself off."

"Wow," I said. It was a good story, and perhaps I'd been a little rash in brushing Natan off so quickly. He seemed knowledgeable and was certainly friendly enough. The man seemed to sense my shift in mood, and so gave me more information.

"Another reason for the name is more mundane. It is perhaps a reference to the tower's strength, and the fact it was never penetrated by enemy fire."

By chance, a couple of people with a child of about ten appeared at the entrance of the old town. They were clearly tourists and seemed lost.

"Ah," said Natan. "If you will excuse me, I think perhaps these people are in need of my help more than you."

I smiled and nodded, fishing out a couple of mantas from my pocket. He took them graciously and rushed off towards the newcomers. After a few moments, he was pointing up at the tower, giving his spiel again. The last thing I saw of Natan was him leading the trio into a medieval market square just along from the tower.

4

Left alone again, I entered the arched entrance to the Maiden Tower and was soon climbing the spiralling stone staircase. A security guard nodded when I stepped out into the open-air platform at the top. As I circled the small area, he lit a cigarette, despite the signs saying no smoking.

The weather was terrible. It wasn't cold but the fog flowing in from the Caspian Sea had bathed the entire city in translucent white.

After stubbing out his cigarette, the guard approached and smiled, revealing a mouthful of gold teeth. Gesturing to my camera, he offered to take a photo of me posing in front of the indistinct background. I handed it to him and stood smiling while the wind ripped about my ears. After thanking him, I climbed back down.

Baku's old town also contained a few other old buildings and ruins, all surrounded by an extensive wall of turrets and battlements. Carpet shops were everywhere, as were mosques, and winding little pathways. I followed my map until I came to the impressively titled Palace of the Shirvanshahs.

5

The Shirvanshahs had been a royal dynasty originating from Persia, who had moved to Baku in the 15th century. Their leader was Ibrahim the First, who had played a crafty little game to save his people's skin. After building his palace, he became aware of an Uzbek warrior called Amir Timur (the same one from the Uzbekistan chapter), who was running rampage around the area, causing no end of carnage in the process. Not wanting this to happen to Baku, Ibrahim allied himself with the bloodthirsty Uzbek, and even participated in a few bloodlust sorties to cement their friendship. It worked. While cites all around were burning, being pillaged and having their populations slaughtered, Baku survived intact. I walked into the palace where Ibrahim had once lived.

Bored teenagers stood huddled around a guide who was showing them a stone pavilion. Two boys at the back were punching each other light-heartedly, with no interest at all in the decorations the guide was describing. I knew how they felt, but unlike the boys, I could walk away. I left them and quickly rushed through the Palace Mosque, Palace Mausoleum, and a room full of pots. After a cursory glance at a few old carpets I left, heading out of the old town and into the heart of the city.

6

I began to pass through a back street of Baku, edging my way past some parked Ladas. Across the road, a large woman wearing a headscarf was leading a small child by the hand, and above me, leaning over an upstairs balcony was a middle-aged man in a string vest, smoking a cigarette. I carried on past them until I came to another narrow street filled with fruit and vegetable shops. It was just near a huge sandstone-coloured mosque with gorgeous golden domes.

I noticed an overflowing bin with a clear plastic bag tied to one end. The bag contained pieces of bread. I'd already read about this strange custom, which had nothing to do with how full the bin was.

Bread was regarded as a holy thing in Azerbaijan, and could not be discarded with other trash; it had to be left separately. As I took a photo for prosperity, I heard a voice and turned to see a middle-aged woman carrying a bag of groceries.

She looked at me quizzically. "Why you take picture of street? It not very beautiful. Mosque beautiful yes, but street no. It very old, maybe more than hundred years. So why?"

I thought it pointless explaining I had been taking a photo of a rubbish bin, and so shrugged and told her I thought the street looked interesting. The woman scoffed and gestured along it. "Not beautiful!"

Just then, a large woman who looked like she knew her way around a turnip stall was walking along. She was wearing a dark-green dress patterned with white flowers.

"Look!" said the woman.

Instead of arguing with her about the relative merits of a Baku street scene, I asked whether she knew the way to the Russian Church.

"Why you go Russian Church? It very old and not very beautiful!" She scrunched up her face. "Photo no good!"

"I just want to see it," I said, smiling.

The woman put her bag of groceries down on the floor. For a fleeting moment, I wondered whether she was going to find a turnip so she could beat me with it. Instead she gestured down a steep path, telling me it was down on the left.

I thanked the woman and walked downhill, wondering why she had been so bothered about my photos only showing beautiful and modern things. Perhaps she wanted to look to the future and not dwell upon the past. Whatever the reason, her directions were good, and I arrived at the church, where I quickly spotted a platoon of old crones sat outside with tins. All of them were staring at me. Between them, they had five teeth. Wearily I approached the entrance as rattling began to an accompaniment of banshee-like babbling.

"I'll give money on the way out," I said as I stepped past them. Most of the women looked blankly at me, but one woman seemed to understand and turned to her friends. I left them to it and entered the tiny courtyard. The Russian Church might not have been very beautiful, but it was still a pretty little thing, with a nice silver onion dome and some fetching red trimming.

A young couple entered after me and once the girl had received a headscarf from a little booth, they both entered the actual church. As for me, I ambled around the courtyard, stopping to look at some religious icons, and then headed back out into the street. The rattling began immediately, and after depositing a few coins, I escaped with my life.

I soon found myself walking through a square dominated by a drama theatre at one end. More interesting were the old men playing nard, a type of backgammon. Groups of them sat huddled around boards flinging dice and moving their pieces while their pals looked on. I approached one group and watched them awhile. They didn't seem to mind. Eventually I headed back to the hotel.

7

After the First World War, Azerbaijan had enjoyed a brief spell of independence. It became the first Islamic nation to grant equal rights to both women and men, and things looked rosy for the fledgling nation. But then the Soviets came knocking on Baku's back door, demanding Azeri oil to power their vast communist machinery. Azerbaijan reluctantly obliged, but less than two years later the Soviets decided it wanted all the oil and invaded the country. After 20,000 Azerbaijani soldiers had died, the nation became the Azerbaijan Soviet Socialist Republic. And that's how it stayed for the next seventy years.

The Soviets also took over Armenia, but relations between the two neighbours were never good. The disputed region of Nagorno-Karabakh was the root cause. As previously mentioned, the problem stemmed from the fact that Nagorno-Karabakh was a region inside Azerbaijan, but with an Armenian-heavy population.

Things came to a head in January 1990, when Armenia announced that Armenians living in Nagorno-Karabakh were eligible to vote in the forthcoming elections for Armenian independence. The Azerbaijanis said they couldn't. The Armenians said they could. Both countries looked to the Soviet Union to sort things out, but Moscow sat back and did nothing.

Rioting started in Baku. Azeris started demanding independence from the Soviets so they could sort out their own affairs, i.e. deal with Armenia themselves. Armenian citizens living in Baku were attacked. The Soviets sent in some troops and warships, but ordered their men not to intervene. Under this backdrop of hesitancy, the capital city of Azerbaijan spiralled into hell.

Mobs of Azeris began hunting down and killing any Armenian Christians living in Baku. A lot of people they found were beaten or stabbed to death. When thousands of Armenians began to flee the city, angry mobs raided and set alight vacant Armenian businesses and homes. Such was the level of violence and hatred that the Azeri authorities could not cope.

Things escalated. Armenian women who had not managed to escape were tortured and killed, some were raped, and others had Christian crosses branded on their backs. Before the week was out, ninety Armenians were dead, but the worst seemed to be over. It was then that Soviet troops entered Baku.

This kick-started the violence again, this time between heavily armed Soviet troops and civilian Azeris. Street battles occurred all over the city, and by the time the Soviets had taken control, more than a hundred Azerbaijanis had died, mostly innocent people caught up in the mess. One was a twelve-year-old girl who had been riding in a bus. This event became known as Black January.

The West seemed largely indifferent to the events in Baku, and those that had noticed actually agreed with how the Soviets had handled things. Meanwhile, in Azerbaijan, anti-Soviet resentment was at its peak, and calls for independence became stronger. By August the following year, Azerbaijan declared itself independent, the ninth Soviet Republic to do so.

In the years since then, Azerbaijan's relationship with Armenia has remained poor, and the thorny issue of Nagorno-Karabakh is still unresolved. Both countries have a ceasefire in place, but it is a fragile one.

8

The next morning the weather was sunny and pleasantly warm, and even better than that, the mist had gone. From the seventeenth floor of my hotel, I found a panoramic view of Baku stretching from the Caspian Sea to the hilltop skyscrapers. Clearly visible were the brand-new Flame Towers, an almost-finished trio of skyscrapers designed to resemble the curves of a flickering fire. They looked fantastic, and added a bit of sparkle to a hill otherwise dominated by a boring old TV Tower.

I headed away from the hotel along a shopping street full of designer shops and mobile phone stores. Young women in high heels strode along with heads held high, while teenagers carrying iPhones stood about laughing and joking. Baku was an affluent city, that much was clear to see, mainly due to its vast oil reserves.

Oil spewed out from Baku's wells at almost a million barrels a day. And the wells had been spewing for a long time. In 1911, Professor Williams of Columbia University noted: *Baku is founded upon oil. Oil is in the air one breathes, in one's nostrils, in one's eyes, in the water of the morning bath – everywhere.*

Before arriving in Baku, I'd expected to see signs of oil all over the city. I honestly believed the Caspian would be full of oil derricks and tanker ships, and that the coast would be black with the stuff. But Baku was nothing like that, at least not in the centre.

I veered left towards a huge Soviet-style building called the Heydar Aliyev Concert Hall. It reminded me of a similar building I'd seen in Tashkent. It had concrete sections dramatically tapering downwards, like a monstrous egg slicer from hell. I loved it, especially since it was located in a square with a statue of Aliyev too. He was standing on a mighty plinth waving at the unseen masses before him.

9

Heydar Aliyev was, and still is, regarded as Azerbaijan's greatest leader. Even the airport was named after him. During Soviet times, Aliyev joined the KGB and quickly rose through the ranks, eventually becoming the communist leader of the Azerbaijan Soviet Socialist Republic in the 1970s.

After independence, due to the bungling incompetence of the first two presidents, Aliyev was elected in 1993, and proved himself more than capable of leading the fledgling nation. He brought about the ceasefire with neighbouring Armenia (over the disputed region of Nagorno-Karabakh), and he secured foreign investment to fuel the country's oil industry. Money flowed in.

Aliyev proved so popular with the people of Azerbaijan that he remained president for the next decade, and then in an almost king-like move, he passed the presidency to his son. I wandered away from his statue towards the Caspian Sea.

10

I began a leisurely amble along Baku's pleasantly airy sea-front promenade, passing a fairground (closed for some reason), as well as people cleaning, painting, polishing and generally making the place look spick and span.

I gazed out at the sea. There was no sign of Baku's famous oil industry anywhere. It looked nice, and I could easily see Baku becoming a popular tourist city. That was if it sorted out its entry visa issues. Young couples sat canoodling along the promenade, and the whole area seemed geared up for tourists, skaters and power joggers, especially with a great view of the Flame Towers in the distance.

I passed a group of teenagers sat on a wall, one of whom pointed at me as I passed. Then he laughed. Others looked and sniggered too. Trying to ignore them, I walked onwards, wondering what they had found so funny. With a sudden change in wind direction, the feeling of air rushing through my gaping flies explained it all.

11

Up in the hills is the Martyr's Lane Memorial. It is dedicated to Azeris killed by Soviet troops in 1990 on Black January. It also contains the graves of those who had lost their lives in the Nagorno-Karabakh conflict.

I wandered to the first two graves and noticed they were of a married couple called Ilham and Fariza Allahverdiyev. Soviet troops shot Ilham dead on 20 January 1990. His wife Fariza had committed suicide soon afterwards.

As well as Azeri graves, there were memorials to Turkish soldiers killed in 1918, and a smaller one dedicated to British troops killed at the same time. There were no memorials to any of the Armenians killed in the events leading up to Black January. With time running out before I had to head to the airport, I left the tombs and headed back down the hill.

12

My short time in the Azerbaijan capital had ended. I checked out of the hotel and caught a taxi back to the airport, once again getting caught up in the ridiculous traffic jams of downtown Baku. Surely there was a better way than this, I thought as we came to another beeping standstill. It seemed every car was changing lanes, forcing their way through, or else simply parked in a stupid place.

But what a trip! A four-country extravaganza that brought my total to seventeen nations. I'd eaten horsemeat in Kazakhstan, and been searched by officials in Uzbekistan. Policemen told me off in Turkmenistan, and I'd been surprised at how nice Azerbaijan was. And I did it all by myself!

Phil might think me mad, but travelling had the power to make me feel alive, especially when it involved visiting places that most people had barely heard of. As I said good-bye to Azerbaijan, I thought about the four months I had remaining before Angela's deadline set in. Four months to visit the final three countries: Tajikistan, Kyrgyzstan and Belarus. All would require careful planning.

19. The Stag Invades Polanski

Interesting fact: In the Middle Ages, Poles drank vodka to awaken lust.

"So which countries are left?" asked Phil. He'd just returned from the bar with a round of drinks that he deposited on a table in front of Michael and me.

"Just a couple more 'Stans, and Belarus, and then I'll be done." I answered. In fact I could hardly believe the Red Quest was almost complete. The final few nations, and I'd be at the finishing line well before the deadline. I was planning on heading to Tajikistan and Kyrgyzstan at the start of the summer holidays, and then Belarus at the end.

Michael looked impressed. He really fancied going to Belarus with me - it was just down his alley - but ever since getting engaged, he'd been saving for the wedding and honeymoon. He'd had to reign in his spending.

Michael picked up his alcopop and took a swig. Working in the soft-drinks factory had left him with a sweet tooth. In fact the last time I'd seen him drink a pint of beer was in Kiev. "What about Poland?" he asked me.

"Poland?" I shrugged. "What about it?"

"Shouldn't you go to Poland too?" I noticed he gave Phil a quick glance.

"I've already been there, and Angela won't let me go again. She says it's a waste of money for me to go somewhere I've already been. I sort of agree with her."

Phil butted in. "But the last time you went to Poland was before you started the quest. I think you need to go again."

Michael nodded in agreement.

"And you can!" said Phil with a grin. "Because we're all going there next month."

I swivelled my eyes in confusion. "Who is?"

"We are. It's Michael's stag do!"

2

In hindsight, it was almost inevitable that one of us would be arrested in Krakow (pronounced Krak-off, and not Krak-cow as some people think). Before that though, the seven of us managed to see most of the major sights on offer, starting with the fabulous central square, which was full to the brim with tourists, and a man dressed as a pint of beer. He turned out to be a sullen individual advertising a bar around the corner, and seemed more interested in talking to another man (dressed as a monster) than in actually doing his job of handing out flyers.

The edge of the medieval square featured a plethora of bars and restaurants, but we bypassed them in favour of Cloth Hall, which stood in the centre. After an amble through the stalls and trinket shops inside, we decided to climb the town hall tower.

After negotiating its spiralling staircase, we found a platform with a decent view of the square below. Beer Man had moved on, I noticed, waddling towards a large statue. We gazed at the splendour below. The square was full of beautifully restored medieval buildings.

In 2005, Krakow's main market square was voted the best in the world. Twenty years before that, it had been the focal point for Solidarity demonstrations, and back even further, in the 1940s, the Nazis had named it Adolf Hitler Platz.

3

"Let's go and see the Barbican," Michael said, consulting his map. And since it was his stag-do, we nodded and followed him towards the oldest surviving fortification of the city.

It had a large archway (which looked like it needed a portcullis) and quite a few pointy spire things on top. We were about to go inside when Phil spotted the entry fee sign. Without further ado, he announced that he wasn't paying to go inside a muscum, and the rest of us agreed, leaving Michael with no choice except to follow us towards Wavel Hill.

Wavel Hill was the heart of Krakow, containing a castle, a large cathedral and a large statue of Pope John Paul II, born not far from Krakow. Built in the 14th century as a royal residence, the complex was located up a slight hill. Because it was a major tourist destination, a few beggars lined the path up to it, all with bowed heads and cowering postures. I gave one man a two zloty coin, and he waved his arms animatedly, thanking me in Polish.

"Is this where King Krak lived?" asked Phil, pointing at the battlements of the huge castle. I shook my head, laughing at the name of the fabled old monarch. We'd read that Krakow had actually been named after the comically sounding monarch. But if it was true, we didn't know.

Further on, we could see a few people looking down at something below the battlements. It turned out to be a fire-breathing bronze dragon. According to legend, a nasty dragon had terrorized the people of Krakow, until someone had come up with a cunning plan. That person turned out to be the local shoemaker.

Filling a dead sheep with hot sulphur, the shoemaker bravely left it at the entrance to the dragon's cave while it was asleep. When the creature woke up and spotted the sheep, it scoffed it down in one greedy helping. With its belly burning, the dragon needed a drink, so dived into the River Vistula and began gulping river water like there was no tomorrow. But alas, the beast ended up drinking so much that its belly burst, and it died.

Being May, tourists were everywhere inside the Wavel Hill complex: sitting in cafes; crawling around the monuments; following guides; or else being carted around inside sightseeing buggies and horse-drawn carriages. There was another stag party wandering around the complex, we noticed, fellow Brits as far as we could tell. They were all wearing white T-shirts with each person's nickname on the back. How one shaven-headed man had earned the nickname *Butterbean,* I couldn't begin to imagine.

4

It was in Poland, of course, that events began which saw the eventual collapse of the Soviet Union. The Solidarity movement started as early as 1980, when a trade union group, supported by the Catholic Church, had formed. A man called Lech Walesa led it.

Communist forces quickly put down the peaceful protests and threw the leaders of Solidarity into prison. When this didn't curtail the movement, they declared Martial Law, which had the desired effect, apart from one major drawback: the country began a spiral into economic crisis. Rationing of food became a way of life.

I was a teenager at the time, and could remember watching news reports from Poland. Footage always seemed to show the same thing: people queuing in the cold for basic necessities. The lines were long, snaking around listless grey buildings. Everything seemed monotone, and it was images like this that cemented most people's impressions of Eastern Europe, including my own, for many years.

Hidden in the shadows, Solidarity continued. When the leaders were released from prison in 1986, the movement grew in such numbers that the authorities had no choice but to acknowledge it. If they hadn't done so, the economy would have collapsed. Without Solidarity, no one would go to work.

All this tied in nicely with Gorbachev's new policy of not intervening in the affairs of its satellite states. By 1989, semi-free elections were held, and Lech Walesa became President of Poland soon after. The floodgates opened across the whole of the Soviet Union.

5

In 2005, when I'd been to Krakow with Angela, we'd stayed in the Kazimierz (Old Jewish) Quarter of the city. Just around the corner from our hotel was a small market square straight from the 1970s. Burly, moustached men were setting up stalls, while large old women spread carrots and potatoes (and of course turnips) out on blankets.

Angela and I also walked past the Church of Saint Mary, located in the corner of the central square. Noticing people milling about, waiting for something to happen, we hung around for a minute, but when nothing did, we began to move off.

An elderly gentleman stopped us. He pointed up at the church spires, then gestured at his watch, making it clear something was about to happen. With a toothy grin, he was off. We decided to wait.

A horde of Japanese tourists, led by a pamphlet-waving guide, suddenly arrived. They gathered and looked up, digital cameras at the ready. And then we heard it, the distinctive sound of a bugle. It was coming from the taller of the two spires.

It was almost eerie the way the whole square went quiet except for the musician. Angela and I stared upwards trying to spot who was playing but couldn't see. Then, half way through the performance, the bugle suddenly stopped. It resumed a few seconds later. Eventually the last note sounded, and a hand waved from a small recess in the spire. Cheers and applause greeted this. Then the crowd dispersed.

"What was all that about?" Angela asked.

I looked in the guidebook. "The spire used to be a lookout point," I said. "A couple of bugle players were stationed there. Their orders were to play a tune if they ever spotted attackers. One day they saw some barbarians and so one of them began to play. Half way through, an arrow pierced his throat, and the other sentry had to take over. Thus the gap."

"That's horrible."

That evening the stag party found a cocktail bar. Phil ordered a drink that looked like it contained a radioactive isotope, but was actually a glowing, green plastic ice cube. It soon became the focus of our attention, with most of us trying to take a photo of the strange cocktail. Phil put an end to it with an angry outburst. "Stop taking pictures, 'cos all I want is to drink the bastard!"

After sinking even more beers, we decided to call it a night. All of us except Dave, who despite being tired like the rest of us, elected to stay out.

Dave was a 6ft 4 ex-nightclub bouncer who had once been a flatmate of Michael's. After enjoying a few more drinks in a bar just across from the hotel, he relocated to a bench where he began to roll himself a cigarette. That was the last thing Dave remembered until he awoke the next morning in a windowless room with six beds. Each bed had a man on it, naked except for his underpants. Dave found himself in the same state. And so his day began.

For the rest of us, with no idea of what had happened to our hapless friend, we decided to do something not usually associated with stag parties and headed to Auschwitz, an hour's drive from Krakow.

The first ominous sign that we were nearing the death camps was the railway tracks by the side of the road. Cattle carts once carried people from as far away as Greece and Norway along these very tracks.

At the tourist entrance, we found out there had been three Auschwitz camps, all quite close together. Auschwitz I (where we were now waiting) had been the administrative centre, Auschwitz II had been the death camp, and Auschwitz III had been a chemical factory. And then the tour began. Harrowing doesn't even begin to describe it.

7

"Auschwitz I is nowhere near as large as Auschwitz II," said the young female guide who was talking to us via electronic headsets, "but they still managed to murder about seventy thousand people here. Originally this camp held political prisoners and Soviet prisoners of war but eventually Polish dissidents arrived too, as did the first Jews. Come, follow please."

After walking under the famous sign (recently returned after being stolen), we passed through the once electrified barbed-wire fence, and then entered the camp itself. The sun was shining and leaves were rustling in a light breeze, the beginnings of quite a nice day.

A few redbrick buildings, separated by narrow areas of grass, made up the camp, with the odd tree thrown in for good measure. The buildings had once been Polish army barracks before the Nazis had arrived and taken them over. Michael who was walking beside me said, "It all looks so normal."

As we passed between two of the blocks, the guide stopped. "Sixty-five years ago there was no grass here, only mud and dirt. Prisoners from each block, about 800 of them, gathered in these gaps for roll call. If any prisoner was missing - perhaps because of an escape attempt – guards made everyone stand for hours, often in the snow. Some prisoners would die. As a further punishment, guards sometimes stripped prisoners, covered them in cold water and left them to freeze to death. Today, in the sun, it is hard to imagine such things happening, and that is why visiting Auschwitz in winter is sometimes better. It is then that you can appreciate the full horror."

We all stood looking at the patch of greenery, trying to picture hundreds of painfully thin prisoners huddled together as SS guards stood over them. Before visiting Auschwitz, I'd read and seen things about what had happened, feeling utter revulsion and disgust, but to actually be in the place was something else entirely;

the whole horror notched up to another level. And I could see from the faces of the thirty or so other people in our group that everyone was experiencing the same thing: nobody was smiling, nobody was talking.

8

As well as our group, Auschwitz had multitudes of other tour groups, either queuing up or trooping past the various blocks. It was clearly a well-oiled machine, with the people in charge making sure everything was running smoothly despite the huge numbers of people present. Sadly, this made me see a connection with how well the SS had run Auschwitz when they had been in command. We followed the guide into one of the blocks, now a museum of artefacts.

"Please look at this photograph," said our guide. It was a haunting black and white shot showing a group of small boys wearing short trousers, and a woman holding a baby. They were all walking past whoever was taking the photo.

"These people had just arrived in Auschwitz II, but were deemed unfit to work by the SS doctors. They are heading for the gas chambers, but do not know that yet." We all stared, some people close to tears.

Suitcases crammed another room, and further along, a room had shoes filling it. And then we walked into the only room where no one could take photographs: the Room of Human Hair.

Plaits, pigtails, blonde, brown and black hair filled the entire room. The guide explained: "After the people had been gassed, all their hair was shaven off. It was then bagged up and sent to factories in Germany where it was used as filling for mattresses or chairs."

One man in our group raised his camera to take a photo, and then stopped when he felt the stares of everyone. He lowered it looking guilty. I stared at the hair, unable to believe people in

Berlin had sat on sofas filled with the hair of murdered people. It didn't bear thinking about.

The next block was the punishment building. In tiny cells, three people had to stand for days at a time. Other cells were for starvation and suffocation. In the latter, prisoners were housed without air vents, slowly dying as the oxygen ran out. It was also in this grim building that the first experiments into gassing people with Cyclone B occurred, the substance eventually used in the gas chambers.

"We will now go to the gas chamber," said the guide. "Even though it was the smaller of the two main camps, Auschwitz I had its own gas chamber and crematorium, which unlike the ones at Auschwitz II, were not destroyed by the Nazis. They didn't have time to demolish it, you see."

9

The windowless gas chamber was dark, and smaller than I'd expected, about the size of a classroom. The rectangular floors, walls and ceiling were bare concrete, giving the chamber a stark appearance. We all gathered around our guide.

"Everyone was stripped naked before entering," she told us. "Most did so willingly because of what they had been told. In Auschwitz II, they thought they were having actual showers, but here at Auschwitz I, they believed they were going to be deloused. After all, they had just arrived by train and hadn't washed for days. Some of them would've been looking forward to it." We considered this awful fact as the guide continued.

"After stripping, the guards herded people into this chamber, packing them tightly to get rid of as much air as possible. Hundreds of men, women and children all pressed together with just a few holes in the ceiling letting some light through."

We all looked up to see a few slits in the roof.

"And when the door was bolted behind them some people must have known things were not as planned, but of course it was too late. From the vents in the ceiling, men wearing gas masks dropped gas canisters containing Cyclone B. Then the vents closed. The lucky ones died almost immediately because they were near the vent. For the rest, it would've taken up to twenty minutes."

During experiments into using Cyclone B gas, Nazi doctors noted that about a third of the victims died straight away. For others, once the shouting and screaming had stopped, their skin began to turn red, their mouths foamed, and blood started seeping from ears.

"After the gas had been cleared," said the guide, "the corpses were ransacked of gold teeth. Then they were shaven. Finally they were cremated."

It felt horrible to be standing in a place where so much death had happened. We were essentially inside a murder room. The vents were still there, and the concrete walls looked dark and dank. I tried to focus my mind away from the hellish images of writhing men, women and children all dying in one of the most gruesome ways imaginable.

As we began to leave the chamber, Phil turned to me, shaking his head. "To think that the last thing those poor people saw was that disgusting concrete room. It's beyond imagination."

Just along from the gas chamber were some wooden gallows. Built after the war had ended, it was the place where Rudolf Hoss (not to be confused with the similarly spelt Rudolf Hess), the camp commandant, had been hanged on the 16 April 1947. In total, Hoss oversaw the murder of almost 1.5 million people.

During his trial, when asked how it was possible that his camp had managed to exterminate ten thousand people a day, he admitted that: 'technically it wasn't so bad...the killing was easy; they just went in expecting showers. It was the burning that took all the time.'

10

Auschwitz II, also known as Birkenau, was the largest of the camps, and the main extermination centre. Birkenau's famous gateway was still there, but instead of Nazi offices, the building now held a bookshop and a small cafe.

Built to ease the congestion of the first camp, Birkenau was massive, featuring row upon row of huts, bisected by the infamous railway track. One cattle carriage remained as a grim reminder.

"When people arrived," said our guide, "SS officers would separate them into two groups. The smaller group were usually the youngest and healthiest individuals, and they would end up as camp workers. The rest went straight to the gas chambers."

We had a walk through one of the huts, looking at the living conditions. "Most of the workers didn't survive long," explained the guide. "Especially during the harsh winters. Some would only live a few days, others for maybe a few months. Those sleeping on the top bunks had snow and ice falling on them during the night, but those at ground level had rats."

I recalled the set of photos we'd all seen in one of the blocks in Auschwitz I. They displayed mug shots of prisoners with the date of arrival, followed by the date of death. A young man named Seweryn Gluszecki aged just sixteen had arrived at Auschwitz in April 1942. The photograph showed the teenager looking fairly healthy, with even a faint trace of a smile on his face. The SS deemed him healthy enough to be a camp worker. Less than two months later he was dead.

On the way back to Krakow, our driver asked us what we'd thought of the visit to the largest of the Nazi concentration camps. We told him we were glad we'd done it, even if it wasn't exactly an uplifting experience.

"Yes," he agreed. "But an important lesson in history, I think. And one everybody should do sometime in their life."

11

Back in a bar in central Krakow, we awaited the arrival of Dave after his day and night of incarceration in a Polish police station. He turned up safe and sound, if a little bit embarrassed.

"Waking up in a room with five other naked blokes was not my idea of a nice day," Dave said as he sat down. "And there was nothing to do - no TV, no books, no phones, not even a window to look out of. But the worst thing was they took all my money, except for the bit to get back here today. They told me it was the price to pay for being drunk in Poland."

We commiserated with his experience but some of us actually thought it was a good idea - a bit of that in the UK would undoubtedly help with the lawlessness of some British streets in the early hours of most weekends.

We spent the remainder of the evening drinking in a few city centre bars. All of us agreed that it had been a strange stag do, certainly not like any others we'd been on. We raised a toast to Michael and Sarah. The next morning we flew back home.

20. Visa Hell in Tajikistan

Interesting fact: Tajikistan is the only country in the world where polio is on the increase.

Angela sighed. "I can't wait for your stupid quest to be over."

It was the day before my trip back to Central Asia, and the start of the summer holidays. I was busy packing my suitcase and making sure I had all the necessary paperwork for the final two 'Stans.

Once again, Stan Tours had helped me out, organising Letters of Invitations, hotels, and airport transfers. It was the end of July, so I had just over a month in which to visit the last few remaining countries on my list. Very tight, but very possible.

"It's getting embarrassing," Angela continued, "explaining why we're not going on holiday like normal people. When I say Jason's going to Tajikistan, and I'm staying at home, I get funny looks."

Technically that was not the whole truth, but I elected to keep quiet. Angela was going to Tallinn with her sister for a few days. The Red Quest was making a pull on her too, it seemed.

"Just three more countries to go now," I answered, packing some sunscreen. According to the weather reports, Central Asia was roasting with temperatures in the forties. "And then it'll all be done."

"Good. Then we can get back on with a normal life."

2

At Manchester Airport, a nice lady working with the UK Border Agency asked where I was jetting off to. It was part of some survey, she informed me. When I told her Tajikistan, she looked confused.

"Sorry, I didn't quite catch that. Where did you say?"

"Tajikistan," I repeated.

She still looked befuddled, clearly not used to countries beyond Spain, Greece and Turkey. "Oh..." she flustered. "I've not heard of that. Where is it?"

"In Central Asia. Not far from China and Afghanistan."

The woman smiled and looked back at her colleague for support, but he was busy with another passenger. "I've got an idea," she said. "Can you write it down in this space here? It'll save me asking you to spell it."

I did so willingly and handed the form back. She peered at the name. "Can you tell me your reason for visiting...Taj-ik-istan?"

Yes. I'm on an insane quest that I need to finish in the next month or so. A madness has possessed me since a trip to Latvia. A madness that will only be quenched when I've visited every former Soviet Republic. A quest that has seen my credit card maxed to the limit. Is that the answer you're looking for?

Before I had the chance to say any of that, the woman answered for me. "Actually you don't need to tell me why you're going, because it must be for work. No one would go to Tajikistan for a holiday."

I nodded and smiled, and with no further questions, the lady wished me an enjoyable trip. I waded into the tide of tourists ambling through duty free.

3

It was 4.15am when I arrived at Dushanbe International Airport. I was knackered and irritable and in the middle of visa hell.

"There is no letter wiz your name," said the despot in charge of visa applications. "Without letter, no visa."

I stared at him through bloodshot eyes and felt like crying. I'd waited in his chaotic queue for twenty minutes, and all I wanted to do was get my visa and go to sleep. The letter he was referring to was the fabled Letter of Invitation (LOI), a nugget of bureaucracy that some former Soviet Republics still insisted upon. Only government-approved tourist agencies could offer a LOI, and Stan Tours had organised mine for me.

I'd had dealings with LOIs before. In both Tashkent and Ashgabat, I'd simply landed at the airport and handed my copy of the LOI to a border official, who had then matched it up with the one in their pile. But things had gone wrong in Tajikistan. From behind my shoulder, someone handed their LOI copy to the despot. The man took it and turned to his precious pile. A few seconds later, he found the matching piece of paper and set to work.

I glared at the hateful pile of A4 paper that was denying my entry to the poorest of all the former Soviet Republics. If I couldn't get a visa to enter Tajikistan, then I'd have to fly back home with the prospect of the Red Quest being derailed, if not crashed to submission. There was no way I could afford to come back again. I pushed that thought to the back of my mind and addressed the despot. "Please can you look again? My letter must be there."

"It is not," he snapped. "Sit and wait. I deal with you later."

I found a seat and silently seethed.

4

The room was thin and ramshackle, and behind the despot, two other officials toiled at computer keyboards. On the back wall was a large photo of the Tajik president, Emomali Rahmon. Etched upon his face was a thin smile as he watched the turmoil his minions had created.

Thirty minutes passed, and nothing happened. The despot continued to deal with other people, so I slumped back in my seat, letting my eyes close for a moment. Then the despot shouted for my attention. I jumped up and approached his small desk.

"Fill forms in," he barked, proffering a couple of A4 pieces of paper at me. I took them, thanking him for this smidgeon of mercy, and returned to my seat with my prize. I filled the identical forms in and handed them back.

Dawn broke, and the people in the visa room came and went. Twenty minutes later, with a quiet period on their hands, the despot, and one of the other officials, took the opportunity to relax. The third man continued typing, occasionally taking large gulps of Red Bull. Suddenly a fourth official entered the room, all dinner-plate cap and golden epaulets. He was obviously the boss, because the two slouching oafs jumped up and busied themselves with hitherto unknown tasks. And then, almost two hours after arriving in Dushanbe, I got my visa.

5

Under Soviet rule, the Tajik Soviet Socialist Republic had experienced some economic progress, but when it became independent in September 1991, things rapidly went downhill. The subsidies from Moscow dried up, trading partners evaporated, and worst of all, a civil war broke out. It was a hellish conflict, lasting until 1997, killing an estimated 75,000 people. Afterwards, Tajikistan's infrastructure was in tatters and its economy virtually non-existent. A decade and a half on, I wondered how Dushanbe, the capital, would look.

Rudaki Avenue, the main drag of the city, was close to my hotel and followed a more or less north to south direction. It was a wide six-lane highway serviced by chugging green and white trolleybuses and battered old taxis. The pavements were a bit cracked, and some of the buildings looked a tatty, but overall it wasn't too bad. Women in fancy headdresses with occasional mouthfuls of gold teeth wandered about, giving the place an almost Arabian feel. But instead of Arabic, the lettering was Cyrillic.

I walked along the tree-lined avenue, avoiding the potholes and gaps, trying my best to keep in the shade offered by the trees. It was bloody hot in Tajikistan, and I was thankful for the foliage above my head. The Soviets planted it all in the 1960s.

6

Despite being an Islamic nation, Dushanbe had little in the way of mosques, but the one I found just off Rudaki Avenue was worth a detour. The Haji Yakoub Mosque, with its mighty pair of blue minarets, had men with long beards, and intricately patterned skullcaps, loitering outside. There was also a long stall selling silver teapots and piles of red and green apples. Without preamble, I walked past the stalls and entered the mosque's quite gorgeous courtyard.

It was empty, apart from two elderly men standing by the entrance. Like the men outside, both sported long white beards. As I walked past them, I said hello, but neither man answered.

While I took a photo of the pastel blue mosque, I overheard the old gents muttering something. I turned and found them both staring at me. I gestured whether it was okay for me to take photos, but again, neither man answered, and so after a few seconds of stalemate I carried on. Satisfied with my little visit to the mosque, I headed towards the exit, but suddenly one of the men grabbed my arm and twisted it.

It didn't hurt, but it did stop me in my tracks. I pulled my arm free, but he grabbed it again, and I considered briefly whether the pensioners were trying to mug me, but neither man seemed interested in me beyond my arm. And then I realised what was going on - they were staring at my watch. After reading the time, the old geezer released my arm. *Buy a bloody watch*, I felt like saying, but instead smiled and went on my way.

7

Dushanbe was in the World Record Books.

Its flagpole was the tallest on earth, and stood higher than two Boeing 747s end to end. An American planned it; engineers in Dubai constructed it, and then truck drivers drove it through Iran,

Turkmenistan and Uzbekistan. Gazing up, I wondered how the designers had managed to make a piece of fabric big enough to flap on the end of the 165-metre pole.

It was located in what looked like a redeveloped park area. New statues were springing up everywhere, all of them overlooking a large manmade lake in the middle. I seemed to be the only person there. I stared up at the flag, which seemed to be moving in slow motion due to its immense size.

At night, powerful lights illuminated the flagpole. It even glowed during Tajikistan's harsh winters, when power cuts were common across the city. Across the lake was the Palace of Nations, the new abode of the Tajik president. It was massive and eye-catching, all white marble and Greek columns, with a gigantic golden dome on the top. It too never suffered from power shortages, and I wondered what the ordinary people of Dushanbe thought of that, while they shivered in their power cut-riddled homes.

Like certain other Central Asian presidents, Emomali Rahmon was just a little bit insane. Within a week of becoming president in 1991, he banned miniskirts. He also banned children from mosques, and like his counterpart in Turkmenistan, made lip-synching at live concerts a punishable crime.

US diplomats have accused Rahmon of gross corruption, claiming he rules Tajikistan for his own personal profit. They say he has offshore bank accounts, and that his family owns most of the nation's businesses. They also claim that he controls the press, rigs elections, and likes to build himself trophy palaces. Yes, Emomali Rahmon, according to them, is a fairly standard Central Asian president.

8

I was wandering along Rudaki Avenue, looking for somewhere to have lunch, when I noticed the strange man.

He was aged about fifty, thin and gaunt, with a terrible expression on his face. He was either angry or extremely unhinged, neither of which were good propositions. As I watched him cross the road towards me, I saw the mad look in his eyes, and slowed my pace. Instead of approaching me though, the nutcase turned and stormed ahead. After about ten metres, he rushed over to a tree and kicked it. Then he kicked it again. The man bared his teeth at his arboreal nemesis and then kicked it once more, before running away.

I stopped for lunch in an outdoor eatery near the Opera House, but couldn't understand the menu. I didn't fancy doing a potluck choice (as I'd done with Michael in Kiev), and so when the waitress appeared, I asked if she could speak English.

"A little..." she said.

I smiled and pointed to the menu with a quizzical look. "I don't understand this..."

"Ah, I see. Perhaps you want shishlik?"

"Shishlik?"

"Yes please. Beef or the chicken?"

"Chicken please." I also managed to order a large Simsim, the local beer.

The other patrons in the cafe were all locals, looking vaguely Iranian, and all chatting to each other good-heartedly while an old man with a small flute wandered around playing a traditional Tajik tune. When he came to me, I handed him a three-somoni note that he pocketed with a smile and a bow. Tajikistan was the first country I'd been where a banknote was a 'three.'

My food arrived and was delicious. Shishlik turned out to be kebabs of meat on a skewer, served with a side portion of raw onion. It also came with a huge circular piece of bread. The beer was refreshing on such a hot day, and when the bill came, I couldn't believe how cheap it was. Less than two pounds for the whole lot.

I decided to look for an old tank. I soon discovered it on a high roundabout, surrounded by a wall. Traffic was charging around it at a hundred miles an hour.

Beep! screamed the car as it swerved past me, missing my foot by inches. Keeping my nerve, I edged along the inside rim of the roundabout and wondered whether to climb the wall. I reckoned I could do it, but the thought of pulling a muscle and then slipping back into the river of cars made me cautious. I carried on walking and found an entry point at the northern end of the roundabout. Weeds poked out from between every crack in the paving blocks, and the place looked like it hadn't been visited for years.

The tank was large and green with a nice red star on the side. Its pointy thing was aimed at some ugly apartment blocks in the distance. Behind the tank were a couple of concrete spikes encrusted with Soviet engravings. The most striking was of a muscle-bound Red Army soldier chopping a Nazi symbol in half with his sword.

My phone rang, which startled me because I hadn't been able to get a signal since leaving the UK. It was Phil.

"Which turnip-eating country are you in now?" he asked.

"Tajikistan."

Across thousands of miles, I could hear Phil snigger. "You really need your head checking. But it's Angela I feel sorry for. She should be sunbathing on a beach in Spain, not sat at home while you're staring at turnips. Anyway, I rang to ask you a favour."

"Oh?"

"Yeah, my nephew has started collecting foreign money. Can you bring some back from Turnipistan or wherever it is you are? He'll be really grateful."

I told him I would.

"Cheers," said Phil. "Well then, I'll leave you alone to do whatever you do in these strange countries. I bet your camera is full of turnip photos. I bet you have a website called *Turnip Porn* or something!" Phil laughed, and I did too. We said good-bye and the line went dead.

I sat on the wall and pondered what to do next. And despite my absolute loathing of museums, I decided to visit one just up the road. The reason was simple: the National Museum of Antiquities of Tajikistan contained the largest sleeping Buddha in Central Asia. I simply had to see that.

10

Under the rule of Buddhist kings, Central Asia had been awash with statues of obese men reaching nirvana. The Buddhist religion had stretched from China in the east, to Iran in the west, and men with spades had found lots of Buddha statues in the 'Stans.

Afghanistan had coughed up a few statues too, but the Taliban didn't care much for them. One statue, at 57-metres long, had been the largest Buddha in the world, yet despite pleas from the world community, in 2001, the Taliban dynamited the 400BC carving to smithereens.

After donning some blue plastic shoe coverings, I entered the darkened museum and paid the entrance fee. I was the only visitor. A stooped, old lady rushed ahead of me to switch on the lights, and then directed me into the first room.

As the lights flickered on, I found it full of the usual stuff – pot fragments, bits of spear, portions of tiny necklaces, and I finished the room in thirty seconds. The next room was more of the same, and the lady had a hard time keeping up with my fast-paced walk. I entered a third darkened room and waited for the flustered woman to find the light switch. When she did, I saw the skeleton.

The bones inside the glass cabinet were in a foetal position, with coloured beads around them, possibly from the robe the woman had been wearing upon burial. The placard on the side said she was *Sarazm's Princess*, the intact skeleton of a wealthy woman who had lived during the Bronze Age. A Tajik farmer had found her in 1976 as he was about to plant some turnips.

Not much was known about the woman, except that she was rich, and lived in a community of around six thousand people. I lingered around the skeleton for a while, finding it difficult to comprehend that she had lived in a time before the Pharaohs of Ancient Egypt had even been born.

Upstairs I came to another pot room, but was delighted to find a comedy item in one of the cabinets. Whether the pot maker had meant it to be funny, I didn't know, but to me, it looked like a five-year-old had moulded it. The clay deer (if that's what it even was) had a pointy gaping mouth, two stuck on horns, and rolled-up caterpillars for eyes. It was nearly as good as the king with a dangling penis I found in the next room.

But then I came to the room I'd been waiting for: the Sleeping Buddha. It was big, thirteen metres in length, and I checked this out by walking its length, counting off my paces. Unearthed in 1966, it was 1500 years old, and to excavate it, archaeologists had been forced to cut the Buddha into 92 pieces. I stared at the giant man; his eyes closed in deep meditation, and then thanked the woman in charge of the lights. After removing my plastic shoe coverings, I left the museum.

11

The next day I decided to brave an old Soviet cable car. This was despite reading that a) it creaked like mad, b) it shook like it was going to drop to the earth, and c) the door often swung open mid-flight, offering passengers a terrifying glimpse of their own demise.

After a half-hour trudge uphill, I reached the lower end of the cable car, but found it shut. Broken windows and a padlocked door suggested it had been idle for quite some time. Just to make sure though, I circled the tall stone building and quickly came across a bunch of men enjoying sips of tea and a fine afternoon chat.

I went to the men and gestured about the possibility of going up in the cable car. One gent shook his head and crossed his arms above his head. *Closed*, he mimed. Just as well, I reflected, it would probably have snapped with me in it. Instead, I commandeered a taxi and in a moment of pure impulsiveness, asked him to drive me west to the town of Hissar, home of Hissar Fortress.

12

The driver was a friendly man, no doubt cheered by the high fare he'd just picked up, but the language barrier proved too much and conversation quickly stalled.

As we hit the outskirts of Dushanbe, I studied my map of Tajikistan because I wanted to double check that the driver was going in the right direction, and not taking me to some kidnappers' lair in Afghanistan.

The Tajik capital, I noticed, was in the far west of the country, with the Afghan border two hundred miles to the south. People had grown rich in Tajikistan because of the opium passing through from Afghanistan. I also spotted the disputed region under Afghan control called Badakhstan, which if it were an actual country would have the best name in the world. I could imagine a hardened bank robber on the run from the law hiding out in Badakhstan.

I waited for a road sign to appear that would indicate we were heading to Hissar, and when one did, I calmed down.

13

Even though it was only thirty kilometres away, the journey to Hissar took ages, mainly due to the poor condition of the road. The driver had to swerve around potholes like a demented rally driver.

Back in Dushanbe, before jumping in his taxi, I'd scoped the vehicle out. From the outside it had looked in good condition, certainly better than some of the other bangers parked nearby. But once we set off, I'd quickly changed my opinion. For a start, there was no suspension, which meant every bump sent me bouncing skywards, sometimes to the point of banging my head on the roof. There was also an unmarked plastic bottle just behind the handbrake. It was filled with an amber liquid that looked suspiciously like urine. Either that or beer, both of which were bad beverage choices, I felt. To take my mind off the bottle, I looked outside at the Tajik countryside.

Men on donkeys, cows with ribs showing, women hoeing fields, and teenage boys pushing carts were just some of the things I saw in rural Tajikistan. We passed plenty of roadside stalls selling watermelons. It seemed the national fruit of the country. We also passed groups of young boys wearing only their swimming trunks, jumping into unseen areas of water beyond the edge of the bumpy highway. Suddenly the driver slowed down, put on his seatbelt, and looked at me. "Police," he said ominously.

Two hundred yards in front, a police checkpoint was in operation. Two baton-waving officers were flagging down vehicles, seemingly at random. The taxi driver looked worried. I already suspected his car was unroadworthy, but maybe my driver was a fugitive from Badakhstan. As it transpired, we passed the police checkpoint unhindered, and as we did so, the driver picked up the bottle of amber liquid and deftly unscrewed the lid. After taking a large swig, he replaced it between the front seats. We soon arrived in the bustling town of Hissar.

14

It was the usual hive of activity, with honking traffic, crowds of people, and policemen pulling vehicles over to check paperwork. More watermelons were on sale, as was other fruit and vegetables, all of them spilling out over sacks. Without the cars, it might have been a medieval village. We stopped briefly so the driver could ask for directions, and then we were off again, driving a few kilometres out of town until we came to the star attraction.

The 18th century fortification did look impressive. It had a couple of tall round towers and a high walled archway. I walked under the arch to see the other side, but found only a few steps and a solitary camel sitting on a hill. As usual with tourist attractions in Tajikistan, I was the only visitor.

I climbed the steps, which took me to the top of one of the towers. In the far distance, almost hidden by haze, was a range of mountains that looked like they had snow on top. Below me were a few other historic buildings, one an old school house. A boy was leading a couple of goats along the road, and as I watched him amble by, I recalled the legend I'd read earlier. It involved a man called Caliph Ali.

Caliph Ali had been passing through Hissar when he'd decided to visit the fort. He wanted to preach Islam to the people inside. After climbing off his horse, Ali knocked on the great big door, asking if he could come in.

"Get lost," the guards shouted. "And don't come back."

Undaunted by this frosty reception, Ali tethered his horse and climbed up a nearby hill. There, he removed a rope from his bag and tied it to a rocky outcrop. Then he threw it to the top of the fortress where it caught on the battlements. After giving it a sharp tug to make sure it was secure, Caliph Ali disguised himself as an acrobat and then rope walked across.

"Greetings," he shouted, as he stepped onto the castle walls. "I am a travelling acrobat!"

"No you're not," said a wily guard, immediately seeing through the flimsy disguise. "You're that preacher bloke from before. You're under arrest. Off to the dungeons with you."

Luckily for Caliph Ali, his cell was within earshot of his trusty steed, and he called for it to come. After untethering itself, the horse trotted past the guards and found its way to the cell door. Somehow it gained entry (even with a clattering sword attached to its back), and then neighed a mighty neigh, signalling the start of battle.

Caliph Ali grabbed the sword and went on an angry rampage through the fortress, killing all the guards as well as an evil magician who owned the castle. Job done, he settled down for a snooze and handed his horse a couple of sugar lumps.

15

Back in downtown Dushanbe, I had another walk around the decidedly leafy and green city centre, sampling another tasty shishlik before heading up Rudaki Avenue to my hotel. Despite the incident with the visa, I had enjoyed my time in Tajikistan.

Dushanbe had turned out to be interesting. True, it was a bit dishevelled around the edges, and some of the pavements were cracked, but overall, it was not bad at all. And it seemed perfectly safe for a tourist too. No one had given me any hard stares, and no policemen had bothered me. In fact the only hassle was from the old geezers at the mosque.

At the hotel, I began packing. After so much travel, I was now a dab hand at this rigmarole and finished in no time at all. I spent the remainder of the evening having a delicious meal (and a couple of glasses of Simsim) in a restaurant near the hotel.

Later, sat in my hotel room, I realised I'd almost conquered the 'Stans. Just Kyrgyzstan to go, leaving only Belarus after that. Two more countries and the Red Quest would be finished. I shut down my laptop and smiled.

21. The Kyrgyzstan Ordeal

Interesting fact: Mountains cover 80% of the country. Which isn't very interesting, I know.

I'd never flown a banned airline before.

The European Union had banned all Kyrgyz airliners from flying in its airspace due to poor safety and maintenance concerns. When the call came to board, my fellow passengers and I trooped out to the knackered-looking jet. I wondered what I'd let myself in for.

I took my seat next to a couple of overweight babushkas. They looked at me briefly before resuming their nattering, handbags on their laps, turnips safely stowed in the overhead bins.

From the inside, the plane looked relatively clean, but when I looked in the seat pouch, I found the safety card ripped into pieces. Never a good omen, I thought. The solitary stewardess was gorgeous though, with the slight Chinese features that most ethnic Kyrgyz people possessed. Soon we were off, rattling into the blue skies of Dushanbe while I grasped my rabbit foot tight enough to turn my knuckles white.

2

The plane made a sickening lurch downwards. Someone screamed, and next to me, the babushkas ceased their chatter. With the engines flaring and the plane heaving earthwards, I closed my eyes. So this was it, I reckoned, the grim reaper had come knocking, and I'd let the bastard in.

Grimly, I opened my eyes and fixed my gaze on the seat ahead as we dropped further through the sky. I waited for the brace command but then, a second later, we stabilised and an eerie calm settled over the cabin. And then we touched down on the runway. My hour in the air with a banned airline ended without death.

3

The difference between Kyrgyzstan and Tajikistan could not have been any starker. Instead of a poky little side room to get my visa, Kyrgyzstan's terminal was modern and bright, and its visa system a breeze. I didn't require a Letter of Invitation, or a rigorous form to be filled in. Instead, I simply presented my passport, some dollars, and a small card to a woman behind a counter. After a few minutes, my visa was issued. Simple, straightforward, and hassle free. It put me in a good mood from the outset.

Heading into the city centre, I noticed other differences between Kyrgyzstan and Tajikistan. For a start, the roads were in better condition, the buildings looked more modern, and the people dressed differently. Gone were the Muslim veils of Tajikistan; they had been replaced by hot pants and crop tops, all very European. Modern cars sped past my taxi, and I sat back thinking I was going to enjoy Kyrgyzstan, even if it did have the hardest spelling of any country in the world.

4

The next morning was hot with temperatures pushing the high-thirties. Trying my best to keep in the shade, I followed the road into the centre of Bishkek.

It was exciting to be in a brand new city, especially one I knew next to nothing about. If anything, I'd expected Bishkek to be down at heel, full of crumbling buildings and broken storefronts. But it wasn't, it was clean and ordered, and even had a sparkle of affluence.

I crossed the road and found myself inside a small amusement park full of bumper cars, shoot the duck stalls and bouncy castles. A few families with small children stood by some of the rides, as did a few teenagers enjoying sly cigarettes. I left the park at its opposite end, just in time to see some goose-stepping soldiers.

Three young soldiers were marching past the State Museum with high kicks, exaggerated arm swinging, and of course, impeccable timing. After they had disappeared, I headed around the back of the museum to see a statue of Lenin that used to be around the front. I stared up at the huge bronze statue, thinking it was easily the largest statue I'd seen of the former Soviet leader. Lenin's hand was outstretched, and his coat open, the classic pose.

Back around the front, in the former Lenin Square, now Ala-Too Square, I found a wide expanse dominated by a huge flagpole and some golden domed buildings. In March 2005, locals had gathered in the square to protest against recent elections. Sick and tired of President Askar Akayev's corrupt methods (the usual thing: friends and family in high office, election fraud, and dubious arrests), 15,000 protesters assembled.

As the protesters made their feelings known, security forces stormed the square. Instead of subduing the protest though, the crowd raged forward, quickly overrunning the police, who fled. With no one stopping them, the protesters raced along the street and stormed the Presidential Palace, causing Akayev to commandeer a helicopter. Without delay, he flew to Kazakhstan and then on to Moscow, never to return.

With President Akayev out of the way, and without any real security presence in Bishkek, mobs began looting shops and raiding cash machines. Other rioters set fire to buildings and fought among themselves. Three people died, and hundreds were injured. When a new president was sworn in a week later, things calmed down.

With the new man in power, the people of Kyrgyzstan hoped for a new start. Alas, it wasn't to be. Kurmanbek Bakiyekhad soon proved himself as bad as his predecessor.

The media accused him of corruption, and so in return, Bakiyekhad censored them. By April 2010, new protests began to break out in Bishkek over the lack of jobs and the news that heating bills were to increase by a staggering 400%. Several protests turned violent. Street battles flared across the capital, and by the end of the day, 76 protesters lay dead. Like his predecessor, Bakiyekhad fled to Kazakhstan, and new elections were hastily organised.

I decided to walk to the Presidential Palace, where many of the deaths had occurred.

5

The palace was huge and white, and at seven stories high, it certainly stood out. I walked along its fence until I got to the gates, the very spot where, in 2010, protesters had driven two trucks at it. This act was the spark causing police to open fire, resulting in the 76 deaths.

Everything looked spick and span now though, with not a mark on the black and gold fence. It was hard to believe that bullets, grenades, burning army vehicles, and scores of deaths had happened where I was standing.

Just inside the grounds was a flowerbed with pink, purple, white and red blooms, a beautiful carpet covering such a grisly episode in Kyrgyzstan's life. I headed back to Ala-Too Square.

6

The Soviets had built Ala-Too Square in the mid-eighties, and they had done a good job, because it looked great - one of the best squares I'd seen in any of the former Soviet republics. In the distance, the snow-capped peaks of the Ala-Too Mountain Range offered a jagged but majestic backdrop.

Suddenly beeping horns sounded as a cavalcade of vehicles sped past, all with flashing headlights. Most of them were Toyota Land Cruisers, but the main one was a white, stretch Hummer with blackened windows. Everyone stopped to stare. When they disappeared from sight, the square returned to normal service.

Underneath the gigantic red Kyrgyz flag was a glass booth where two guards stood to attention. Both looked barely old enough to have left school, a sure sign I was getting old. Just along from the guards was a huge monument that had replaced Lenin. I stared at it in confusion. According to my guidebook, the statue should have been a woman with wings, but unless she had dropped the feathers, acquired a horse, and had grown a beard, it was not her.

I consulted my map to see if I was in the right place, but I was - Ala-Too Square. It was all very mysterious. At that moment, a man's voice caught my attention because he was addressing me. He was in his fifties and looked like a local gent. He continued speaking and pointing to the statue, but I couldn't understand a single word. I asked him if he spoke English, and he nodded. "Of course."

Hamid turned out to be a local lecturer and had seen me staring at the map, and then up at the statue, and had guessed at my confusion.

"This statue is new," he told me. "It replaced the Erkindik Monument last year. In 2010, during the revolution, some people tried to bulldoze the woman down."

This was interesting, I thought. I wondered why the local populace had wanted to do that, because according to the picture I had, the winged woman looked far better than the standard man-on-horse job. Plus, it had been a relatively new statue anyway. I asked Hamid if he knew.

"Yes. There are some possible reasons. One was that the woman was dressed inappropriately – she was wearing a loose robe. Another reason was that she resembled the ousted President's wife. But I think the main reason was that she was holding a tunduk. According to tradition, a woman should never touch a tunduk, so people began to think she was bringing bad luck to the nation. And Kyrgyzstan is a very superstitious country. In the end, the government dismantled it and replaced it with Manas, the man you see here. He is a local Kyrgyz hero."

After thanking Hamid, I found a bench to find out what a tunduk was. It turned out to be an integral part of a yurt that allowed sunlight to enter. As such, it was an important symbol of the country, even featuring in the middle of the Kyrgyz flag. As for Manas, he was not a real person at all, but a hero of Kyrgyz legend. A 16th century poem with half a million lines described his many deeds.

His usual companions were a tiger, a lion and a giant black bird. With them, he battled monsters and vicious dragons. When he was annoyed, his eyes turned red (the same as mine in the visa section of Dushanbe airport a few days previously), and he liked to drink human blood. I looked again at the monument and conceded it was a good replacement.

7

I headed east towards one of Bishkek's big league attractions, Victory Park. With a name like that, it came as no surprise that it dated from Soviet times. The main thrust of the park was a WWII monument and eternal flame. A sombre looking statue of a lady, symbolising the millions of women who had waited in vain for their menfolk to return from fighting the Germans, stood proud. Above her, three giant granite ribs, representing a Kyrgyz yurt, cast long shadows across the ground.

Despite the sad context, the park was popular with wedding parties, even with brides who had been kidnapped for the wedding.

I was astonished to learn that bride snatching was common across Central Asia, especially in Kyrgyzstan. According to one researcher, half of all marriages in rural Kyrgyzstan were because of kidnap.

For a Kyrgyz man, snatching a bride was much easier than courtship, and could potentially save his family $800, plus the price of a cow. And the great thing for a potential bride snatcher was the fact that in Kyrgyz society, it was considered an acceptable way to go about things.

8

Here's how it works. A young man, often accompanied by his male relatives, will scour the local area in search of suitable young women. In the old days, they did this on horseback, but nowadays it is by car.

The kidnap party will watch a potential bride for a few days - to establish her routine - and then they will strike, bundling her (usually kicking and screaming) into their getaway vehicle. At top speed, they will drive to the young man's home where the future mother-in-law will try to calm the girl down. She'll also try to persuade the young woman that her son is a decent, law-abiding man, and it would be best if she accepted the marriage proposal.

If the young woman declines this offer, the kidnappers may return the girl home, but more often than not, they hold her hostage in an attempt to break her resolve.

As the hours slip by, the girl knows one thing for sure: if she stays the night, her virginity will be shrouded in doubt. And while this terrible thought is going through her mind, her future in-laws might threaten to put a curse on her. In a country deeply beset by superstition, this is no laughing matter, and so most girls agree to the proposal before the day is out. The rest stay the night, often not eating and drinking, refusing to entertain the idea despite the shame it will bring to their family. By morning though, almost all will have succumbed.

Consider this true story. A female university student learns that kidnappers are scoping her out. At the apartment she shares with her sister in Bishkek, there is a knock on the door. Ten men are there, the kidnap party. She slams the door and locks it, refusing to leave. Many hours later the men give up and depart.

The next morning the girl drops out of university and moves back in with her parents. Soon she secures herself a job in a nearby factory. On the way home one evening, a man approaches, wanting to make acquaintances. She quickly brushes him off and the man leaves. A few days later, she is waiting at a bus stop with two female friends when a car pulls up with two men inside. One of the girls knows the men, and so it's all right. All three women get in the car, with the kind offer of a quick trip home.

After depositing the woman's two friends, the car makes a detour, and the man she'd met a few days previously jumps in. She realises straightaway they are a kidnap posse.

As the car drives off with a screech of rubber, she tries to strangle the driver but another man subdues her. In desperation she tells a terrible lie. She informs the men that she is not a *girl* anymore. The men exchange looks and stop the car. They get out to discuss the admission – after all, no Kyrgyz man wants to marry a bride who is not a virgin. Eventually, they climb back in and drive the girl home. They set her free.

But the girl's life is now different. Despite being young and attractive, no man wants anything to do with her. The people she works with mock her, and her father is angry at the lie she told. Grimly, the girl accepts that she may remain unmarried for the rest of her life. Then unexpectedly, kidnap attempt number three springs into action, with a brand new set of men this time.

The kidnappers drive the girl to the groom's home. Soon her own parents arrive and urge the girl to accept the marriage proposal. Her in-laws help with the decision by telling the girl that other kidnap plans are afoot if their proposal fails. And some of the men in the new plots have criminal pasts. *Bad men*, they tell her. Finally she agrees to marry her kidnapper.

I stared at the photo of the woman, now in her thirties, sixteen years on from her kidnap ordeal. She was sitting down smiling, next to her husband, who was affectionately kissing her cheek.

Surrounding them were the couple's young children, three girls and one boy. A happy Kyrgyz family in every way possible.

Although illegal, the police largely ignore bride kidnap because they see it as an accepted Kyrgyz tradition. Besides, like the example above, many marriages forged in this way turn out to be successful. A quote states that if a Kyrgyz wedding starts with tears, then it is a good omen for a happy marriage.

9

My final stop of the day was the Statue to the Martyrs of the Revolution, a name that only communists could have cooked up. Built in 1978, it was another gigantic monument with a proud and valiant lady standing on top of a ridiculously high plinth. She had her arms wide apart in a sweeping gesture of heroism. Her name was Urkuya Salieva.

Urkuya was born in 1910 in a village in southern Kyrgyzstan. When the Soviets took over, she embraced them and actually joined the Communist Party, quickly rising up through its ranks. By the time she was eighteen, she was the leader of her village, which must have raised some eyebrows, especially when she began to promote feminist issues.

Particularly irked were the peasant men folk. After toiling in the turnip fields all day, the last thing they wanted was to arrive home to find their wives demanding that they should also peel and cook the damned things.

"We are equal to you men," the ladies would chorus. "Urkuya has told us so!"

In the end, a few men gathered, picked up their pitchforks and turnip-pulling apparel, and went off to find the young upstart. When they found Urkuya, they murdered her and killed her husband too. In her memory, the Soviets named streets and schools after her, and someone even made a film about her life, but the statue was her greatest monument. I stared up at the woman who had dared to cross turnip wielding peasants and had lost.

10

The next afternoon I headed towards Osh Bazaar, one of Bishkek's largest markets.

The arched entrance to the bazaar had large, red Cyrillic letters spelling out its name. A huge billboard advertising *Beta Tea* was just underneath. I followed a man pushing a wooden cart filled with watermelons under the large arch, unaware that two policemen were watching me.

Osh Bazaar was a hive of activity with endless arrays of fruit and vegetables, clothes and mops, and everything else the people of Bishkek could possibly want. Bunches of delicious grapes dangled from some stalls, but then I spotted what I was looking for - a stand peddling kumis, fermented mare's milk.

Even though I'd tried the hideous stuff in Almaty, I was eager to give it a second chance. Perhaps the Kazakh kumis I'd drunk was from a bad batch. Peering into the large urn, I mimed to the lady in charge that I wanted a cup of Kyrgyzstan's national drink.

After the usual confusion, she produced a bowl and ladled some white liquid in for me. I handed over thirty som and took my brew to the side where I could sample it unhindered.

After swirling it around for a few seconds, I deemed it lump free and raised the bowl to my lips. And then I took a sip. The taste hit me immediately - a horrible vomit flavour mixed with curdled cheese. Kazakh and Kyrgyz kumis were one and the same. In the resulting convulsions, I spilt some down my shirt, and so put the bowl down and fled.

I decided to seek out a stall that sold water, so I could rid myself of the vile taste.

And then they pounced.

Two blue-uniformed policemen with massive black and red caps blocked my path. One looked about thirty, the other was younger, barely out of his teens. Both were unsmiling and looked like they meant business.

"Passport," the older of the two stated bluntly. He had a wispy black moustache that I reckoned he could quiver at will for sinister effect.

This was just my luck. The only day I'd left my passport at the hotel was the day someone actually wanted to see it. I told them this, and they conferred for a moment. Mr Moustache shook his head. "We need to see. Otherwise big problem." He'd emphasised the word *big*, stretching the vowel out.

Fortunately, I had a photocopy of it in my wallet and so fished it out while a group of young boys hovered nearby. They were watching me suffer with barely disguised glee. I handed the piece of paper over, hoping it would suffice.

"Eeengliz?" said Moustache Man after staring at the photocopy.

I nodded and smiled. I didn't want to annoy them in any way. Both men studied it and then conferred again. The patrons of Osh Bazaar were all giving us a wide berth, except for the boys who still lurked nearby.

"Visa?" Mr Moustache said eventually.

I'd expected this request, but without my passport, there was no way I could show them it. But I reasoned they already knew this.

"Without visa, big problem." said Mr Moustache, faintly quivering his facial hair.

Both men stared at me for a long while, and I began to feel a little unnerved. Finally Mr Moustache spoke. "Come," he stated. He pointed through the market.

I pretended I didn't understand, and pointed in the opposite direction and grinned an inane grin, hoping the men would think I was a simpleton and let me go. They didn't. Mr Moustache put a hand on my shoulder in an attempt to get me moving, but I stood my ground.

"No," I said, still grinning. "I'm going that way. Bye."

Both men blocked my path. The older man shook his head and tutted. "No. You come so we deal with things."

What choice did I have? I could hardly flee through the market with some rancid mare's milk sloshing about in my innards. Besides, they were the police! People like me didn't run away from the law. Finally, I acquiesced and allowed the officers to lead me away. Some people stopped to watch me leave, but most averted their eyes and carried on with their business. The only people enjoying my torment seemed to be the group of boys.

12

As we made our way through the market, we passed the stall where I'd bought the mare's milk. My bowl had gone, I noticed, and Mr Moustache stopped to mime someone drinking and then grimacing. Then he pointed at me and laughed. I wondered where they had watched me from. The boys were shouting and laughing, causing some people to stare. Mr Moustache turned around and yelled. They swiftly scarpered.

Policeman number two, the youngster, began speaking to me in broken English. "Kyrgyzstan good? Yah?"

I nodded enthusiastically and the man smiled for the first time. He seemed the friendlier of the two. He also decided to mime me drinking the kumis and laughed uproariously at his own impersonation. I laughed too because the situation was utterly absurd. It got even worse when he followed it up with a chillingly accurate impression of a horse neighing. He then mimed someone milking it, presumably educating me about where the kumis came from.

We rounded a bend and came to a dark little part of Osh Bazaar. Fewer people were here, and it crossed my mind that I might be about to receive a beating. I considered making a dash for it, but for all I knew, there could be security cameras everywhere, making escape impossible. Shaking my head resignedly, I followed the policemen into a cramped and stuffy windowless room filled with three desks.

A few other policemen were sitting doing nothing in particular. All looked up when I entered. I quickly became the centre of attention. A quick conversation erupted, but I didn't understand any of it. A fly buzzed by the low ceiling and Mr Moustache directed me to an empty chair. I sat down, awaiting my fate in my first Kyrgyz police station.

13

Mr Moustache sat opposite while Mr Friendly stood by his side. Bad cop, good cop. "Why you in Kyrgyzstan?" asked the man in charge.

"I'm a tourist from England."

Mr Moustache waggled his whiskers at me. "Where hotel?" he asked.

I pulled out a card the hotel had given me when I'd checked in. It clearly stated I was a guest there. I handed it over. Both men studied it and put it on the table between us.

Mr Moustache gestured to my bag, and decided to do some mime again. He acted out a strange scenario that looked like he was injecting himself with something. His sidekick nodded like a galoot. I quickly worked out that they wanted to know whether I had any drugs.

"No," I stated.

They got me to empty my bag and remove everything from my pockets. Mr Moustache immediately picked up my wallet and began leafing through the Kyrgyz som and US dollars I had, but Mr Friendly was more interested in my camera. He picked it up and tried to turn it on. After failing to do so, he handed it to me to do the job. I powered it up and he started flicking through all the photos and videos I'd taken that day: a Mig fighter jet I'd seen on a plinth in a downtown street, the entrance to Osh Bazaar, and me drinking the kumis. He seemed particularly interested in the latter and asked me to play the video. Within seconds he was laughing furiously, pointing at the camera and then at me. He showed it to Mr Moustache who smiled but continued to poke about inside my wallet. After watching the clip a third time, the strange policeman did his horse neighing impression again. Maybe he was insane.

Mr Moustache finally placed the wallet with the rest of my stuff on the table, and said I could pack it all away. I did this while his pal still fiddled with my camera. In another moment of unreality, he asked me to pose for a photograph with my own camera. I did so, and he handed the camera back. When I'd finished packing, I looked at Mr Moustache, wondering whether he'd helped himself to some cash in the confusion.

"Finish," Mr Moustache said. "You leave." He stood up and offered his hand, which I shook involuntarily. The other man did the same, and I left the room, sweating and wondering what had just happened.

Outside, I counted my money, but it was all there. Then I looked at the photo the young policeman had taken. It was rather good. If it hadn't been for the photo, I might have thought I'd dreamed the whole episode.

14

To settle my nerves I left Osh Bazaar and headed back to Alo-Too Square. I found a bench and wondered what to do next. The episode with the police officers had shaken me somewhat, and I was now wary of venturing too far. I decided I would wander around the square again, and then head back to the hotel to pack. I was putting my guidebook away when a young woman approached.

Her name was Ainura, a 23-year-old university student. She had guessed I was a tourist, and gambled that I'd be able to speak English. When she found out I was actually from England, she grew really excited.

"I have never before spoken to anyone from England! This is amazing for me to practice my speaking of the English! My friends will be big jealous!"

I couldn't help but like her straightaway. Like most other Kyrgyz women, she looked vaguely Chinese, with shoulder length black hair and a slender figure.

Beaming, Ainura produced a piece of paper from her handbag and proudly showed it to me. "This is exam result for English! I only do this morning. I get 66 points, and pass mark was 60! It is my favourite language to learn, and I much prefer it to German. Where you go?"

After I'd told her of my plans to walk around the square, she asked if she could walk with me a while, to practice speaking. I could hardly refuse, and to be honest, talking to someone friendly was a refreshing change after my experiences with the policemen at Osh Bazaar.

We set off, and she jabbered away, wanting to know whether she was pronouncing things correctly and whether her grammar was correct. It all sounded fine to me, and I told her so. She smiled sweetly and I wondered whether I should kidnap her. But then I remembered I was already married. At the next block, we shook hands and said good-bye.

I headed back to the hotel to pack my bags. I had completed the five 'Stans, something I never imagined I would do. The next morning I was flying back to Manchester, safe in the knowledge that I only had one more country to tick off on the Red Quest: Belarus.

One more to go!

22. The Last Dictatorship in Europe

Interesting fact: Belarus has more buried treasure than any other country in Europe.

"Where the hell is it?" I screeched after the postman failed to deliver my passport back from the Belarus Embassy yet again. With just two days to go before my flight to Minsk, my nerves were in tatters. Without my passport and visa, there was no chance of getting on a plane, let alone stepping foot onto Belarusian soil. I paced into the kitchen.

"It'll come tomorrow," said Angela, trying to calm me down.

"But what if it doesn't?" I snapped. "What then, eh?"

Angela remained silent.

"I'll tell you what happens. I'll have wasted £75 pounds on a visa, and God only knows how much on flights and hotels, and the quest will never be finished. The aggravation I've had with organising this trip...I don't know whether I can go through it again."

I'd arranged my Letter of Invitation in good time. I'd sent off my passport and forms with easily enough time to spare. But something had gone wrong. Perhaps the embassy had refused my visa application, or maybe the post office had lost my envelope. Or could the postman have delivered it to the wrong address? Whatever the reason, if it didn't turn up the next day, I could kiss good-bye to Belarus.

I stormed out of the kitchen and into the living room, switching on the TV to watch the news.

The next morning it arrived, once again proving that the *Law of Obtaining a Visa* was true and correct. Quite simply, this law states that anyone wanting a visa will have to endure a series of nail-biting mornings as their passport fails to arrive, until it finally does, the day before travel.

The Air Baltic Fokker 50 landed like a World War II bomber and taxied past the usual assortment of old Soviet-era airliners that had been left in a huge field.

МИНСК written in large Cyrillic lettering above the terminal confirmed I had indeed landed in Minsk. As I stepped onto Belarusian soil, or rather tarmac, and entered the passenger terminal, I wondered what the country the Americans had described as Europe's last dictatorship would be like.

To be honest, I'd not heard many good things about Belarus, and the things I had heard were mainly to do with its president, Alexander Lukashenko, a man renowned for his poor human rights record and his fondness for rigging elections. This man had once famously stated that if any of his citizens joined in with protests against him, his regime would 'wring their necks, as one might a duck.'

The border official deemed my visa okay, and I was soon in a taxi through the countryside. The Belarusian landscape was filled with forests so vast that it reportedly harboured wolf, bear, elk, boar and even the heaviest land mammal to roam Europe, the mighty bison.

It was a miracle that any bison had survived. During World War I, with food scarce, the people of Belarus hunted the creatures to near extinction. By 1919, no bison were left in the wild. Some remained in zoos, and in the 1920s, someone wondered whether they could be bred and let loose. But with only four bulls and three cows of the original European stock remaining, this was going to be a tall order.

Amazingly though, one of the bulls got lucky, and then got lucky again. And again after that. In the end, this single bull became responsible for over ninety percent of the current stock of European bison.

The Hotel Minsk was located along Nezalezhnastsi Avenue, the main thoroughfare of the city. My room overlooked some grand buildings festooned with hammers and sickles, which made me smile. I'd read that Minsk was like stepping into Moscow from the 1980s, and now I could see why.

After I'd changed some dollars into Belarusian roubles, I wandered towards Independence Square, taking in the ambience of downtown Minsk. Despite the hammers and sickles, the city was not in the grip of communist fever. Instead it looked affluent and normal. Modern cars and buses plied the busy avenue, and with the sun shining, the people of Minsk looked happy and carefree. Large billboards advertised casinos and electrical goods, and plush shops lined the street. And according to my city map, a McDonald's and a TGI Friday were just down the road. Hardly 1980s Soviet Union.

Independence Square was also known as Lenin Square. This was due to the giant statue of Lenin in front of the government building, one of the few buildings in Minsk to survive the bombing of World War II. Unlike other Lenin statues I'd come across in my quest, this one didn't feature the classic - arm thrust forward - pose, Instead, Lenin was leaning against a rail, looking pensively to his right.

Almost all towns, villages and cities in Belarus have statues of Lenin. In 2009, one of them killed a man. The 21-year old had been with some friends, in the town of Buda-Koshelevsky, when he had drunkenly stumbled across the seven-metre tall statue. Thinking it would be great to climb it, the hapless man managed to scale the legs but then, as he tried to swing onto Lenin's outstretched arm, he'd caused the statue to topple. It crushed him to death.

4

During World War II, Belarus suffered badly at the hands of the Germans. For a start, 209 of the country's 290 cities were destroyed, not to mention the ten thousand villages that were also sacked.

After the war, the Soviets began a rebuild, putting up Stalinesque buildings everywhere. They made Russian the official language, and the Belarusian Soviet Socialist Republic became the most Soviet of all the republics. And then, like neighbouring Ukraine, it became one of the powerhouses of the Soviet Empire, most notably with its production of farm machinery and large trucks.

Fast forward to the late eighties, and with neighbouring countries such as Latvia and Estonia already in full throes towards independence, Belarus made movements too. The discovery of thousands of bodies in a wood just outside Minsk fuelled this drive. The bodies belonged to Belarusians executed by the Soviet secret police between 1937 and 1941. Belarus declared itself independent on the 25 August 1991, one day after Ukraine and two days before Moldova.

Despite going it alone, Belarus maintained close links with Russia, and even kept some of the old Soviet systems in place. One of them was the KGB.

The large yellow KGB Headquarters was along Nezalezhnastsi Avenue. It had four great columns at its entrance, and a high wooden door to keep people out. Unlike every other former Soviet Republic, Belarus still used the KGB as its secret police, and for all I knew, its agents were watching me at that very moment.

I stationed myself across the road from the yellow building and pretended to look at a restaurant menu. When I was sure all surveillance cameras had swept past me, I spun around, took a couple of photos and returned to the menu. With my camera safely in my pocket, I moved on.

The Red Stork flies at midnight.

5

In December 2011, three young Ukrainian women had stripped off and bared their chests in front of the KGB Building. They had been protesting against the tyranny of Alexander Lukashenko, and judging by the photo I saw, two of the women must have caused quite a stir, because they looked like supermodels, despite the false moustaches. The third lady was a different matter, large and stout, possessing humongous drooping breasts, but all three quickly attracted the attention of the KGB.

Agents arrested them. According to the women afterwards, men from the KGB blindfolded and herded them aboard a bus. Then they drove the women to a remote forest and poured oil over them, threatening to set them alight if they caused any fuss. At knifepoint, the KGB made all three remove their clothes and then cut off their hair. Finally they were set free.

The girls had no choice but to flee through the forest until they came across a village. What the villagers thought of a set of nude young women intruding upon their homestead, the article did not say, but the women soon returned to Kiev to tell their story. The Belarusian KGB denied any of this happening, of course.

6

The next morning I was heading down Nezalezhnastsi Avenue again, once again passing the KGB Headquarters, but this time noticing a large statue I'd somehow missed the previous evening. It was Felix Dzerzhinsky or Iron Felix as people who angered him knew him by.

Felix had been a Belarusian revolutionary who had attracted the attention of Lenin. Lenin offered Felix a job in Moscow. There, Felix quickly rose through the communist ranks to become director of Cheka, the forerunner to the KGB. He soon established himself as a ruthless leader, executing people without trial.

I headed away from his statue, passing groups of people waiting for marshrutkas, the battered minibus taxis that were always a feature of the former Soviet Union. Street side kiosks peddled magazines, cigarettes, beer and vodka, often with sullen babushkas sitting inside. Unlike the babushkas though, I was in high spirits. I was actually in the last country of the Red Quest!

I turned left and then headed up a slight hill until I arrived at The Pit.

7

The Pit was a memorial to Belarusian Jews shot by the Nazis. Its location was in the heart of the former Minsk ghetto. Around 100,000 Jews lived in horrific conditions in the ghetto. Virtually all of them would die at some point, but one particularly nasty day was the 2 March 1942. That day, Nazis shot five thousand Jews and brought the bodies (some still alive) to the pit I was staring at.

I wandered down a set of steps leading into the pit, passing a sombre bronze sculpture called *The Last Way*. It featured a line of thin individuals huddled together. It was one of the most depressing monuments I'd seen on my travels.

At the bottom of the actual pit (now a grassy lower level), I walked towards a small obelisk covered with Russian and Yiddish engravings. Someone had placed flowers at its base. A small Israeli flag lay next to them.

I stood in silence, contemplating the horror humankind could unleash on one another. Later, inside the Great and Patriotic War Museum, I would see more horror, but for now, I walked silently back up the steps.

8

Not far from The Pit was a tall concrete spike with a golden star on the top. Next to the spike was a large statue of a woman holding an automatic weapon. Looking deliciously Soviet, I consulted my map but found no mention of it. Undaunted, I headed along a busy road flanked by the River Svislach until I arrived at the monument. It looked like a building site.

A platoon of workmen was toiling under the obelisk with a couple of JCBs. A trio of teenagers on skateboards were messing about on some steps leading up it. I decided to take a photo.

"Are you journalist?" said a voice behind me. I turned to see a young man with dark hair smoking a cigarette. How he knew I was an English speaker was strange. Maybe he'd spotted the map in my hand.

I shook my head. "No. I'm a tourist."

The man considered this and then nodded. "I see. We get not many tourists in Minsk, and fewer still who come to this part of the city. That is why I think you were journalist, maybe covering the construction work happening here. My name is Artem, and I am studying engineering at the Belarusian State University. What is your name?"

"Jason," I said and we shook hands.

Artem pointed at the obelisk. "You know what this monument is for?"

"No, but I assume it's from Soviet times?"

"Yes of course. It is Obelisk to Hero City. In 1974, the Soviet regime awarded Minsk the status of Hero City - one of only twelve cities to receive this. If you look at the top of monument, you will see a gold star and wreath - the Order of Lenin. It is recognition of heroic deeds Minsk played in war."

I was impressed. The young man was probably aged about nineteen, yet his grasp of English, not to mention his knowledge of Belarusian history, was impressive. I could not imagine many nineteen-year-olds in Britain being quite so articulate about a fading piece of architecture in the middle of their city. I asked him about the statue next to the obelisk, the woman firing a machine gun into the air.

"Ah," laughed Artem. "I see what you mean, but it is not a weapon she is holding, it is a trumpet."

I peered closer at the thing, but to me it still looked like a machine gun.

"This place will be the new premises of the Great Patriotic War Museum. It is to be opened soon."

I nodded. That made sense. I thanked Artem and wished him all the best in his studies. From what I'd seen, he would do well.

9

I still couldn't believe I was in the final country of the Red Quest. Three years it had taken to get this far, and even though the financial cost had been horrendous, I still felt it had been well worth it.

A couple of days before setting out to Minsk, I'd met up with Phil and Michael in the pub. Both had praised my determination in reaching my goal. Michael especially was impressed, wishing he'd been able to accompany me on a few more trips. Both had wished me well for Belarus, even toasting the fact it was the final stop on the adventure.

I walked along Nezalezhnastsi Avenue until I found the street where Lee Harvey Oswald had once lived.

Before Oswald became famous for shooting John F Kennedy, he'd defected to the Soviet Union. In 1959, aged just twenty, the Soviets sent him to Minsk, where he got a job working in a factory. He then met a local girl, got married, and had a child with her. Two years later, he grew weary of the Soviet Union, saying his job was drab. A year later, Oswald and his young family were back in America, where he made history.

I stared at Oswald's former apartment. It looked quite nice actually, located along a leafy street with a great view of the river. Oswald had probably walked along the pavement where I was presently standing, perhaps stopping occasionally to gaze into the park opposite. Next door to his apartment was a fashionable ladies' clothes shop. I wondered what Oswald and his wife would have thought of that. All he'd probably been able to spend his money on were turnips and tractor parts.

10

My guidebook said the Minsk Metro could be confusing for first-time travellers. Despite this, I headed down some steps until I came to the usual array of gates and booths. I wandered up to the nearest booth and simply held up one finger to the babushka behind the counter, indicating I wanted a one-way ticket. The woman nodded and produced a small plastic counter and gibbered at me in Russian. I nodded in turn, passed her some roubles and waited for my change. Transaction complete, I walked towards the barriers and slipped the counter in the slot. Hey presto, the bar allowed me in. Simple, straightforward and cheap as hell.

The little plastic counter had cost me 1500 roubles, which was about 12 pence, and after descending further via some escalators, I found myself on a platform with the locals of Minsk. None paid me any attention, and after deciphering the signs written in Cyrillic, I calmed down and waited. The train quickly arrived, and was packed, but I squeezed aboard, and a few minutes later was rattling through the darkness.

I exited the train at Oktyabrskaya metro station, the place where in April 2011, someone had detonated a bomb. At 6pm that day, during the usual evening rush, 300 people were waiting for trains to arrive. Without warning, a nail bomb exploded, causing a scene of pure carnage. The ornamental features that the Soviets had fitted did not help things either. Due to the force of the blast, they were blown from the walls, sending deadly shards in all directions. Decorations on the ceiling came crashing down too, causing even more injuries. Fifteen people died, and over a hundred were injured.

The next day, Belarus declared a day of mourning, and the authorities arrested two men. A firing squad executed both in March 2012, once again establishing Belarus as the only country in Europe with the death penalty.

11

After negotiating my way out of the metro station, I found myself staring at the gigantic Presidential Palace. Soldiers were guarding the building at every corner, and I wondered whether Alexander Lukashenko was in residence, scheming up new ways to piss off Europe.

I walked around the side of the palace, passing a few policemen until I arrived at a tank on a plinth. After a few moments of staring, I retraced my steps, found a doorway to hide and produced my camera. Fully expecting to hear a whistle, I took a photo of the Presidential Palace (something not allowed) and scurried away. It was time to visit a museum.

12

I was hoping to see lots of Soviet imagery inside the *Belarusian Great Patriotic War Museum,* and I was not disappointed. The huge building was full of red stars, hammers and sickles, and Soviet-era artwork, but the bulk of the displays were uniforms, weapons, battle scene mock-ups, and photos of Red Army troops fighting in the Second World War.

The only problem was that all the information was in Cyrillic, and I soon gave up trying to decipher it. But then I came to a section that stopped me in my tracks. It was photos of the nasty deeds the Nazis had done when they had conquered Minsk. For this area, I didn't need to read anything. The photos told everything.

They showed piles of bodies with gunshot wounds, twisted corpses dumped like garbage, people waiting for execution, and one particularly harrowing photo of two small boys weeping. I was glad I couldn't read anything because looking at them was bad enough.

The next section was worse. On the wall was a series of photos showing executions. Some showed people being hanged; others showed dead and dangling bodies, often with Nazi soldiers smiling for the camera near them.

A voice addressed me in Russian. When the woman realised I couldn't speak Russian, she switched to fluent English. Her name was Anna, and she was a museum guide.

"The girl in this photo is Maria Bruskina. She is aged just seventeen," Anna said, pointing at the first photo in a grim set of six. "And the person next to her is Volodia Shcherbatsevich, a sixteen-year-old boy. The man with the beard is Kiril Trus, a veteran from World War 1. All are about to be hanged. The plaque around Maria's neck reads: *We are partisans and have shot at German troops.*"

I stared at the image, wondering how they had felt being marched through the city towards the gallows. All three looked afraid, but defiant. I couldn't imagine how I'd have felt had I been one of them. Hanging, to me, was one of the most barbaric and horrific ways to die. It made me feel sick just thinking about it.

The second photo showed a German officer putting a noose around the young woman's neck. Behind her, a few German troops were watching, clearly enjoying themselves. Photo number three was horrible to look at; showing Maria actually being hanged. There was a dreadful expression on her young face, and I just hoped she was already dead, because if she wasn't, then it didn't bear thinking about. The next photo carried on with the horror, showing sixteen-year-old Volodia getting a noose around his neck. Then it was the turn of Kiril, and with his two friends already limp, his expression was haunting. It was something I didn't want to look at. The final photo showed three bodies hanging lifelessly.

"The Germans left them three days," said Anna soberly. "But these hangings were not isolated. They were happening all over Minsk."

I shook my head, staring at a photo of what looked like an elderly couple hanging together. I left the museum soon after, depressed at what I'd seen, knowing that the terrible images would flicker back to life whenever I thought about the museum.

13

My short time in Minsk was almost at an end: the final Soviet republic on a seemingly never-ending jaunt around Europe and Asia. I opened the door of TGI Fridays, and found a seat.

It seemed strange to be nearing the end of a trip that had seen me travel to twenty-one different countries (not to mention a breakaway state). During that time, the quest had taken over my life, as well as my bank account, but now it was over. Done and dusted. All countries ticked off the list. Time to get back to normality.

My chicken fajitas arrived, and I took a mouthful. The food was delicious, but I couldn't help feel a twinge of disappointment. My last meal in a former Soviet Republic should've been something more traditional, maybe boiled herring and mashed turnip. But then I thought of all the places I'd been to, the things I'd seen and the people I'd met, and I smiled to myself. How many people could honestly say they had visited every country in the former Soviet Union? How many people could say they had sampled goulash in Hungary, bear sausage in Estonia, horse steak in Kazakhstan, and fermented mare's milk in Kyrgyzstan? Well I could. And I'd also been chased by hounds in Kiev, chastised by policemen in Ashgabat, and had seen a man kick a tree in Dushanbe. Not bad for an escapade that began with a wintry trip to Latvia. Not bad at all.

Afterwards, as I walked to my hotel, gazing about at the Cyrillic lettering I'd probably never see again, I felt a twinge of sadness. This really was it. I had visited all the former Soviet Republics, and there was no more to do.

Except my adventure was not over. Unbeknown to me, there was a sting in the tail waiting back in England. It came from my friend Phil.

23. Checkpoint Charlie

Interesting fact: 171 people died trying to cross the Berlin Wall.

"You're an idiot," said Phil with a fiendish grin. "Do you want to know why?"

I looked at him and smiled. It was less than a week after my victorious return from Belarus, and I was riding the crest of the Red Quest wave. Angela and I were already planning trips to normal places, where sun loungers and swimming pools featured.

"Well I'll tell you. It's because you think you've finished your Turnip Quest, but you haven't. There's still one more country to go?"

"No there isn't."

"Yes there is!" Phil had the satisfied look of a leopard that had just dragged an impala up to the branches of a tall tree. "And its name is Germany."

I picked up my drink and took a sip. Australian lager just couldn't compare to the lager over in Eastern Europe. I stared at Phil. "We've been through this already. Germany doesn't count because I've been there before."

"So you've been to East Germany?"

"I've been to Germany." I felt the first stirrings of alarm.

"Have you been anywhere in *East* Germany?"

"No…" I admitted.

"So your quest isn't finished. How can it be? Yes, you've been to Russia, yes, you've been to Kazakhstan, and yes, you've even been to Moldavia..."

"Moldova," I corrected.

"Moldova. Whatever. But you've not been to East Germany. That's where you need to go…where you have to go! Without seeing the Berlin Wall and Checkpoint Charlie, you can't say you've been to all the old Soviet countries, can you? And that's why you're an idiot."

2

I burst into the living room, interrupting Angela watching TV. I told her about East Germany, and the fact that I had to go there. "It'll only be for one night, and then I'll be back! And it's cheap. I can get a return flight on Lufthansa for less than it costs to fill up my car." I'd already checked out flights in the taxi home.

Angela turned to me. She had an incredulous look on her face. "Did you say you want to go to Berlin this weekend? And you've actually checked flights already? Even though the deadline has passed?"

"I know. But it's Phil's fault. He's the one who pointed out I haven't been to East Germany. You should be angry with him."

"Why would I be angry with Phil?" Angela snorted. "Is he going with you? Is he wasting his money flying to Berlin? Is he leaving his wife for the weekend while he gallivants off to Europe? Is Phil's wife going to drop him off at the airport and then pick him back up? No, I thought not. Phil must be laughing at how stupid you actually are."

"I know...I'm sorry. I won't go. I shouldn't have even asked; it wasn't fair." I then produced the glummest and the most pathetic face I could summon.

"No it isn't fair." Angela turned back to the TV. With nothing more to say, I went upstairs to sulk on the computer. After a while I began to think about things.

Did it actually matter if I didn't get to Berlin? It wasn't as if I'd missed out on say, Russia or Armenia. Besides, East Germany had never actually been part of the former Soviet Union - it had only been part of the Warsaw Pact. Not going there wouldn't count as cheating, would it?

I could hear Angela coming up the stairs. I turned around to see her staring at me. "Go to Berlin," she said. "Book your stupid flight and finish the quest – and I can't believe I even said that word - it sounds like something a twelve-year-old boy would say -

and then that's it. No more idiotic trips around the world so you can collect passport stamps. No more flights to countries that no one has ever heard of. I'm not having any more. Okay?"

3

When Germany surrendered after the Second World War, the four conquering allies split the country into four occupation zones. France, the United Kingdom and the United States controlled the three Western sections, and the Soviets controlled the Eastern sector. All nicely divided up, thank you very much.

Berlin, located in the centre of the Soviet Sector, was more problematic. In the end, the four nations hammered out a deal whereby the city was divided into four sectors, one bit each. The West could transfer goods and people into West Berlin by road, rail and river, and the Soviets could do what they liked with their bit. That done, they all settled down and began the rebuild.

Then in 1948, France, USA and the UK fell out with the Soviet Union over some currency reforms. The upshot was that the Soviets blocked all access points around Berlin. West Berlin was cast adrift inside a sea of Sovietness. The Soviets refused to provide food and coal for the people living in West Berlin and thus began the famous Berlin Airlift.

A constant stream of cargo aircraft delivered supplies to West Berlin, initially causing bemusement to the Soviets, who claimed that the airlift could not supply everything. But as the planes kept landing, the Soviets had to concede that it possibly could, and so they changed tactics. They offered free food to anyone in West Berlin who crossed over to their sector. No one did. Next they tried disrupting the flow of aircraft, by shining bright lights into pilots' eyes, or buzzing planes with fighters. None of these measures worked either, and the cargo kept coming.

With winter arriving, the Soviets sat back, confident that the Western powers would not be able to provide enough fuel and food to cope with the cold and snow. But they were wrong. The Berlin Airlift coped fantastically well, and the Soviets realised that it could go on indefinitely, humiliating them in the process. They cut their losses and reopened Berlin to the West. But even though the Berlin Airlift had ended, the Cold War had effectively begun.

4

With only one full day in Berlin, I decided to concentrate on the section once under Soviet control. The Berlin transport system quickly became my best friend, offering an efficient system that was both easy to navigate and cheap as hell. My first stop was Treptower Park, located just along from the River Spree.

Treptower Park was notable for two reasons. The first was because it had been the site of the first open-air concert by a Western rock band behind the Iron Curtain. British progressive rockers, Barclay James Harvest, had played there in 1987 to a crowd of over 170,000. But the other reason was that it contained a massive Soviet War Memorial.

It was just as I'd hoped it would be - large, heroic, overstated and unashamedly Soviet in every aspect. A concrete archway full of hammers and sickles set the scene, as did a couple of giant Soviet flags made of red granite, but the focus was most certainly the enormous Red Army soldier. He was holding a sword in one hand, a child in the other, and his booted foot was trampling a broken swastika.

As I stared up at the statue, the sheer brilliance of Soviet War Memorials once again struck me. The communists got many things wrong, but they definitely knew how to knock up a good monument. Even the sixteen white marble carvings that lined the way to the statue were impressive, each featuring reliefs of brave Soviet deeds. What I didn't know was that they were actually sarcophagi, the final resting place for about 5000 Red Army troops.

5

I felt the vibrations first, and then heard the sound of my phone ringing. I fished it out of my pocket, wondering who it was. Phil.

He said, "How's it going?"

I began to walk to the exit of Treptower Park. "Quite well actually. Right now, I'm inside a Soviet War Memorial. You'd love it. And the weather's great. Nice and sunny."

"Have you been to see the Wall yet?"

"No. But it's on the list. I'm heading to Checkpoint Charlie next."

Phil paused on the other end of the phone. "Actually, I have to hand it to you. A few days ago, we were sat in the pub and you thought you'd finished the Turnip List, and now you're in Germany. I actually wish I were there with you; Berlin is somewhere I've always fancied. Anyway, I'm just ringing to say well done. I think you're going to finish the quest."

I was shocked. Phil had always derided my mission, making digs at every opportunity. But here he was wishing me luck, and actually hinting that he was almost jealous. "Cheers, mate. See you when I get back."

6

During the Cold War, Checkpoint Charlie was one of the few available crossing points between East and West Berlin. Nowadays it is a tourist trap full of gaudy stalls, overpriced cafes, and even a booth with a man dressed as a soldier trying to flog East German passport stamps. Next to him was a stall selling bags emblazoned with *I Love Checkpoint Charlie*.

Where the actual crossing point had once stood, a reconstructed guard post (complete with sand bags, and a couple of actors dressed as Allied military policemen) wowed the crowds. The guards were posing with tourists for a handful of euros, and a long queue had formed to take advantage of this. Masses of sightseers and a never-ending parade of tourist buses plied the intersection, and so I decided to head into a museum dedicated to the checkpoint, but the horrendous queue put me off. Instead, I headed back into the underground.

I could not fault the historical significance of Checkpoint Charlie, but I could fault the amount of tourists, even though I was one myself. All it needed was a balloon stall, a man selling hotdogs, some people dressed as spies, and the circus would be complete. I decided the best thing to do was visit an actual section of the infamous wall. A minute later, a train pulled up, and I climbed aboard.

7

It was hard to believe that the Berlin Wall had stood while I was a student at university.

The authorities in East Germany claimed the wall was to stop the West conspiring against its people, but the real reason was much simpler: it was to stop people escaping. By the time construction began in 1961, twenty percent of East Germany's population had already crossed over, most of them young, intelligent and skilled. The communists wanted to put a stop to the brain drain.

The wall's construction began at midnight on the 12 August 1961. Soviet soldiers tore up streets and placed barbed wire along the border. Then they flattened large areas running parallel to it, raking sand on top so anyone trying to cross would leave footprints. Over time, this section received the name Death Strip. As people woke up on the morning of the 13th, the border between East and West Germany was closed.

Four days later, the first concrete sections of the wall appeared, and troops received orders to shoot anyone who tried to defect. The effect was immediate. The barrier split families. Any East Germans who had jobs in West Berlin now couldn't get to work.

8

I ascended the subway stop and found myself walking towards a section of Death Strip, now a grass field with information boards and metal columns signalling where the strip had once been. Also notable were small placards with names etched onto them. These were the spots where people had died trying to cross. Some sections of the wall were visible too. They were ugly, grey concrete segments that had once traversed huge swathes of the city. It was interesting to note that unlike Checkpoint Charlie, this section of East Berlin had few tourists.

The road I was walking along was Bernauer Street, and a large photo of a soldier painted on the side of a large grey building caught my eye. It was Conrad Schumann, a young East German soldier who had been guarding the fledgling wall.

Conrad had the distinction of being the first man to cross, and did so two days after the wall began its life. He jumped the simple barbed-wire fence.

A week later, border guards shot and killed their first defector, another young man (as indeed most of the escapers would turn out to be) called Gunter Litfin.

Twenty-four-year-old Gunter had been a tailor with a job over in West Berlin. He'd even managed to find himself a flat near to where he worked, and had been driving back and forth to furnish it in preparation for his imminent move. Then the barriers and roadblocks went up, and things changed.

Seeing little choice, Litfin waited a few days, and then scaled a wall near the banks of the River Spree in an attempt to swim across. Unfortunately, border guards spotted him and shot him in the back of the head.

9

Thousands of people did manage to cross however and one of the most dramatic escapes involved a 19-year-old East German soldier called Wolfgang Engels. Wolfgang stole an armoured car and simply rammed the wall. His vehicle ended up stuck in the barbed wire, and as he tried to flee, he got tangled up in it. Border guards managed to shoot him, but West Berliners intervened and pulled him to safety. He made a full recovery in hospital.

Other escape attempts included tunnels, sewers, and even hot-air balloons. And sometimes people almost made it across, only to fall back into the Death Strip. One infamous incident involved a young man called Peter Fechter.

On the 17 August 1962, eighteen-year-old Peter and his friend Helmut Kulbeik rushed across the Death Strip near Checkpoint Charlie and managed to reach the wall. Border guards spotted them and started shooting. Helmut managed to clamber over the top but Peter wasn't so lucky. Guards shot him in the hip, and he fell back onto the Death Strip on the East German side. It wasn't a fatal shot, but as Peter lay screaming and crying, the guards in the West did nothing, because they feared it would invoke reprisals from the East, and the East German guards did nothing either, possibly worried about being shot at by the West. In the end, it took one hour for Peter Fechter to bleed to death.

10

I walked along Bernauer Street until I came to the Berlin Wall Commemoration Centre. It comprised of a small museum and a viewing platform. I climbed the steps to the top. There were already a few people up there, mainly elderly American tourists with a guide.

I squeezed past them to look down. From my vantage point, it was possible to see what the Death Strip had once looked like because there was a reconstructed section of it below. A large rectangle of raked sand, with a series of fences, and even a watchtower, gave an indication of just how hard it must have been to cross. There was a long section of the Berlin Wall too, completing the grim picture, but on both sides of the reconstruction, Berlin looked normal, with greenery, bus stops and people merrily crossing between the old border like it had never existed.

"Soberin' ain't it, son," said an American man standing next to me. "I was here between '74 and '77 with the United States Army. Not here at this actual part you understand – this was the French Sector – I was mainly around Tempelhof. I got used to seeing the wall every day of my duty, but there's not much left now. What brings you here all by yourself?"

"I just wanted to see what it was like behind the Iron Curtain," I explained, "and to see a bit of the Berlin Wall. And you're right, it is sobering. I can't imagine that Death Strip being all along this street..."

"And much more besides. I used to patrol it. Our side was full of graffiti and colour, theirs just grey concrete. I was so glad when it came down."

11

The demise of the Berlin Wall actually began in Hungary. The authorities there had already disabled its borders, meaning East Germans could escape through Austria. Then the same thing happened in Czechoslovakia, which kick-started protests in East Germany. By November 1989, half a million people were gathering in East Berlin's public squares, demanding that soldiers open the border. And then some classic miscommunication occurred.

With growing dissent, the East German authorities decided to offer a concession. They said they would allow *private* travel between the borders, but only after it had been signed off with copious amounts of paperwork and rubber-stamping. It would put most people off, they hoped.

No one bothered to tell the politburo spokesman about to appear at a TV press conference this though. When a journalist asked him when the border would open, he floundered for a while before stating the borders were open right now.

The result was electric. East Germans gathered by the wall demanding that guards let them through. With a possible riot on their hands, the soldiers hastily rang their superiors. With the clock ticking, no one would make any decisions. At 10.45pm, with the crowds at dangerous levels, the guards on duty took action for themselves. They simply allowed people to pass freely. East and West Germans hugged each other and danced in the streets.

People began demolishing the wall almost immediately, with many chipping away small pieces to keep as souvenirs. Soon these chippings turned to gaps, then into holes, and then into unofficial border crossings. By June the following year, the official dismantling of the wall began, leaving only a few sections that are visible today. East and West Germany united on the 3 October 1990. I was nineteen years old at the time.

12

I entered Friedrich Street Underground Station. During the Cold War, this particular subway stop was an important transit point between East and West Berlin. For the Soviets, the station was a massive headache, and to combat it, they installed a border crossing inside, and added a few cells for good measure.

As I walked along a bricked corridor towards the platforms, I noticed that it still looked as it had during the Cold War. Old-fashioned lettering told visitors which platform to go to, and the place reeked of a spy novel. In fact, a scene from the *Bourne Supremacy* was filmed in front of Friedrich Station. I headed down the steps to the platform. With a whoosh of air, a train arrived, and I was soon on my way to the Brandenburg Gate.

13

The giant, columned edifice topped with the famous four-horsed chariot was an icon of Berlin. It stood at the end of a large rectangular square. Like Checkpoint Charlie, tourists packed the place, many scoffing ice-creams or posing in front of the gate. A parade of horses and carriages lined the square, waiting to take people on tours, and just next to me, was a man blowing giant bubbles.

During the Cold War, the Soviets sealed off Brandenburg Gate, but if I'd wanted to, I could've walked underneath it. After taking a few photos, I was back in the tube on my way to East Berlin.

As I travelled through the subterranean world of East Berlin, it struck me how easy it was to jump on a train and cross between a now obsolete border. Less than twenty-five years ago, it was so different. Checkpoints here, barbed wire there, numerous guard posts, and of course a 12-feet high concrete wall to contend with. All was the grim reality of life in a Germany split in two.

I exited Alexanderplatz Station into a large square dominated by a Soviet-built TV Tower, the tallest building in Germany no less. The square was a hive of activity, with the young and trendy of Berlin hanging around the famous World Clock, or else taking a drink and a chat in the bars and restaurants that dotted the area. Nearby I could hear a band banging out modern rock tunes, and I wondered what East Berliners from the 1970s would think of how their square had changed.

I found a bar near the town hall, and when the waitress arrived, I ordered a beer. The weather was fine, and so was my mood. So this really was it, I mused: the absolute final stop on the Red Quest. But unlike in Belarus, where I'd experienced a slight melancholy about the quest ending, here I was in acceptance. And perhaps out of the all cities I could've finished my adventure in; I thought Berlin was the most fitting. Put simply, it was where East had really met West.

14

My beer arrived and I looked up at the TV tower. I had considered going up to the observation deck, but the snaking queue had put me off. Besides, the view from where I was sitting was good enough, a view that spanned the square and the people within.

As I took a sip of my drink, I thought back to the cities I'd visited, and tried to pick out a favourite. Surprisingly, my mind quickly settled on Ashgabat, capital of Turkmenistan. To me, it was a city all on its own, not only in terms of its fantastic Gulf State architecture, but also because of the way it seemed so deeply paranoid, policing its citizens (and outsiders) like the Cold War had never ended. In fact, I suppose, that was why I had enjoyed Ashgabat so much – I had felt a little bit like a spy – and that had excited me.

Minsk had been a little like that too, but almost everywhere else was fairly normal. Countries moved on, I knew, and times changed. Young people were born who had never known communism, or reacted with fear at the mere mention of the KGB. And in twenty years' time, what would it be like then? What would remain? Would anyone care?

I finished my beer and paid the waitress. Ten minutes later, I was sitting on a train back to my hotel. My mission to visit every nation of the former Soviet Union had finally ended. Twenty-two countries, stretching from Austria to China, from rich to poor, from Christianity to Islam, from democratically free to the regimentally oppressed - all of them ticked off the list.

And do you know what? I'd loved every one of them.

If you have enjoyed reading *The Red Quest*, then head over to www.theredquest.com for exclusive photos and information about Jason Smart.

By the same author:

The Red Quest
Flashpacking through Africa
Take Your Wings and Fly
The Balkan Odyssey
Temples, Tuk-Tuks and Fried Fish Lips (Coming soon)

Made in the USA
Lexington, KY
11 August 2015